THE TRANSCENDENTAL CIRCUIT:

OTHERWORLDS OF POETRY

Joshua Corey

MadHat Press
Asheville, North Carolina

MadHat Press
MadHat Incorporated
PO Box 8364, Asheville, NC 28814

Copyright © 2017 Joshua Corey
All rights reserved

The Library of Congress has assigned
this edition a Control Number of
2017960096

ISBN 978-1-941196-59-5 (paperback)

Cover art and design by Marc Vincenz
Book design by MadHat Press

www.madhat-press.com

First Printing

To Reginald

Table of Contents

Introduction   vii

I. New Versions of Pastoral

I Say a Flower: The Nature of Writing	3
Modes of Pastoral, Modes of Modernism	13
Tansy City: Charles Olson and the Prospects for Avant-Pastoral	38
The Poetic Thing: The Challenge of Francis Ponge	57

II. Three for Duncan

The Dungeon Master: Robert Duncan	77
Robert Duncan's Visionary Ecology	82
Robert Duncan's Polysemous Turn	108

III. The Poet in the Worlds

New American Writing and the New Establishment	117
Phantasmagoria of Authorship	124
The Tripod: Three Modes for Twenty-First-Century American Poetry	131
Richard Hugo's Constructivist Moment	137
Return to *Howl*	141
Baroque Nation	146
The Transcendental Circuit	153

IV. Reginald Shepherd: A Dialogue

Reginald Shepherd: A Dialogue	177

V. The Poet's Novel

My Poet's Novel	229
The Poet's Novel: On Ben Lerner's Fiction	233
Horizontal Hold: Poetry and Narrative	239
Poetic Fictions and Fictional Poets	241
Ambience, Consecration, the Open: Poetic Fictions	245

A Little Endarkenment: Poetry's Outside — 249
Nekuia: The Novel — 252

VI. NOTES AND THOUGHTS ON VISION

Elegy, Arcadia, Apostrophe — 257
Notes Toward the Dramatic Lyric — 260
Notes Toward the Postmodern Baroque — 266
Notes Toward a Cosmological Realism — 271
Poetry and Silence — 275
A Lyric Cosmology — 278
Stay-Puft: On Secret Knowledge — 280
Six Dimensions — 283
Theses on Visionary Materialism — 285
The Moths — 293

Acknowledgments — 299
About the Author — 301

Introduction

I. *"Blogspot was our Montparnasse" –Robert Archambeau*

This book, the heart of this book, began as a blog, focused mainly on poetry and poetics, that I launched along with a thousand others in the early 2000s, and which petered out, along with most of its fellows, about ten years later. The era of poetry blogging was a brief one, more like a moment than an era. It was preceded, in the 1990s, by the SUNY Buffalo Poetics List, founded, according to its archival site, by Charles Bernstein in late 1993.[1] A simple listserv that predated widespread access to the World Wide Web, it was the first Internet-enabled network by which poets connected directly or tangentially to the Poetics Program could discuss, argue, cajole, and harangue one another without having to congregate in Buffalo itself—or in New York City or the San Francisco Bay Area or in any other conurbation. One of the consequences of this lineage was that the first poetry blogs, including the one I created in January 2003, emerged from the structures of thought and feeling around Language poetry; it is no coincidence that it was the blog of Ron Silliman, which launched about four months before mine, that quickly became the de facto center of the new movement. The critical project of Language poetry was thus in a sense baked in to poetry blogging: most of us who started blogs in that period were acutely aware of the material conditions of production that surrounded poetry, were conscious of ourselves as outsiders to a poetry mainstream organized at that time around MFA programs and the major New York and university presses, and saw our blogs, therefore, as a kind of minor insurrection, an opportunity to bypass institutions hostile or indifferent to the kinds of poetry and discourse around poetry that we valued. There was an undeniable feeling of the frontier, a new territory that we could configure as we wished, potentially infinite in its virtual scope, rendering turf battles superfluous. This view would, of course, prove to be naive, and many younger poets came to see blogging as just one more means by which to try to make a mark and advance their careers, most quickly and easily by starting some sort of flame war with a poet perceived as more senior and established than themselves.

---

1 https://listserv.buffalo.edu/cgi-bin/wa?A0=POETICS

Joshua Corey

And yet I felt at the time and still feel that there was something genuinely new about blogging and the discursivity it enabled: rigorous yet casual, critical yet inclusive, inherently digressive, personal, quirky, goofy. It was a genuinely new literary form, located somewhere between the intimacy of the personal letter, the rawness of the diary, the miscellany of the commonplace book, and the wit of the better sort of newspaper column or *feuilleton*. Comparatively few of us posted much in the way of actual *poems*; the blogs instead fed a seemingly unquenchable hunger on the part of poets for the sort of talk and gossip and position-taking that has always happened around poetry but had previously been limited to local scenes. The influence of the Poetics List meant that a quasi-scholarly tone was struck early by myself and many other poetry bloggers; a tone that was imitated, deconstructed, and occasionally mocked by the next "generation" (by which I mean those who started their own blogs in late 2003 or early 2004). In my own case my status as a PhD candidate at Cornell was also a major factor: I was a poet whose first book, *Selah*, would be published later that year; but I was living in the skin of a grad student, with a student's enthusiasms as well as a student's anxiety about standing too nakedly in my ignorance. Blogging, I am happy to say, helped inoculate me somewhat against that anxiety; it was a form of thinking in public that felt less exposing, more fluid, and friendlier than what happened in the seminar room or the creative writing workshop. Above all it was a *conversation*: when I look at my early blog posts I see myself constantly riffing in response to what others were saying on their blogs, and responding to their responses to me. In the earliest days there were no such things as comments sections, which in hindsight strikes me as possibly the most utopian dimension of blogging. If someone wanted to say that something I had written was asinine or had missed the point—and someone very often did—he or she had to either send me an e-mail or start their own blog, thus claiming ownership of their thoughts. There was a personal quality to this, a sense that we were all in the same poetic boat, even when we disagreed with each other. The dawn of the comments sections, and the anonymity they enabled, led very quickly to a coarsening of the discourse, or else forced the blogger to become a kind of policeman, regulating and approving each individual comment. I never could understand or appreciate those who chose to vent their spleen in my virtual backyard, rather than frolicking in virtual backyards of their own.

Not the least appeal of platforms like Blogspot was how easy they were to maintain and use, and how simple and stripped-down they were in their visual presentation; few of the early poetry blogs bothered much with images or videos, aside from the occasional author portrait or book cover. The form of blogging, in which the newest entry is always the one at the top of the page, and one scrolls down into the past, offers a sense of dailiness that helps to promote a casual, everyday tone. While the experience of writing a blog is diaristic and chronological, as a reader one always moves backward, gradually picking up on the endlessly ramifying web of references and allusions that have built up to the blogger's present moment. Inevitably one makes lateral moves, clicking on links that take the reader to other posts and others' blogs, as well as to Wikipedia, YouTube, and every other imaginable site. Blogs are also searchable, making it easy for a reader or the author to pick up on particular themes and threads; by tagging one's entries one could create a kind of virtual index or concordance, and there are automatic features built into the software highlighting the most popular posts. At the height of their proliferation, when there were dozens if not hundreds of poets blogging, skimming their blogs felt very much like an encounter with the web of experience described by Henry James in "The Art of Fiction":

> Experience is never limited and it is never complete; it is an immense sensibility, a kind of huge spider-web, of the finest silken threads, suspended in the chamber of consciousness and catching every airborne particle in its tissue. It is the very atmosphere of the mind; and when the mind is imaginative—much more when it happens to be that of a man of genius—it takes to itself the faintest hints of life, it converts the very pulses of the air into revelations.

The imaginative mind, in this case, was a collective one. When I look back at the posts from 2003 to 2005, what I see is a tissue woven by a

Joshua Corey

variety of minds: of Ron Silliman, first of all, the home page of the poetry Internet; of Jonathan Mayhew's Bemsha Swing and John Erhardt's The Skeptic; of Ray Davis's Bellona Times (now called Pseudopodium) and Kasey Mohammad's Lime Tree; of Robert Archambeau's Samizdat Blog and Mark Scroggins's Culture Industry, Nick Piombino's fait accompli and Stephanie Young's the well nourished moon. As this necessarily extremely partial list suggests, male bloggers outnumbered female bloggers to an enormous extent; perhaps men in general are more comfortable with, or more oblivious to, the consequences of making fools of themselves in public. It's more likely the case that the women were deterred by their exposure to ghastly verbal and sexual abuse when they dared to speak publicly in a forum without regulation or gatekeepers; as far as I can tell this problem hasn't been much alleviated by the advent of Facebook and Twitter. It's also true that even as individual poets' blogs have declined, there has been a corresponding rise in collective literary blogs sponsored by groups, institutions, and magazines such as the Poetry Foundation's Harriet, HTMLGIANT, The Best American Poetry, and Montevidayo, and women tend to be far better represented on those blogs. Nevertheless the stark gender imbalance of poetry blogging is another indication, should one be needed, that the seemingly unlimited virtual frontier that blogging seemed to offer some of us in the early 2000s was by no means detached from the same material conditions as the rest of our society.

Poetry blogging got its start in the charged political environment of the George W. Bush years, and that charge lent a certain sense of urgency to our larger project. Ron Silliman started his blog almost exactly one year after 9/11, and when I started mine the run-up to the Iraq War was already well underway. The left-leaning tendencies of the poetry blogosphere led some of us contribute some incisive commentary to the political situation; but as the wars dragged on, and especially after John Kerry lost his bid to unseat Bush in 2004, cultural politics began to crowd out the global and national variety. Many bloggers, including myself, devoted far too much time to drawing lines in the sand demarcating the right sort of poets from the wrong sort; the most notorious and persistent line was drawn by Silliman between the "School of Quietude"—the "bad" poets behind what Charles Bernstein likes to call Official Verse Culture—and the "post-avant" poets, the "good guys" of the blogosphere. The tendency to equate cultural conservatism with political conservatism was criticized incisively by Reginald Shepherd, a late addition to the blog scene who began his contributions in the form of e-mails to myself and other bloggers; he began his own blog in 2007 and maintained it until his untimely death a year later. That dialogue is reproduced here in *The Transcendental Circuit*'s central section, which comes as close as any book can to reproducing the dialogical spirit of blogging at its best.

Poetry blogging probably peaked in the middle of the second George W. Bush administration, when *Publishers Weekly* took notice of the phenomenon with an April 2006 article, "Poetry Off the Books," in which Silliman is quoted as having "had over 616,000 visitors to my Web log," while I admitted to a more modest 200,000, a number that was to more than double before I stopped updating the blog in 2014. The preceding year I had logged 373 individual posts, more than one a day, a small decline from my busiest year, 2004, when I posted 410 times. By the time of Reginald Shepherd's passing in 2008, the form seemed to be entering its decline. This may largely be attributed to advances in technology: so-called "microblogging" in the form of Twitter, Facebook, and Instagram posts came to fill the space that long-form blogging had once occupied, driven largely by the omnipresence of smartphones, which have become many people's primary means of accessing the Internet. The economic crash of 2008 may also have played a role, simultaneous with the election of Barack Obama: the one event perhaps deprived some people of the sense of leisure that blogging requires, while the other might have sapped some of the oppositional political energies on which poetry blogging seemed to thrive. (The advent of Donald Trump might just possibly lead to some sort of revival, but I have my doubts.) In my own case, I had personal reasons for blogging less often. I was no longer a graduate student but a fledgling professor at the small liberal arts college where I still teach; I was a new father as well. I found I had less time and energy to spend on writing that seemed by its nature to be not just ephemeral but ill-equipped to compete for attention with 140-character tweets.

Still, I never entirely abandoned the form, and found it especially helpful when I began navigating the fraught transition from poet-critic to poet-critic-novelist. The blog was like the rock on which I rubbed off one skin and prepared myself to inhabit another; it permitted a kind of experimental literary self to precede my actual, embodied self into what felt like a new world. And yet—with my first novel at least—I had by no means left poetry behind. The experience of writing *Beautiful Soul: An American Elegy* was more or less coterminous with the transformation of my blog from a space for discussion and controversy into something more like a dream annex, where I could post the sorts of pieces that had no obvious home elsewhere—manifestos, prose poems, theories, and the occasional review (of films and music as well as books). In 2014 I stopped updating my original blog with its absurd name (I always intended "Cahiers de Corey" to be self-deflating, but I'm not sure others got the joke, aside from those who insisted on spelling the first word "Cashiers") and started a new blog on my permanent website, www.joshua-corey.com, which I update only infrequently. But blogging remains a resource to me, still very close to the idea expressed by my original blog's pretentious title, as a form of note-taking. "To note" as a verb, after all, means to write down or record; but its primary meaning is to notice, to pay attention to some object, if only one's own thoughts.

II. Worlds and Poetry

The majority of the pieces collected in *The Transcendental Circuit* made their first appearances on my blog, but others were published in magazines, many of them online and some of those short-lived. Others had their first lives as peer-reviewed journal articles, which I have re-edited in an attempt to draw some of the academic torpor from their sentences. This book for me represents a kind of reckoning, a scattershot intellectual autobiography that catches up the many casual and occasionally more formal pieces of poetry criticism and commentary that I've written over the past decade and a half. For a number of years I harbored grandiose dreams of developing some sort of grand unified theory of poetry, or at any rate of pastoral poetry, or at least of a personal poetics caught between spirit and skepticism. That ambition has waned, in large part because I now discover looking back at these writings how consistent I've been in spite of myself. The same themes recur upon the same ground: utopia as figure and possibility, centered largely though not exclusively on the genre of pastoral and on the grouping of writers and artists associated with Black Mountain College; an internal struggle, projected outward, between a species of sociological rationalism and a neo-Romantic fascination with the visionary and transcendent; the politics of the North American poetic field and the value or bankruptcy of "innovative" poetries; the potential of creative writing as a discipline to go beyond the affirmation of existing identities; and a Stevensian longing to meet "reality" with some equal and oppositely violent force of "imagination." The different sections of the book track, more or less, these continual preoccupations.

 Early in my scholarly career I fell into an *idée fixe,* namely the notion that the apparently nostalgic mode of pastoral and the techniques of modernist and postmodernist poetry intersected more interestingly than they diverged. This idea carried me through a doctoral dissertation on the "avant-pastoral" poetry of Ezra Pound, Louis Zukofsky, and Ronald Johnson, and eventually to my co-editorship, with G.C. Waldrep, of *The Arcadia Project: North American Postmodern Pastoral,* an anthology published by Ahsahta Press in 2012. Writings assembled in the wake of those projects populate this book's first and most "academic" section, "New Versions of Pastoral"; they present, in what I hope is not too repetitive a fashion, my evolving fascination with the persistence and complication of the pastoral fantasy by the critical spirit of postmodernism. The most recent pieces in that section refer to my translation (with Jean-Luc Garneau) of Francis Ponge's first book *Le parti pris des choses*; they try to account for the skeptical and materialist version of pastoral that Ponge's work represents for me, and stand for the moment at the center of own notions of poetry as a means of negotiating ideological encounters with the nonhuman and with nature.

Joshua Corey

One of the pieces in the first section explores the urban pastoral of Charles Olson, an immensely generative figure for poets concerned with how layers of history and landscape might be explored and rendered via the adaptation of modernist open forms. Reading Olson led me to the more *récherché* figure of Robert Duncan, who has since assumed a surprising centrality to my sense of what's most vital and untimely in contemporary poetry. The pivot between Olson and Duncan is one way to analogize the shift I underwent from the first decade of the twenty-first century to the next. Olson worried over the difficulty of being "both a poet and, an historian" (the comma is immensely telling); at Cornell, I was under the spell of critical theorists like Theodor Adorno and Frederic Jameson, convinced that the highest justification for modernist and postmodernist poetry was that it enabled the "cognitive mapping" of otherwise overwhelming and not directly perceivable fields of social force, so-called late capitalism pre-eminent among them. At the same time, I found the Language poets fascinating but off-putting in their cliqueish self-importance; the grandparental generations of Black Mountain and "Objectivist" poets were far more attractive to me as models for poetic thought. Olson assumed a natural prominence for this project. But there was another pole that made itself felt for me in the figure of Duncan: the appeal to an esoteric history of the imagination, of a visionary lineage extending back through H.D. and Blake, a more comprehensive vision of histories and theories of knowledge that dismissed nothing as false consciousness and was thus, as it still seems to me, more truly scientific and empirical, if not materialist, in its stance toward poetry's possible objects than the latter-day Marxianisms of the Language poets. I struggled against Duncan, much as Olson does in his essay, "Against Wisdom as Such," but in the end he became one of my touchstone poets, and the pieces collected in "Three for Duncan" show how that came to be the case.

The plurality of "worlds" is for me an imaginative necessity, even as I also admit the moral necessity of return to the one and only world in which we meet the enemy that is invariably us. The third section, "The Poet in the Worlds," brings the reader closer to the day-to-day conversation that took place in what I like to think of, with gentle irony, as the heroic age of poetry blogging. In these essays, I engage with differing styles and movements of poetry and examine frequently the figure of the poet itself and the possible worlds that poetry as a fundamentally open and inclusive form can give rise to. The last pieces in that section connect most explicitly to the still-evolving political moment of the present, a moment that I feel has ripened both the possibilities and contradictions for poetry, in which the mask of ideology has come loose like never before in my lifetime, revealing the ugliest impulses of the state. I refer primarily to the Black Lives Matter movement that formed after the murder of Michael Brown by white police officers in 2014 and to the hardly unrelated election of Donald Trump, a man for whom language has proven to be a horrifyingly pliable weapon that may not be as remote from poetry as we might wish.

The fourth section is devoted entirely to the dialogue with Reginald Shepherd that I mentioned above, and functions in many ways as the continuation and apotheosis of the essays in the preceding section—it represents, for me, the shift I underwent from eager partisan of innovative poetry to someone who, if not much wiser, has at least cultivated a somewhat slower reaction time to whatever controversy of the day is stirring in American poetry. The fifth section, "The Poet's Novel," is a series of speculations on the often-fraught relationship between poets and prose, and between creative writers and the academy—as a poet with a PhD, I have often looked askance at what I see as the anti-intellectual tendencies of the discourse around creative writing as an academic discipline. It is also a reckoning with how being a poet taught me, slowly and haltingly, to become a fiction writer. Poetry, it has long seemed to me, is a species of thought, a way of "thinking with the things as they exist," as Louis Zukofsky said. Only belatedly, after twenty years identifying as a poet, have I discovered that storytelling, character, and plot can also be thought-full, a mode of cognition that can be a means of encountering and experiencing in a rich and saturated way. If I have made myself into a novelist, it is only because I was a poet that I was able to find a way into the satisfactions and beguilements of that largest and baggiest of literary forms.

The sixth and final section, "Notes and Thoughts on Vision" (the title is a nod to H.D.), in a way re-encapsulates the journey I've undergone between 2001 and now, beginning with early essays that constitute my search for a sufficient theory of the lyric, ending with a pair of manifesto-like pieces that try to articulate a poetics flexible yet sharp enough to cut along the twinned biases of skepticism and romance. If there can be a "new materialism"—a concept that led me to and through a new translation of Ponge—can an ethical vision of transcendence be so far behind?

The title essay, in the course of a review of Ben Lerner's *The Hatred of Poetry* and Reginald Gibbons's *How Poems Think*, tries to account for poetry as a means of achieving transcendence, and concludes that an ethical poetry of today, a poetics of the multiple, can never have such transcendence as a goal. Transcendence is always local and specific—the transcendence of particular historical conditions—and its primary function must be that of returning to those conditions refreshed and, as it were, re-armed for doing battle with them. Without saying so expressly, I unite here my fascination with Romantic transcendence with my more pragmatic sense of the pastoral poem as a kind of temporary refuge—"Back out of all this now too much for us," as Robert Frost puts it in "Directive," using a curiously Robert Duncan-esque turn of phrase. From the convulsive energy of the world and its surfaces, the world that is too much with us, derives a counter-movement, a pull away that begins as self-preservation and ends as something ecstatic, an Emersonian push into loss and compensation. Duncan, that untimely Freudian, is forever calling his reader's attention to what lies behind or beneath or "back of" the drive he summarizes so beautifully in "Poetry, a Natural Thing." Having begun by commenting, "Neither our vices nor our virtues / further the poem," he insists:

> The poem
> feeds upon thought, feeling, impulse,
>   to breed   itself,
> a spiritual urgency at the dark ladders leaping.

The Transcendental Circuit

The poem leaps up to breed itself like the salmon leaping their ladders, an impossible artifice demanded by its nature. And where does it land? In the "place of first permission," the pastoral meadow to which the poet is "often" permitted to return, to gather strength from "a given property of the mind / that certain bounds hold against chaos" before returning to the political and social world of the poet's responsibility: "Responsibility is to keep / the ability to respond." That is the transcendental circuit I seek to follow, a progress I hope the reader will discern, however fitfully, in the pieces collected in this book.

These writings thus collectively constitute a kind of narrative, a movement away from the chiefly academic concerns with which I began—including the young academic's concerns with turf-claiming and self-assertion—toward an impulse more generously speculative, bred in part by blogging. If I continue with the essay form, it will be to push even further in this speculative direction, uniting at hazard impulses of poetic association and intensely subjective feeling with the thought I address to the poems of others (and to novels, paintings, films, and other forms of art). There is no pattern, path, or plan, only the quick of my responsibility to the languages of our world.

I
NEW VERSIONS OF PASTORAL

I Say a Flower: The Nature of Writing

Why speak of a postmodern pastoral? What relevance can an obsolete genre preoccupied with the mating games of shepherds in an imaginary Arcadia have in an era in which ecocriticism and ecopoetics are rapidly becoming mainstream modes of critical and creative thought? And why invoke postmodernism at this late date, when its fundamental moves have come to seem obvious, if not exhausted and clichéd? Well, we are still living in what Frederic Jameson called the cultural logic of late capitalism, even as the larger irrationality of that logic threatens to destroy the conditions of life itself. "Postmodernism" cannot be disassociated from capital's obsession with novelty, with continuous expansion, with "creative destruction," and with the generation and exploitation of new markets in psychic as well as geographic territories, not to mention the Colbertian "truthiness" that has come to condition our profoundly degraded political discourse. If the concept is to retain any truth-value we must reclaim it as an implement of critique; it's my belief that juxtaposing it with pastoral reclaims both terms' potential for a critical effect—and Marxian affect.

As postmodernism as a concept ought to call attention to the ideological formation of cultural reality, pastoral brings into the foreground our mythic and ideological relation to nature, even and especially because nature, scientifically apprehended, provides the broadest and most fundamental horizon for what we term "the real." As the critic Greg Garrard writes, "The challenge for ecocritics is to keep one eye on the ways in which 'nature' is always in some ways culturally constructed, and the other on the fact that nature really exists, both the object and, albeit distantly, the origin of our discourse.... Ecocritics remain suspicious of the idea of science as wholly objective and value-free, but they are in the unusual position as cultural critics of having to defer, in the last analysis, to a scientific understanding of the world." It's that suspicion of scientism (faith in science as objective and value-free) that distinguishes the postmodern pastoral from the broader category of "ecopoetry" that is the counterpart of ecocriticsm.

It's not enough to "decenter" the human as the deep ecologists claim to do, or as the reverse of the medal would have it, deify or demonize human agency by universalizing it as "Anthropocene." Discursive moves, as such, can never provide nonideological direct contact with "nature" or "the real." Postmodern pastoral remembers, with Paul Celan, that reality is never simply "there," but neither is it entirely constructed. With language, the poet "tries to measure the area of the given and the possible.... Reality is not simply there, it must be searched and won."

Postmodern pastoral reminds us that "nature poetry" is always a social text. It puts environmentalism and socialism in an unresolved dialectical relationship, rather than simply presenting one as the replacement as the other. As William Empson put it in what is still one of the most influential books on the genre, "The essential trick of the old pastoral, which was felt to imply a beautiful relation between rich and poor, was to make simple people express strong feelings (felt as the most universal subject, something fundamentally true about everybody) in learned and fashionable language (so that you wrote about the best subject in the best way)." Empson's phrase "the old pastoral" is the image of a reconciled social order, an imaginary resolution of real social contradictions, and an accession to hierarchy. The ideological function of pastoral in this sense is still very much with us, as for example in the characterization of American rural and exurban whites as living in the "heartland," in possession of authentic American values that render them morally and spiritually superior to coastal "urban elites." But just as "postmodernism" must be reclaimed so that it is no longer a term that conceals the cultural contradictions it was coined to point out, so too can the post-pastoral become an instrument for diagnosing and critiquing the contradictions it has historically been used to smooth over.

Such a pastoral offers us a privileged vantage point from which to discern the conflict between environmentalism and postmodernism as the latest manifestation of the cultural dynamic that Max Horkheimer and Theodor Adorno called the dialectic of enlightenment. The cultural logic of late capitalism encounters, in the deepening environmental emergency, its limit condition: the endless play of the signifier and the proliferation of discourses of difference turn out to have been subsidized by cheap fossil fuels. Peak oil and global warming are the ultimate eruption of the Real into the Arcadia of signifiers, the postmodern capitalist space in which all that is solid melts into air. The postmodern poetic that seemed so liberating in the late twentieth century, that in its Black Mountain and Language poetry incarnations provided acutely critical cognitive maps of American "SPACE," is now confronted by the limits of what ecocritic Andrew McMurray calls "the environmental actual." We stand now on the precipice of the environmental actual and the void that looms before is dizzying and appropriately uncanny. This is the end of postmodernism as discursive play, just as it threatens to be the end of modernity itself.

Yet pastoral persists in several ratifying, sometimes mutually exclusive forms. On the one hand a kind of rear-guard Romantic nature poetry continues to ascribe numinous properties to a persistently "natural" "outside" world. Such poetry may or may not directly acknowledge the precipitous decline of nonhuman biomes and species, but either way its critical capacities are subordinated to a desire to maintain the cycle of Wordsworthian call-and-response between a beautiful landscape and *les belles âmes* that wander there. On the other hand there has been the rapid rise of environmental poetics and ecocriticism, the mainstream of which attempts to found its discourse on the decentering of the human and the empirical description of plants, animals, and biotic systems. That decentering gives ecocriticism much of its critical and ethical force. But as a self-described "realist" discourse, ecocriticism risks blinding itself to its own ideological impulses. On a pragmatic level as well, the scientific-descriptive stance of some ecopoets may lack the affective and imaginative power that the older Romantic mode once mustered. Wordsworth and Thoreau effectively created an entirely new imaginative relationship between human beings and nature at the dawn of the industrial age; can it be said that environmental poetics is doing the same necessary labor as that age is perhaps coming to a close?

Joshua Corey

I return often and often to Virgil's Ninth Eclogue, in which dismayed shepherds learn that their land, their commons, has been expropriated by the state, and that they are now in exile. The first shepherd says disbelievingly (in David Ferry's translation):

> But I was told Menalcas with his songs
> Had saved the land, from where those hills arise
> To where they slope down gently to the water,
> Near those old beech trees, with their broken tops.

Notice how song—pastoral poetry—is here ascribed the power of boundary-making and boundary-keeping. But the reply is disillusioning:

> Yes, that was the story; but what can music do
> Against the weapons of soldiers? When eagles come,
> Tell me what doves can possibly do about it?
> If the raven on the left in this hollow oak
> Hadn't warned me not to resist, I might have been killed.
> Menalcas himself might very well have been killed.

In this early moment of self-consciousness, pastoral acknowledges its own weakness in the face of military and political power. "The weapons of soldiers" cannot be countered or even replied to by poetry: when poetry confronts power, silence is the result; and as we were taught not so very long ago, silence equals death. And yet Virgil here ascribes a scrap of what Heidegger calls "saving power" to a poetry capable of imagining an alliance with the natural world against power: it is the raven, a speaking bird, a scavenger, not so easily lent to the symbolic as the eagle or the dove, that saves the poet's life for other risky engagements with power, and for future song.

Et in Arcadia ego—I, Death, am also in Arcadia. Arcadia, like Robert Duncan's meadow, is a made place, constructed on an unstable boundary or ecotone between the shepherd and the soldier, the human and the nonhuman, the country and the city, the margin and the imperium. It was the Romantic poets who introduced the notion of the sublime into that boundary—making the pastoral safe for a half-domesticated species of terror. In the twentieth and twenty-first centuries our sense of unease has persisted and deepened. Are we destroying and degrading the environment, or are we energetically and unsystematically erasing the imaginary boundary between foreground and background, human and nature, upon which the pastoral relation depends?

Pastoral will not be subsumed or discarded by ecopoetics, as useful as that latter category has proven to be. Pastoral is the memory of affect and ideology—of utopia as it emerges in relation to the nonhuman. Since there is no subtracting affect and ideology from our approaches to nature, I believe pastoral will continue to play a crucial role in that project. Postmodern pastoral well describes the affect proper to our encounter with what Timothy Morton calls "hyperobjects": entities that blur the boundary between human and nonhuman, whose reality is undeniable but which evade our senses as phenomena: global climate change and the half-life of plutonium are Morton's chief examples of hyperobjects, but consider also your relation to genetically modified organisms in the food chain, to the quasi-religious ritual of dropping a plastic bottle in a recycling bin, or to the "selfish genes" of your own DNA. That is why the title of the anthology I helped to edit with G.C. Waldrep, *The Arcadia Project*, playfully alludes to Walter Benjamin's unfinished masterpiece. "Nature" has become an archive of hyperobjects concealed by increasingly archaic, and therefore increasingly historical, images of animals, wilderness preserves, English country houses, and the increasingly belligerent, uncertain, and uninnocent weather that can no longer serve as anyone's conversational neutral ground. Postmodern pastoral is your all-access pass to this archive, to the junk heap of "Nature" that has become inseparable from the junk heap contemplated by another Benjaminian construct, the Angel of History. Call it the opening of the Möbius field: a surface with only one side and only one boundary, though the illusion of doubleness and separation persists.

After all, we still refer to clean air or clean water or arable earth as "natural resources," implying that they are somehow separate from us, that they do not surround and envelop us, that we could somehow live without them. Our very language operates as an act of enclosure, privatizing a common good while disavowing common responsibility. As with air, water, and earth, language itself is becoming polluted, unusable, uninhabitable. Sometimes their abuse goes hand in hand, as in the case of corporate "greenwashing," in which the language of environmentalism provides a veneer of respectability for oil companies and industrial agriculture. But more often than not we separate our thinking about language from our thinking about nature. Poets have often been guilty of using language as a means to access nature or an idea of nature that somehow serves the poet's egotistical sublime. If ecology means an attitude toward nature that decenters the human being and insists on seeing our lives as components of a larger organism, then I want to consider the possibility of a poetic ecology that is similarly oriented not toward the needs of isolated individuals (much less institutions or corporations) but toward the needs of the whole organism: that is, language as the transcendental precondition for human being as such. For that reason it can be useful to return not only to postmodernism but to the even more discredited idea of the avant-garde—a category rarely if ever associated with what we usually think of as "nature writing." In her book *Dreamworld and Catastrophe,* Susan Buck-Morss describes the desired effect of the avant-garde artwork: "What counts is that the aesthetic experience teach us something new about our world, that it shock us out of moral complacency and political resignation, and that it take us to task for the overwhelming lack of social imagination that characterizes so much of cultural production in all its forms." When the pastoral meets the avant-garde, we can emend that sentence to read "that it takes us to task for the overwhelming lack of social *and ecological* imagination that characterizes so much of cultural production." The expansion of imagination is not fundamentally about new new subject matter but a question of form. The poetry that can teach us, shock us, and take us to task will do so not by recovering nature in poetry but by recovering the nature *of* poetry: as language wild in the streets of our sociality.

When we speak today of the "nature poem," we are still likely to be speaking of poetry modeled on the Wordsworthian, Romantic sublime. The poet inserts him or herself into a landscape, looks out into it, and re-encounters that same self, refreshed by its momentary contemplation of the nonhuman. The spectacle of nature offers consolation, comfort, and an affirmation of the speaker's unique subjectivity. There is barely any distance to travel between Wordsworth's "I Wandered Lonely as a Cloud" and virtually any poem of Mary Oliver's you would care to name. As Oliver writes in "Morning Poem":

> there is still
> somewhere deep within you
> a beast shouting that the earth
> is exactly what it wanted —

Whether or not we agree with this sentiment will depend more upon our own existing presuppositions about the relationship between external nature (in Oliver's shorthand, "earth") and our inner nature (the "beast") than it will upon the vigor or strangeness of Oliver's language. In fact I would describe Oliver's poetry generally as a kind of Wordsworthian shorthand, through which she ventures out into the landscape to discover exactly what she expects to find—herself. This is a formal problem as much as it is an ethical one: Oliver's plainness of speech, while serving as a marker of her accessibility and authenticity, represses the strangeness and vitality of language beyond its usefulness as a resource. Her language gestures at "your one wild and precious life," tries to terrify you like a lion at the end of a leash—but it is tame, and we never lose sight of the lion tamer's whip and chair. In their labored attempts to reveal capital-T Truth and capital-N Nature, Oliver's poems present us with predigested pieties with all the comforts of home. Wildness is concealed, the self—an isolated self—revealed. The Lucretian swerve of nature and the *physis* or self-becoming of language are quietly suppressed.

Against "nature writing" as such I oppose a version of post- or postmodern or avant-pastoral that, in its patent artifice, may come much closer to the experience of wilderness than a transparently "natural" language that affirms an unthought boundary between nature and culture. Immanuel Kant describes the pleasure of natural beauty as deriving from the sense of encountering a design whose purpose we cannot fathom: "purposiveness without purpose." Before it can mean anything to a botanist or a lover a tulip simply *is*, and it is that isness that astonishes and delights us. We do not need to ask what the tulip means for it to have its effect on us. When Mary Oliver tells us about the peonies, she *signifies* them and the meaning she intends to associate with them: "their red stems holding // all that dancing and recklessness / gladly and lightly." Compare "Peonies" to one of Louis Zukofsky's *80 Flowers,* "Dandelion":

> No blanch witloof handbound dry
> heart to racks a comb
> lion's-teeth thistlehead *golden-hair earth nail*
> flower-clock *up-by-pace* dandle lion won't
> dwarf lamb closes night season
> its long year *dumble-dor* bumbles
> cure wine *blowball* black fall's-berry
> madding sun mixen seeded rebus

Zukofsky's credentials as a nature poet may appear to be pretty weak: he lived his whole life in New York City and was never part of any environmental movement that I know of. His notoriously thorny writing, rife with intertextuality, puns, and manic energy, is about as far as you can get from the earnest simplicity that we associate with contemporary nature poetry. He was not particularly interested in either rural life or the concern for conservation we associate with organizations like the Sierra Club. Yet I get more dandelion from "Dandelion" than I get peony from "Peonies." Zukofsky's "flower" inscribes itself on our nerves with a language that manages to be precise and unfamiliar at the same time. Before it sends us to the dictionary after the meaning of words like "witloof" (an endive), "dumble-dor" (a bumblebee), and "mixen" (a compost heap or dung-pile), "Dandelion" makes a sound, echoing with traces of meaning unpacked from the image of the flower joined with its name. This "Dandelion" is a "seeded rebus": a puzzle in which pictures and symbols are used to make up a word, and Zukofsky's poem wants its words to strike you as immediately as pictures do. His poetics radically extends the conflation of word with natural object suggested by Whitman's *Leaves of Grass*—the poet who further insisted that "This is no book / Who touches this touches a man." Language matters because language is matter: for Zukofsky, language is one face of the Spinozan divine substance from which all being derives. If language is a picture that holds us captive, as Wittgenstein suggests, Zukofsky's poem at least refracts that picture so that it appears to us as it might through a bee's multifaceted eyes, exploding possibilities for pollination.

Zukofsky's stubbornly linguistic imagination suggests an ecology for words: a desire to present them, if not in their natural habitat, then at least with their history intact: their roots, their flowers and seeds, all visible. The American poet who has taken this notion the furthest is probably Ronald Johnson, whose magnificent long poem *ARK* is both a Poundian intertextual collage and a garden of linguistic play. His early poem "Shake, Quoth the Dove House," lays out a poetic program for the blending of language and life, elaborating on Heidegger's claim that "man dwells poetically on the earth":

> This is the Garden, where all is a poet's
> topiary. Where even the trees
> shall have tongues, green aviaries,
> to rustle at his will.
>
> And as I sit here, my pipe
> alight, coos like a turtle-dove in the wood—
>
> its smoke a live-oak, in still air.
>
> Where the smokes curl up, the moss hangs down:
> let us call it Arden
>
> & live in it!

Joshua Corey

Playful, lyrical, crammed with exuberant images of light and seeing, Johnson's poetry constitutes the most complete pastoral retreat imaginable; his *socius* is intimate and indirect, derived as much from Frank Baum's Oz books as it is from the company of naturalists, painters, and fellow poets like Zukofsky, Lorine Niedecker, Jonathan Williams, and Charles Olson. But a more expansive social imagination can be found in the work of contemporary avant-garde pastoralists as diverse as Eleni Sikelianos, Donald Revell, and Lisa Jarnot (it is parenthetically worth noting that some of the most vital and interesting work with pastoral today is being done by Canadians such as Lisa Robertson, Steve McCaffrey, and Christopher Dewdney). These poets have little in common when it comes to verse technique or specific aesthetic goals: they are not a "school." They do not approach nature in the same way: some are invested in empirical and scientific naturalism, while others are more fascinated by the idea of nature as a force for the destabilization of ideology. All, however, demonstrate an acute consciousness of the ways in which nature and culture are inextricably implicated in one another. Their sometimes thorny, sometimes deceptively simple language serves as a site of mediation (in Leo Marx's terms, a "middle landscape") between wilderness and civilization. In their work, "pastoral" does not connote a particular landscape or subject matter: their Arcadia is their language, a retreat from the imperatives of proposition and production, a powerful renewable resource with which new social and environmental possibilities might be conjured, while the existing catastrophic conditions are unconcealed.

Modes of Pastoral, Modes of Modernism

In the twenty-first century it is only a short leap from civilization and its discontents to the postmodern pastoral. *Postmodern* and *pastoral*: two exhausted and empty cultural signifiers reactivated by forced proximity, united by the logic of mutual and nearly assured destruction. With gas and food prices climbing, with the planet's accelerated warming, with the contraction of our cheap-energy economy and the rapid extinction of plant and animal species, both the flat world of global capitalism and the green world of fond memory are in the process of vanishing before our eyes. As Frederic Jameson has remarked, "It seems to be easier for us today to imagine the thoroughgoing deterioration of the earth and of nature than the breakdown of late capitalism; perhaps that is due to some weakness in our imaginations." His claim was anticipated two centuries earlier by Percy Bysshe Shelley, who in his "Defence of Poetry" lamented that "We want the creative faculty to imagine that which we know; we want the generous impulse to act that which we imagine; we want the poetry of life: our calculations have outrun conception; we have eaten more than we can digest." Shelley's revolution of the imagination was that of Romanticism, the intersection of "The everlasting universe of things" with the human mind, each enlarging the other; Jameson is the prophet of a postmodernism that historicizes Shelley's impulse by tracking the entanglements of "things" with the ideology of late capitalism, by which the uncanny liveliness of the commodity observed by Marx gets turned up to eleven. Postmodernism, in other words, is anti-transcendent, and yet in its frantic diffusiveness is more corrosive of the historical than the Shelleyan sublime could ever be. The two categories of thought need each other; we need them in order to understand the North American lineage of pastoral poetry and its interactions with modernist, late modernist, and postmodern modes and forms. In this essay, originally conceived as an introduction to *The Arcadia Project; North American Postmodern Pastoral*, I attempt to track that lineage and to make those interactions legible.

> Modern life has expanded our conception of nature and along with it nature's role in our lives and our art—a woman stepping on a bus may afford a greater insight into nature than the hills outside Rome, for nature has not stood still since Shelley's day. In past times there was nature and there was human nature; because of the ferocity of modern life, man and nature have become one. A scientist can be an earthquake. A poet can be a plague.
>
> —Frank O'Hara, "Nature and New Painting"

The terms "pastoral" and "modernism"—both of which seem to name large swaths of cultural practice while resisting close definition—are only apparently incompatible. We associate the pastoral with a vision of harmony between humans and the natural world—what Leo Marx called "the middle landscape," outside the city without being entirely outside civilization, and natural without being wholly wild or inhospitable to human beings. Modernism and postmodernism, meanwhile, are closely associated with urban and with virtual experience: whether we name its latter-day form the information age, the society of the spectacle, or globalization, it would seem obvious that nature has nothing to do with it. The most fundamental categories of nature, after all, are space and time, both of which are severely abridged in an age in which consumption as well as production have been outsourced, so that our clothes come from Bangladesh, our computers from China, and our customer service representatives answer the phone in India. Not only space and time but our capacity for attention is fragmented, as we hunt and gather e-mails, videos, tweets, and other primarily visual data on multiple and simultaneous screens. It all seems a far cry from Tityrus piping on his oaten reed while reclining on an Arcadian hillside in Virgil's *Eclogues,* or Wordsworth questioning the leech-gatherer, or Frost's lonely swinger of birches, or even the consumerist pastorals reproduced by Restoration Hardware catalogs and *Cooks Illustrated* magazine.

As O'Hara suggests in the quotation above, the site of modernity's intersection with the pastoral can be located at the moment that "nature" becomes recognizable not as outside history but part of history, a discourse in itself. Yet this does not re-inscribe the modern divorce between nature and humanity that we can date at least as far back as Descartes' *cogito*: for O'Hara, the (post)modern condition means that "man and nature have become one." This merging, as he is aware, creates the potential for catastrophe on an unprecedented scale: "A scientist can be an earthquake. A poet can be a plague." But it also suggests the potential for a fully postmodern poetry to enter this zone of the pastoral—the vision of humanity undivided from nature—and activate its ambiguities, making readers more fully consciousness of the discursive and social reality churning beneath the surface of either idyllic or appalling images.

Pastoral manifests humanity's oldest fantasy of *otium*, leisure, liberation from Adam's curse and the need to sweat for one's bread. Postmodernism represents the bankrupt culture of consumer society: it is the nightmarish or farcical realization of the pastoral fantasy, a world in which meaning(ful) production is not so much obsolete as out of reach. Through its attention to the physical world, postmodern poetry can become something other than a glib or cynical celebration of our culture's fragmentation. And by passing through postmodernism's focus on the materiality of language, the historicity of discourse, and the constructedness of subjectivity, pastoral sheds its naivety and tactically refocuses our attention on the strategies of greenwashing and obfuscation by which the corporate powers that be work to hide, quite literally, our own nature from us.

In the wake of nature's disenchantment by the progress of capitalism and modern science, the word "nature" becomes more ideological than ever: drained of its mythic content, pastoral comes rushing in to fill the vacuum. We do not often think of high modernist poets as maintaining close associations with pastoral or the natural world: the major exception is Robert Frost, whose modernist credentials are often questioned precisely because of his preoccupation with natural phenomena and the New England landscape, not to mention his adherence to traditional English poetic forms. More significant for the purposes of this discussion would be T.S. Eliot in his most radical phase, the phase of *The Waste Land*: for Eliot, nature is at best an uncanny supplement to the brave new world of industrial capitalism and mass political movements, a ghostly absence or zombie presence ("'That corpse you planted last year in your garden, / 'Has it begun to sprout?'"). The very title of his poem is enough to suggest this, as the poem traces a "dry," disturbingly de-natured nature in which April, with its showers sweet, has mutated into "the cruelest month." The inhuman world of Eliot's poem is corrupt and slimy when it is not desiccated and empty: it is a negative, an anti-pastoral, and only the *deus ex machina* of myth derived from a non-Western context, the Hindu Upanishads, is able to produce *otium* or at least stasis in the poem's last gasping line: "*Shantih shantih shantih.*" The poem does therefore achieve something like pastoral closure, but only by turning away from the implications of a disenchanted modernity toward a peace that literally passeth understanding; a retreat from rationality that foreshadows Eliot's conversion to high Anglicanism. A mythified and tentative pastoral returns to manifest itself in *Four Quartets,* in which he writes, "I think that the river / Is a strong brown god.... Unhonoured, unpropitiated / By worshippers of the machine." But Eliot's Anglo-Catholic version of pastoral is neither persuasive nor useful to poets who are wary of an undialectical reversal of the progress of disenchantment.

Ezra Pound's diagnosis of a diseased and decadent nature was similar to Eliot's, but his prescription for its cure was more radical and more sinister. Pound writes an explicitly Fascist pastoral conditioned by his rigid idealism, which renders landscape as a once-beautiful artwork corrupted by usury, to be purified by the labors of Il Duce, the supreme "artifex." The "history" that Pound's epic "includes" proves to be an unstable mix with pastoral (traditionally a zone of escape from history and politics), so that his attempt to construct "*un paradis terrestre,*" collapses into shards and fragments, as did Mussolini's regime: "I cannot make it cohere." This is the most most fortunate of failures, from a poetic as well as a political perspective, since the most moving of Pound's poems are the Pisan Cantos in which fragmentary images of nature offer an implicit critique of the madness of ideology. "When the mind swings by a grass-blade an ant's forefoot shall save you," a chastened Pound writes, placing himself at the epicenter of postmodern pastoral. Politics and nature collide in Pound's work and dirty each other up in ways his successors have continue to explore and exploit.

The problem of nature as repository of mythic value was engaged by most of the American modernist poets at one time or another. H.D. was more benign than Pound in her attempt to re-invest the natural world with the sacred qualities of her beloved Greeks, but the path she forged was narrow and by her own characterization, hermetic—though her influence on Robert Duncan and, through him, a visionary tradition in postwar American pastoral cannot be underestimated (more, much more, on Duncan below). Marianne Moore's poems engage playfully and prankfully with the animal world, layering precise observations within the witty constraints of syllabic verse, but those she influenced were less radical. Gertrude Stein's writing often flirts with pastoral tropes (the abstracted French countryside of *Stanzas in Meditation,* or the eroticized domestic interiors of *Tender Buttons*) in language that manages to be at once deliberately impoverished and ceaselessly elaborative. We must also not neglect the influence of Wallace Stevens, who, particularly in the poems of *Harmonium,* characteristically juxtaposes a deliberately ascetic, anti-Romantic vision of the natural world ("One must have a mind of winter") with a lush, intoxicated, aestheticized, manifestly artificial diction in pursuit of what we might call the skeptical paganism of a poem like "Sunday Morning":

> Supple and turbulent, a ring of men
> Shall chant in orgy on a summer morn
> Their boisterous devotion to the sun,
> Not as a god, but as a god might be,
> Naked among them, like a savage source.

The so-called "Objectivist" poets—among whom we include George Oppen, William Carlos Williams, Louis Zukofsky, and Lorine Niedecker—are significant practitioners of a late modernist pastoral.

Following Pound, they are responsible for opening the field of the poem to research and the document, integral to later practices of poetic postmodernism and ecopoetics. Williams is perhaps best known for the variations he rung on pastoral in *Spring and All*: the anti-pastoral of "The pure products of America / go crazy," the *ars pastora* of "The Farmer," the elliptical pastoral of "The Red Wheelbarrow." His long poem *Paterson* might well be described as a pastoral epic or even a pastoral elegy writ large, as the figure of the title personage sprawls across the New Jersey landscape that Williams portrays as much through the collaged inclusion of ethnographic reports, newspaper articles, and private letters as he does through lyric evocations of picnickers and waterfalls. Louis Zukofsky, though a quintessential poet of New York (and not just any New York, but the New York of Jewish immigrants on the Lower East Side—a locale much closer to Jacob Riis' images of tenement squalor than the wide-open spaces typical of North American pastoral), nevertheless resorted often to pastoral images and ideas. *"A"*, his "poem of a life," devotes much of its length to the development of an idealized domestic pastoral centering on himself, his wife Celia, and his son Paul, while one of its late sections, "A"-22, is a kind of Mallarmean natural history. His last work, *80 Flowers*, reads as an attempt to permit language itself to bloom spontaneously through the intensive collage of homonyms, puns, citations, and fragmentary references to the "flowers" that each poem imitates in its mode of becoming, laying the groundwork for the mode that G.C. and I labeled "textual ecologies" in our anthology.

Of all the poets associated with the Objectivists, Lorine Niedecker's work is the most consistently pastoral in its subject matter, yet recognizable late modernist in its collage of geological, historical, and personal details, creating a portrait of the artist inseparable from a portrait of the rural Wisconsin landscape in which she lived. Living and writing for decades on Black Hawk Island in Wisconsin, Niedecker adapted Zukofsky's emphasis on "sincerity and objectification" and "the clear physical eye" for her own life and physical environment. One of Niedecker's best-known longer poems, "Lake Superior," is emblematic of her practice in its fluid combination of lyricism and research. It distills more than three hundred pages of notes into just five pages, compressing its extensive range of reference into intensive packets of short lyrics. The career of seventeenth-century French explorer Pierre-Esprit Radisson, who discovered Hudson's Bay, is encapsulated in six lines:

> Radisson:
> "a laborinth of pleasure"
> this world of the Lake
> Long hair, long gun
> Fingernails pulled out
> by Mohawks

Niedecker referred to her own "Poet's work" as "this condensery," a play on Ezra Pound's famous equation DICHTEN = CONDENSARE: a condensery is a factory for manufacturing condensed or evaporated milk, the sort of business Niedecker the Wisconsinite had an intimate familiarity with. This combination of high modernism with more homely and local concerns is emblematic of Niedecker's practice and of a historicized version of pastoral committed to negotiating with everyday activities and landscapes. Her poems are an intensive collage of natural phenomena, the personal, and what she called "the real world of history, wars, depressions, art and science." She is a major practitioner of what I call *ecolage,* a neologism intended to bring the terms "collage" and "bricolage"—the most characteristic and significant techniques of twentieth-century art, the latter with an emphasis on improvisation and *détournement*—into contact with a concern for ecology and environment. (There is an inherent and useful tension between the frame-breaking logic of collage and the supposed integrity of the *oikos,* the "home" that ecology seeks to study and economy to manage.) Niedecker's ecolage comes close to realizing the promise of what Olson called "page as field" writing: the poem as environment, in a complex, more-than-descriptive relation to actual places, ecotones, habitats, and histories that does not erase the tensions between those varying discourses and their normative contexts.

But the pastoral spirit is hardly the possession of any one movement or group. Even as the "Objectivists"—Niedecker aside—pursued their largely urban and suburban poetics of the object, the postwar poets associated with the Beats, the San Francisco Renaissance, and Black Mountain College were in diverging ways bringing the techniques and preoccupations of an emerging postmodernism to bear on pastoral themes. I will single out a few crucial figures from each movement to evaluate their impact and persistence in the postmodern pastoral poetry being written today.

The career of Gary Snyder towers like a colossus over the landscape of twentieth-century American writing concerned with ecology and nature. His stature as an environmental activist and the popularity of his writing over decades may have served to obscure how innovative his poetry can be, and how deeply, formatively engaged it is with the historical and ecological conditions of the post-1945 world. Snyder's influential early poems may appear to offer naive portrayals of unmediated oneness between humans and nature; but as Nick Selby has argued in his essay "Poem as Work-Place: Gary Snyder's Ecological Poetics," even an apparently straightforward nature poem like "Mid-August at Sourdough Mountain Lookout" from Snyder's first book, *Riprap* (1959) demonstrates an almost Creeley-esque anxiety regarding the necessary mediation of nature through language. The poem documents Snyder's work as a lookout watching for wildfires—an eminently pastoral, shepherd-like form of work that blurs labor and leisure in the act of looking.

> Down valley a smoke haze
> Three days heat, after five days rain
> Pitch glows on the fir-cones
> Across rocks and meadows
> Swarms of new flies.
>
> I cannot remember things I once read
> A few friends, but they are in cities.
> Drinking cold snow-water from a tin cup

The Transcendental Circuit

Looking down for miles
Through high still air.

In its brevity, apparent clarity, and meditative tone, the poem seems almost to bypass Imagism, Objectivism, and other -isms, instead harking back to the Chinese nature poems and Japanese haiku fundamental to Snyder's poetics. Snyder himself writes of these models that they do "the work of seeing the world without any prism of language, and bring that seeing into language." But there is a complexly pastoral dialectic operating between the poem's two stanzas: the first, which registers the presence of the landscape and the speaker's work, as fire lookout, of interpreting that landscape; and the second, which introduces the "I" as remote and alienated from culture ("things I once read") and civilization ("A few friends, but they are in cities"). Crucially, this "I" is also remote from the landscape he reads for signs of fire; he is "Looking down for miles / Through high still air" and as Selby remarks, "Clear as this air may seem, it is still a medium through which the landscape must be read."

From his earliest poems, therefore, Snyder demonstrates a consciousness of the slippage (what Selby calls "anxiety") between word and world that characterizes a postmodern writer's approach to nature, though he is often mistaken for the sort of naive nature writer that the larger literary world responds to with piety at best and condescension at worst. (In a 2005 interview in Jonathan Skinner's invaluable journal *ecopoetics*, Snyder remarks that his book *Danger on Peaks*, which combines restless formal experimentation with highly charged political speech, was dismissed by critics as "another nature book about nature.") Snyder has spoken out in his essay, "Is Nature Real?" against "high-paid intellectuals trying to knock nature and trying to knock the people who value nature and still come out smelling smart and progressive," warning that the notion of nature as "social construction" risks re-inscribing the Western Enlightenment view of nature as a resource requiring human administration: "Deconstruction without compassion is self-aggrandizement." Nature is really *there*, Snyder reminds us: "Wild is the process that surrounds us all, self-organizing nature: creating plant-zones, humans and their societies, all ultimately resilient beyond our wildest imagination." His vision of wilderness is discursive without being entirely reducible to discourse, and even as discourse it is not reducible to a single interpretation, a single narrative. The wild, for Snyder, includes and penetrates the human mind and human body, as he writes in another essay, "The Etiquette of Freedom": "There are more things in mind, in the imagination, than 'you' can keep track of—thoughts, memories, images, angers, delights, rise unbidden. The depths of mind, the unconscious, are our inner wilderness areas.... The conscious agenda-planning ego occupies a very tiny territory, a little cubicle somewhere near the gate."

Two of the more significant poets for the lineage of American pastoral to emerge from the San Francisco Renaissance, Robert Duncan and his protégé Ronald Johnson, are often committed to exploring what Snyder calls "inner wilderness areas," albeit with different tools and with a far greater emphasis on the "inner." Duncan, like Pound, invests his natural imagery with mythic significance, re-enchanting the world as it appears or disappears into his characteristically episodic or series-structured poems of esoteric knowledge. Unlike Pound, the mythic references of this self-consciously "derivative" poet function, as Michael Davidson has written, "not as privileged signs of cultural order ... nor as allusions but as generative elements in the composing process." For Duncan, as mid-twentieth-century recuperator of the rhetoric of late Romanticism and the ambition of the modernists, pastoral manifests in its highest and most idealizing mode. But that idealization is rarely simple. Consider for example one of his most famous shorter poems, "Often I Am Permitted to Return to a Meadow." As Peter O'Leary has written of the poem's eponymous meadow, "it's an ambiguous place, neither made up by the mind ('as if it were a scene made up') nor belonging to the poet, but an actual 'made place' that he claims as his own." For O'Leary, the meadow is primarily "an apocalyptic battlefield" of the spirit; but I would argue that the poem consciously creates, exploits, and depends upon the tension between the pastoral associations of the word *meadow* and the monumental or epic "architectures" and warlike "hosts" of the poem's mythic "Lady" for its full effect. The poem's conclusion suspends the meadow between its pastoral associations and its role for Duncan as the site of mystical initiation and danger:

> Often I am permitted to return to a meadow
> as if it were a given property of the mind
> that certain bounds hold against chaos
>
> that is a place of first permission,
> everlasting omen of what is.

The meadow acts *as if* it were a "property of the mind" but by those words is implicitly both more and less than this: real meadow, ideal meadow, meadow of revelation. The "that" of the penultimate line, a pronoun referring back to the meadow, implies that it is only this ambivalent and manifold meadow (epic, idyllic, actual) that can be "a place of first permission" and an omen—a sign, a foretelling—of being. The prophetic pressure that Duncan puts on the pastoral is a mark of his commitment to a Romanticism that operates nevertheless under postmodern conditions, though by doing so it risks losing contact with a recognizable natural world altogether.

Ronald Johnson's increasingly influential poetry is more concerned than Duncan's with bringing the observed and particular phenomena of the actual natural world into his poems, while at the same time following Duncan into realms of ecstatic and transcendental knowledge. Like Duncan's, Johnson's poetry takes the form of a generative mosaic of "everyday fragments of phrase, words plucked out of context, trouvailles to be worked and knitted and sawn or welded in." His models include not just Pound, Duncan, and the Objectivists, but also naïve artists like Simon Rodia, the creator of the Watts Towers (an image of which graces the cover of the Living Batch Press edition of Johnson's masterwork, *ARK*), who constructed visionary "gardens of revelation" (the phrase is John Beardsley's) out of bottle caps, broken glass, wire, and other fundamentally unvalued materials to achieve what Johnson wonderfully terms "scrapture."

Johnson's own visionary gardens often take the form of concrete poetry, as in this poem from his 1970 sequence "Songs of the Earth":

> earthearthearth
> earthearthearth
> earthearthearth
> earthearthearth
> earthearthearth
> earthearthearth

In this deceptively simple poem, an entire chorus of words pulses in and around the central word *earth: hearth, heart, hear, ear, art, the, he,* as well as fleeting combinations and homophones formed by the eye: *hearth he, earthy, ear the art, hear the heart.* The visual play instigated by the form transforms the apparently solid block made from a single word into a highly compressed and intensive collage. Johnson's *ARK* can itself be conceived as a concrete poem on a much larger scale, its construction structured by architectural metaphors (its three major sections are "The Foundations," "The Spires," and "The Arches"). At the same time *ARK* is "a garden of the brain," a "made place" in Duncan's phrase, that marks for Johnson the location of the human body as sharer and perceiver of nature. For Johnson, the brain, the eye, and the sun are all points on a great chain of perceiving and being, so that he seeks to efface the difference between physical vision and the visionary, or rather to mark that transition, that boundary, as the territory proper to poetic language: "A is the fulcrum, I, the lever (eye). Out if it ray these three: L F E – single, double, triple vision: L I F E."

The poetic neighbors of Duncan and the San Francisco Renaissance poets are the Black Mountain Poets, closely associated with the experimental college in rural North Carolina that gave them their name. Founded in 1933 by the innovative American educator John Andrew Rice, from his stewardship it passed into the hands of artists Josef and Anni Albers before Charles Olson, who had taught there occasionally, became rector in 1951. Financial woes led to the college's shuttering in 1957, but not before it had been a utopian gathering place for a who's who of innovative American artists and writers, including Merce Cunningham, Willem DeKooning, Robert Creeley, Ben Shahn, Robert Motherwell, Franz Kline, Buckminster Fuller, and many others. The college was a self-consciously Arcadian institution, where writers and artists at odds with the repressive atmosphere of the 1950s could explore alternative means of expression (in their personal lives as well as in art). The college was also an experiment in agricultural self-sufficiency, with students and faculty alike doing the manual labor required to keep the facility going. At best modest success was achieved in this regard, but this utopian-agrarian dimension remained a signal part of the college's self-image and legacy.

Olson, the official or unofficial "boss poet" of Black Mountain, has perhaps done the most to integrate the collage tradition of Pound with a concern for the local, place, and the environment: *The Maximus Poems,* like Williams's *Paterson,* could well be described as a pastoral epic that attempts to integrate the particular and specific history of a town (in Olson's case the fishing village of Gloucester, Massachusetts) with world history and prehistory. But just as significant for some of the more radical strains of late modernist pastoral is the work of another writer associated with Black Mountain, the poet and composer John Cage. You will find little nature imagery per se in Cage's music or writing. Rather, Cage's work offers a kind of ecological *via negativa,* through an ethics and aesthetics of subtraction that leaves readers and listeners acutely conscious of their immediate environment (a state we might call "environ-mentality"): the sound, in *4'33",* of no music being played instead discloses the wilderness of the mind (what does the listener expect?) and of the concert space itself (seemingly silent but really filled to the point of cacophony with creaks, coughs, nervous laughter, and what recording engineers call "room tone"). Like Gary Snyder, Cage was deeply influenced by Buddhist philosophy and thought, and pieces like *4'33"* and texts like "Lecture on Nothing" are intended to be "a means   of experiencing   nothing." Put another way, Cage's is a pastoral of abstraction, that is nonetheless in his work connected to an active consciousness of and concern for the environment as something inseparable from humans, that requires, as Joan Retallack remarks, "silencing the ego so that the rest of the world has a chance to enter the ego's own experience."

While few (though a notable few) have followed in the visionary tradition of Duncan and Johnson, and others have assembled a documentary ecopoetics that owes much to Pound, Olson, and the Objectivists, the most influential figure for a properly postmodern pastoral, as for postmodern lyric generally, has to be John Ashbery. Hardly a nature poet, closely associated with (yet unconfined by) the urban poetics of the New York School, claimed by avant-garde and establishment alike, Ashbery nevertheless consistently engages the division of word and world fundamental to postmodern pastoral in a manner that has proven to be highly generative and suggestive.

The ego is not so much silenced in Ashbery's work as it is rendered multiple and fragmentary; the poet Evelyn Reilly has described his poetry as representing "the inner polyphony of ordinary consciousness." Ashbery presents the reader with the constant chatter of a mediated world meeting an equally mediated self, endlessly deferring and teasing the false pastoral of authenticity. Consider for example this excerpt from his well-known poem "Into the Dusk-Charged Air" from the 1984 book *Rivers and Mountains*:

> If the Rio Negro
> Could abandon its song, and the Magdalena
> The jungle flowers, the Tagus
> Would still flow serenely, and the Ohio
> Abrade its slate banks. The tan Euphrates would
> Sidle silently across the world. The Yukon
> Was choked with ice, but the Susquehanna still pushed
> Bravely along. The Dee caught the day's last flares
> Like the Pilcomayo's carrion rose.
> The Peace offered eternal fragrance
> Perhaps, but the Mackenzie churned livid mud
> Like tan chalk-marks. Near where
> The Brahmaputra slapped swollen dikes

Was an opening through which the Limmat
Could have trickled.

The rule of the subjunctive over this passage ("if," "Perhaps," "could") and the ironic play of the poem's constraint (nearly every line includes a river's name) belies the gesture of its pastoral descriptions: like Duncan's meadow, these are and are not real rivers in restless motion. As Angus Fletcher has written in his magisterial study *A New Theory for American Poetry: Democracy, the Environment, and the Future of Imagination*, "With Ashbery the typical lyric uses its being written down, its textuality, to carry the reader away from the focused materials into a flux whereby those materials are processed." Ashbery's mediating "flux," like the rivers of his poem, propels pastoral away from the static "middle landscape" described by Leo Marx and into the dynamism of postmodernism at its most robust and regenerative. The point is less the conjuring of an ideal landscape than involving the reader in the flux between word and image, foreground and background—to conjure, in short, a specifically poetic environment or "environment-poem": "these environment-poems aspire to surround the reader, such that to read them is to have an experience much like suddenly recognizing that one actually has an environment, instead of not perceiving the surround at all."

A genuinely postmodern pastoral poem such as Ashbery's, therefore, turns the refuge of the "middle landscape" into an experience of the liminal, presenting a marginal representation of "nature" that threatens continually to collapse into the cacophonous mainstream of cultural discourse. Such poems are perhaps more to be encountered, in the manner of art installations, than read. But the emerging tradition of postmodern pastoral asks more of its readers than merely surfing the zeitgeist. It demands distinction, recognition, and criticism of the pastoral boundary between word and image, city and country, culture and nature. Most radically, it demands what Timothy Morton, in tune with ecopolitical theorist Bruno Latour, might call the end of nature itself as a category of thought. Nature, along with the older, ideological modes of pastoral, must give way to politics: a new "Constitution," in Latour's view, that recognizes both human and nonhuman entities as deserving and requiring voice and representation, so that the poetry of the earth might give way to a poetry of a radically inclusive and democratic world.

Something of this is suggested by the progress of Ashbery's *Flow Chart*, a book-length poem whose title suggests that the poem is intended to function as a kind of decision-making technology (a closely related device has a name that's highly suggestive for our purposes: *decision tree*). Of course all decisions as to the poem's meaning are left to readers confronted by dizzying ramifications of syntax, ambiguously proliferating pronouns, and sudden shifts in topic and mood; "The remarkably long lines just keep rolling in one after another, nonchalantly bringing more litter onto the shore," writes Evelyn Reilly, and this requires of the reader "a kind of reading more like drifting than swimming." Though not overtly a "nature" poem, *Flow Chart* resorts recurringly to images of the natural world, particularly images of water, while constantly undercutting their mimesis, producing a simulacrum of the old Romantic relation between poetic word and natural object: "poetry scarcely drips from vines" while "The breeze that always nurtures us (no matter how dry, how filled with complaints about time and the weather the air) pointed out a way that diverged from the true way without negating it, to arrive at the same results by different spells." The reader dwells in the poem, or more likely in and out of it: one of the not-insignificant characteristics of an ambient poetry like Ashbery's has to be in the way it resists constant and focused attention but constantly repels the reader out and away from the page up into his or her own thoughts and perceptions, even as its murmurous flux or flow invites the reader back in again to continue the journey. And if the reader cannot choose, any more than Pound could, to make it cohere, there is nevertheless a mood, an elegiac atmosphere (the poem was written in the aftermath of Ashbery's mother's death and so constitutes a form of pastoral elegy), that circles back again and again to the circumstances which give rise to poetry itself:

> Any day now you must start to dwell in it,
> the poetry, and for this, grave preparations must be made, the
> >walks of sand
> raked, the rubble wall picked clean of dead vine stems, but what
> if poetry were something else entirely, not this purple weather
> with the eye of a god attached, that sees
> inward and outward? What if it were only a small, other way of
> >living,
> like being in the wind? or letting the various settling sounds we
> >hear now
> rest and record the effort any creature has put forth to summon its
> >spirits for a moment and then
> fall silent, hoping that enough has happened?

Nature and the poem are equally inauthentic and equally inescapable—as inescapable as the social-historical world that the poem's "creature," "hoping that enough has happened," must return to from the momentary stay of the poem's pastoral landscape (or flowscape). When the reader is returned, once again, to herself, she may find herself newly attuned to that relationship, dis- or re-oriented from the environment-poem to the poetic ecology in which poems and plants and people are participants—a diverse collective and assemblage, far from the fantasies of transcendent wholeness that characterize traditional pastoral. This poetry, instead, manifests as "a small, other way of living." In this manner postmodern pastoral attunes its readers to the possibility of what Bruno Latour calls "the Republic," a raucous democracy of human and non-human beings, in which ecology is indistinguishable from politics.

> Ontology is the luxury of the landed. Let's pretend you had a land. Then you "lost" it. Now fondly describe it. That is pastoral. Consider your homeland, like all utopias, obsolete. Your rhetoric points to frightened obsolescence.... What if for your new suit you chose to parade obsolescence? Make a parallel nation, an anagram of the land. Annex liberty, absorb her, and recode her.
>
> —Lisa Robertson, from "How Pastoral: A Manifesto"

The proto-politics of postmodern pastoral cannot be separated from the history and subject positions of its practitioners. To fully grasp its possibilities, we must also be conscious of feminist pastorals, queer pastorals, black pastorals. Even the Canadian poets in this anthology are positioned by virtue of their marginality to American empire as outsiders, attentive to the ways in which their geography and history have conditioned their sense of what nature is and does. The Canadian poet D.G. Jones has said, in an interview with Philip Lanthier: "Most of us in English Canada tend to see ourselves in terms of land and space while for a long time French Canadians saw themselves in terms of language, word, realities represented by symbols or signs." That division usefully repeats, with a difference, the division that the poets of this anthology are keenly conscious of: the pastoral of "land and space" versus what we might call Language pastoral (or "textual ecologies). It then reframes that division in explicitly political terms, fundamental to the problematic project of poetic "nation-making."

Lisa Robertson has given sustained attention to the pastoral-utopian genre and its vexed relation to questions of politics and gender. In the prologue to her first book, Xeclogue, titled "How Pastoral: A Manifesto," Robertson challenges the "obsolete" genre that a significant portion of her career, as poet and chief representative of the Vancouver-based "Office for Soft Architecture," has been dedicated to "recoding": "I'd call pastoral the nation-making genre: within a hothouse language we force the myth of the Land to act as both political resource and mystic origin." "I needed a genre for the times that I go phantom": Robertson's writing becomes the ghost in the machine of pastoral, de-hypostasizing feminized abstractions like "Land" and "Liberty" so that they are restored to the always political possibilities of a female subject's desire.

Queerness and the urban are as closely linked as the former is to "the unnatural" in right-wing ideology; it therefore follows that the paradoxical subgenre of urban pastoral should, for this anthology, be nearly inseparable from a queer or camp sensibility. The poetry of Frank O'Hara is once again exemplary in this regard: his "personal poems" reimagine the streets of Manhattan and the *otium* of the lunch hour as pastoral cruising ground, turning almost everything he sees into an object of delight for the desiring eye:

> It's my lunch hour, so I go
> for a walk among the hum-colored
> cabs. First, down the sidewalk
> where laborers feed their dirty
> glistening torsos sandwiches
> and Coca-Cola, with yellow helmets
> on. They protect them from falling
> bricks, I guess. Then onto the
> avenue where skirts are flipping
> above heels and blow up over
> grates. The sun is hot, but the
> cabs stir up the air. I look
> at bargains in wristwatches. There
> are cats playing in sawdust.

"A Step Away From Them" is a nearly classical pastoral elegy, in which the poet passes from the delights of the flesh and fields (or in this case, the beauty and warmth of "Puerto / Ricans on the avenue") to a search for consolation in the face of death: "First / Bunny died, then John Latouche, / then Jackson Pollock. But is the / earth as full as life was full, of them?" With a seemingly effortless recall of the landscape of same-sex desire evoked by Virgil's *Eclogues,* O'Hara in his poetry acts as a shepherd-flaneur, and turns New York into a garden of self-fashioning: "My heart is in my / pocket, it is Poems by Pierre Reverdy."

O'Hara's compatriots John Ashbery and James Schuyler have their own means of queering the pastoral. If O'Hara seems intent on making same-sex desire seem beautiful and "natural," Ashbery as we have seen is bent toward sublimity and the anxious jouissance of indeterminate subjects and syntaxes, so that the reader is asked to navigate his indeterminate environment of flows. Schuyler's queer pastoral manifests principally through his painterly details and beautifully modulated, occasionally campy tone, which can turn on a dime from archness to abjection. At the same time, like Ashbery, his finest poems skate on the distinction between word and world, so that descriptions of natural objects are never just "natural":

> *if the touch-me-nots*
>   *are not in bloom*
>   *neither are the chrysanthemums*
> the bales of pink cotton candy
> in the slanting light
>   are ornamental cherry trees.
>   The greens around them, and
>   the browns, the grays, are the park.
> It's. Hmm. No.
>   Their scallop shell of quiet
>   is the S.S. *United States*.
>   It is not so quiet and they
>   are a medium-size couple who
>   when they fold each other up
>   well, thrill. That's their story.

The object of attention in the poem, the "It," slips and slides, enabling a paratactic blurring of the distinction between metaphor and metonymy, even as the genders of the erotically enfolded "medium-size couple" are left indeterminate. "That's their story": the shagginess of the poem's narrative is the whole point story, by which the *locus amoenus* of Schuyler's pastoral attracts erotic possibilities of combination to itself.

Another major version of outsider pastoral to consider is Black pastoral, a field made more visible by Camille Dungy's anthology *Black Nature: Four Centuries of African American Nature Poetry*. African Americans have an especially complex and fraught relation to a Southern pastoral tradition in which black slaves were just another part of the scenery when they were visible at all, their forced labor underwriting a white plantation lifestyle that has loomed large in the

American imagination. Even more sinister is the close association between pastoral fantasies of a "pure," "authentic" American landscape and lynching, as depicted by the song "Strange Fruit," (originally a poem by the white Marxist songwriter Abel Meeropol), sung so memorably by Billie Holiday:

> Pastoral scene of the gallant South,
> The bulging eyes and the twisted mouth,
> Scent of magnolias, sweet and fresh,
> Then the sudden smell of burning flesh.

Richard Wright wrote searingly of the troubled, subservient relation Blacks have had to the American landscape in his book *12 Million Black Voices*:

> To paint the picture of how we live on the tobacco, cane, rice, cotton plantations is to compete with mighty artists: the movies, the radio, the newspapers, the magazines, and even the Church. They have painted one picture: idyllic, romantic; but we live another; full of fear of the Lords of the Land, bowing and grinning when we meet white faces, toiling from sun to sun, living in unpainted wooden shacks that sit casually and insecurely upon the red clay.

The Great Migration of the early twentieth century from the South to northern cities did much to seal the common association made today between Black people and the "urban"; many Black writers have understandably worked hard against the tendency to see Blacks as "closer to nature"—that is, as objects to be subdued and dominated. As Dungy's anthology shows there is a rich, varied, and often critical relation between African Americans and nature poetry, with a history ranging back to Phyills Wheatley, the first Black American to publish her poetry. Many Black poets in the pastoral mode understand "nature" both as the real, non-human world and as a complex social discourse that they are called upon to interrogate and revise. As C.S. Giscombe has written, "I tend to 'read' cities and locations as though they were poems—ambiguous, contradictory, riddled with echoes of other poems and other places.... How might *all* a town's populations work their way into the big poem, the epic, of a particular location?" His book *Prairie Style* demonstrates Giscombe's attempt to "read" (or to borrow Jed Rasula's neologism, *wread*) his native Midwest as the complex collectivity of racial, natural, economic, and literary histories that it is.

Perhaps most strikingly marginal to traditional pastoral—and therefore, most central to a postmodern pastoral committed to blurring and blending the ideological boundary between nature and culture— is what we might call the pastoral of excess, of the sublime or the grotesque. Traditional pastoral poems are fundamentally Apollonian, even Cartesian; the landscapes they conjure may be tame or rugged, but they are either beautiful in themselves or else function as pressure release valves, sites of difference from civilization and its discontents. Such pastorals refresh, recuperate, return their readers to a fantasy of authenticity, and naturalize (or neuter) desires that otherwise resist social usefulness. Even Thoreau's paeans to "wildness" fall under this traditional pastoral logic: his cry "in Wildness is the preservation of the world" in "Walking" is fundamentally progressive, and he quotes without irony the idealist philosopher George Berkeley's line, "Westward the star of empire takes its way." Elsewhere in that essay he writes, "I think that the farmer displaces the Indian even because he redeems the meadow, and so makes himself stronger and in some respects more natural." Even the most visionary of writers—and Thoreau was certainly a visionary— cannot escape the conditions of their time.

Counter to this tendency would be a Dionysian pastoral of excess and expenditure, a direct challenge to the carefully groomed boundary between culture and nature, individual and collective, policed by traditional pastoral poems. A postmodern pastoral of excess refuses even Thoreauvian notions of preservation and redemption: this is the pastoral of negative affects like the abject and incalculable ones like jouissance and the sublime. This is the zone of what Joyelle McSweeney has brilliantly termed *necropastoral,* which reimagines nature poetry as a zombie genre, lurching on in spite of the manifest death of nature under postmodern conditions, leaving a trail of crumbled ideology in its wake:

A key factor of the necropastoral for me is not just the way it manifests the infectiousness, anxiety, and contagion occultly present in the hygienic borders of the classical pastoral—i.e., the most celebrity resident of Arcadia is Death—but also its activity, its networking, its paradoxical proliferation, its self-digestive activity, its eructations, its necroticness, its hunger and its hole making, which configures a burgeoning textual tissue defined by holes, a tissue thus as absent as it is present, and therefore not absent, not present—protoplasmic, spectral.

Necropastoral entangles the reader in what Timothy Morton, in *The Ecological Thought*, has described as the dark side of ecology, what he calls "the mesh": "a vast, sprawling mesh of interconnection without a definite center or edge. It is radical intimacy, coexistence with other beings, sentient and otherwise—and how can we so clearly tell the difference?" What is human, what is animal, what is dead, what is alive? Necropastoral is the limit case of pastoral, its degree zero, by which poets like McSweeney seek to de-nature and de-purify the pastoral poem, so that everywhere and nowhere becomes not *locus amoenus* but *locus solus,* the only possible place of the present, from which we must venture clear-eyed and free from nostalgia, so that pastoral becomes indistinguishable from the wilderness of now.

The Arcadia Project was published in 2012, a date that was for a time the object of much hysterical speculation regarding Mayan prophecies about the end of the world. And yet before as well as after the fact, "the world," as humanist or technological "enframing" (Martin Heidegger's *Gestell*: a way of looking or understanding that is also a demand, a challenging, domination) has already ended, is no longer possible. As Olson once remarked, "Man must rediscover the earth or leave it." Postmodern pastoral dwells in that fatal boundary between rediscovery and departure.

The pastoral dream of harmony with the environment, of rest from labor, of a return to Eden, is predicated on the fundamental alienation of human beings from the natural world. From the strife and corruption of the urban everyday, from the turmoil of the city, from the hell of modernity glimpsed by Blake as "every charter'd street" and "dark Satanic Mills"—throughout the long tradition of pastoral, poets have created visions of gardens and wildernesses to which readers might repair for refuge. But a refuge is not home. Sooner or later we must turn away from these visions, whether pastoral or anti-pastoral, and return to the compromised cities, suburbs, small towns, and rural counties where modern life actually takes place.

If pastoral has an end—in the double sense of termination and goal—it must be the end of environmentalism. The very word "environment," with its attendant hints of degradation and entropy, carries with it the notion of something we as humans and individuals might somehow separate from, stand aloof from, manipulate and defer with the Archimedean lever of technology. As well separate ourselves from death—but that of course is the hygienic dream of modernity in its most American form. As John Cage reminds us in his "Lecture on Something," "life without death is no longer life   but / only self-preservation." The inscription on the tomb in the famous painting by Poussin, attributed to death—"I too am in Arcadia"—is a statement of the pastoral's limitation, but also of its immanent promise: to return us to life, refreshed, prepared to renew the struggle, without losing sight of the fact of limitation: of self, of the body, of bioregions, of the earth itself.

Possibilities. Beyond pastoral—for Virgil as well as for us—lies the georgic: the poem of and as production in complex interrelation with nature, which sees no daylight between human life rightly lived and care for the land. In more contemporary terms we might speak of eco-economy, the theory of steady-state economics which rejects capitalism's ethos of permanent growth in favor of seeing economics as one subsystem of the larger ecosystem, whose larger goal is sustainability (in a very different sense than the buzzphrase "sustainable growth," an oxymoron with more than a touch of pastoral ideology at its core). And beyond georgic is epic, the poetry of nation-building. Might not a paradoxical "epic pastoral" become possible, in which "nation" is reimagined as a *polis* in which women and immigrants and gays and animals and plants and bioregions are all represented politically, as contenders and subjects? And might such a pastoral of "nation-making" open a path beyond the State, hold open place as a space of contention, refuse technological fixes and New Age cure-alls, re-mark and reconcile us to our woundedness, to living in history?

Beyond the comforts of pastoral, of that which subdues the excesses of wilderness and civilization, a wilder poetry is possible.

Tansy City:
Charles Olson and the Prospects for Avant-Pastoral

Pastoral is never only the poetry of the natural world: it is profoundly ideological, embedding within itself a nostalgic stance of yearning for a past as vivid as it is imaginary. In the pastoral vision, human beings inhabit a gracious "middle landscape" (the phrase comes from Leo Marx) between nature and civilization, taking the best of both while being spared their deprivations and depredations. The practices of postmodern poets, on the other hand, are oriented toward a present in flux, derived from what Andrea Huyssen calls the "technological imagination" of the modernist avant-garde, "best grasped in artistic practices such as collage, assemblage, montage, and photomontage." Postmodernism is oriented toward the cultural fragmentation characteristic of an urbanized, late-capitalist modernity, a fragmentation these poets tend to celebrate as the unwriting of oppressive, hegemonic narratives, and therefore grounds for new modes of representation. In the context of twentieth-century American poetry, the poets we are used to thinking of as pastoralists are proportionally distant from postmodernism—not only in the latter's overt preoccupation with a hyperurban, mediated reality, but in the former's rejection of avant-garde artistic technique in favor of the nineteenth-century usages of John Clare, William Wordsworth, and Henry David Thoreau. Some twentieth-century American pastoralists, such as Wendell Berry or Mary Oliver, celebrate human harmony with nature as found through working the land or simply being in the presence of animals and their habitats; others, like Robert Frost and Robinson Jeffers, still see nature as red in tooth and claw but all the more antimodern (or in Jeffers' case, antihuman) because of it, and therefore as a site of refreshment, of renewed contact with the nature within oneself. In a recent poem, Wendell Berry accuses "cause theorists and bigbangists" for tying up "ignorance with a ribbon"; science is attacked for its failure to account for value, meaning, and mystery, and the poem ends in a paean to pastoral opposition to modernity:

> Prove to me that chance did ever
> make a sycamore tree, a yellow-
> throated warbler nesting and singing
> high up among the white limbs
> and the golden leaf-light, and a man
> to love the tree, the bird, the song
> his life long, and by his love, to save
> them, so far, from all the machines.

Postmodernists, on the other hand, are suspicious of the very category of "the natural," seeing it as an ideological mask worn by power for the purpose of suppressing difference (women, homosexuals, ethnic and linguistic others) as unnatural. Frank O'Hara's satire of the reactionary ideology associated with pastoral in his prose poem "Meditations in an Emergency" may be read as emblematic of the postmodern stance toward pastoral:

> However, I have never clogged myself with the praises of
> pastoral life, nor with nostalgia for an innocent past of
> perverted acts in pastures. No. One need never leave the
> confines of New York to get all the greenery one wishes—I can't
> even enjoy a blade of grass unless I know there's a subway
> handy, or a record store or some other sign that people do not
> totally *regret* life. It is more important to affirm the
> least sincere; the clouds get enough attention as it is and
> even they continue to pass. Do they know what they're missing?
> Uh huh.

O'Hara here affirms the postmodernist stance that sees nature as simply another discourse: there is no daylight here between nature as such—the Whitmanian "blade of grass"—and the ideological uses people might make of it. O'Hara tweaks the expectations tied to pastoral poetry by reminding readers of its affiliation with non-normative sexualities (the male shepherds pining for each other in

Virgil's *Eclogues*), but in a more emphatic moment rejects the basic pastoral premise of nostalgia for a fuller state of being lived in contact with nature. Far from associating the natural world with a fuller sense of life, O'Hara insists on its emptiness unless it can be brought into the modern, cosmopolitan context of New York City, affirming through signs of urbanity "that people do not totally *regret* life." Meanwhile the passing clouds, by implication, don't "know what they're missing"; they do not participate in the erotic text of the city that O'Hara's poetry romps playfully in and around. A nature that cannot be eroticized or otherwise incorporated into his discourse is dismissed with an ironic wave of the hand.

Yet the urgency of the human-caused crisis in the natural world—the Anthropocenic fact of what Bill McKibben calls "the end of nature"—has made both the backward-looking practices of pastoral and the postmodern obsession with the social as the ultimate human horizon seem increasingly untenable. *Do* "the clouds get enough attention as it is" in an era of rampant pollution and global warming? But pastoral also has cultural implications, when read against the grain, that can transform its nostalgia into a differential utopian horizon capable of transforming and "greening" postmodern poetics. The work of Charles Olson suggests one possible pathway by which both nature and the utopian energies of the avant-garde can be restored to a formally and politically progressive "avant-pastoral."

Normative American pastoralists bring a formal dimension to their rejection of modernity that inversely corresponds to postmodernism's embrace of the age of mechanical reproduction: their poetry centers on a language that is felt to be somehow mimetic of nature and that rejects the postmodern universe of discourse in favor of a universe centered on natural phenomena, whose authenticity of presence or aura their poems seek to transmit directly to their readers.[1] The avant-

---

[1] Walter Benjamin's concept of the aura is described in "The Work of Art in the Age of Mechanical Reproduction" through reference to a pastoral image: "If, while resting on a summer afternoon, you follow with your eyes a mountain range on the horizon or a branch which casts its shadow over you, you experience the aura of those mountains, of that branch." For Benjamin, artworks differ from natural objects precisely in the degradability of their presence via their mediation through

garde techniques associated with postmodernism, which include collage, fragmentation, and intertextuality, are seen as foreign to the spirit of a poetry intended to provide the least obstructive possible mediation between human beings and nature. Wendell Berry emphatically rejects any claims that the postmodern condition might have on him when he writes, "Devotion to order that is not poetical prevents the specialization of poetry." Berry's statement implicitly rejects Derrida's infamous claim, "There is no outside the text" and instead adheres to the metaphysical pastoral that Leo Marx, a founding scholar of American pastoralism, finds in Virgil's *Eclogues*. Writing of the relation to nature implied in the first Eclogue when the shepherd Tityrus is described "teaching the woods to echo Amaryllis," Marx writes, "It is as if the consciousness of the musician shared a principle of order with the landscape and, indeed, the external universe. The echo, a recurrent device in pastoral, is another metaphor of reciprocity. It evokes that sense of relatedness between man and not-man which lends a metaphysical aspect to the mode; it is a hint of the quasi-religious experience to be developed in the romantic pastoralism of Wordsworth, Emerson, and Thoreau." The balancing "echo" puts culture and nature, subject and object, on equal terms by granting nature a human legibility. Berry declares his allegiance to a nondiscursive world whose order the poet translates through "Song ... a force opposed to specialty and to isolation. It is the testimony of the singer's inescapable relation to the world, to the human community, and also to tradition." His Virgilian pastoral insists on a mystical community or consonance between the traditional values of the poem (its rhythm, its capacity for narrative) and the traditional values of the land: a fundamentally religious idea, based on the idea that "the existence of the world is rooted in mystery and in sanctity."

---

photographs, film, and audio recordings. In the case of the reproduced art object, "a most sensitive nucleus—namely, its authenticity—is interfered with whereas no natural object is vulnerable on that score." The American sincere pastoralists seek to preserve and transmit the aura of nature, whereas postmodernists have tended, like Frank O'Hara, "to affirm the least sincere," denying authenticity to nature as though it were simply another cultural formation whose will to hegemony must be sapped and undermined.

Whether traditional formalists or free-verse writers, the writing styles of the pastoralists reflect their nostalgia not only for a precapitalist natural world but for the pre-modern poetic and discursive practices felt capable of describing that world. Both antimodern and antimodernist, the poems of these pastoralists take what Peter Bürger, in *Theory of the Avant-Garde,* calls "organic" form: "In the organic work of art, the political and moral contents the author wishes to express are necessarily subordinated to the organicity of the whole. This means that whether the author wants to or not, they become parts of the whole, to whose constitution they contribute." As an organic artwork the well-made pastoral poem seeks "to make unrecognizable the fact that is has been made; it imitates nature or a "natural" reaction to nature. However forceful the protest of an organic poem, or sincere in its desire to set up a reciprocal, "echoing" relation between culture and nature, it becomes a necessarily false image of reconciliation by virtue of its form: "The man-made organic work of art that *pretends* to be like nature projects an *image* of the reconciliation of man and nature" (my emphasis). As Bürger writes elsewhere, "To consider the work of art as an organism, or an organic totality, means to separate it from the area of normal human production and to assign to it a quasi natural status." This is "a reaction to the increasing importance of rational patterns of action" (what Berry calls "specialization") and as such contributes to the bourgeois notion of art as "a functional equivalent of the institution of religion."

Postmodern poetry, on the other hand, deploys variations on parataxis and montage that foreground the poem's artifice, so that "it no longer creates the semblance (*Schein*) of reconciliation" between the made and the unmade, between nature and culture. While Bürger cautions us that "It is fundamentally problematical to assign a fixed meaning to a procedure," he does go on to quote a remark from Adorno's *Aesthetic Theory* about anti-organic technique: "the negation of synthesis becomes a compositional principle." In such poems any pastoral images and tropes are ironized by the anti-organic context a montage creates for itself; their textuality is not permitted to dissolve into any gestures toward mimesis or authenticity. One of the effects of this is to convert nature into a function of the social, as in the Frank O'Hara passage quoted above. Postmodern poets are capable of a good deal of interesting play with the pastoral, but they rarely commit to representing nature as normative pastoralists do: the nondisursive totality of all human and non-human life. Their utopian commitments are based in the negativity of the historic European avant-gardes from which their fundamental poetic techniques are drawn, and there is no real place in a poetics of negativity for a nature that is not solely an ideological construct.

For a critic like Adorno, positive images of nature can only have bad ideological effects. As he writes in *Minima Moralia*, recalling Brecht's 1939 poem "An die Nachgeborenen" ("To Those Unborn"), "Even the blossoming tree lies the moment its bloom is seen without the shadow of terror; even the innocent 'How lovely!' becomes an excuse for an existence outrageously unlovely, and there is no beauty or consolation except in the gaze falling on horror, withstanding it, and in unalleviated consciousness of negativity holding fast to the possibility of what is better." This is the negative utopianism expressed by avant-garde form, which is inherent even in the so-called "post-avant" practices of postmodern poetry. As Frederic Jameson has argued, utopian texts refuse the representation of a utopian, reconciled reality in favor of an allegorical critique of the world as it is. This contradicts the function of the pastoral, which imagines a "return to some earlier precapitalist form" and constitutes "an appeal to a generalized and global nostalgia.... This kind of idyll or fantasy, in other words, is, unlike Utopia, precisely a representation and musters its narrative resources in order to impose the fullness of an image of a different form of life, an image the fascinated contemplation of which includes both anxiety and longing within itself."

It therefore falls to postmodern artists to turn their backs on the goal of creating images of nature that can only fascinate; instead, they must take up the tasks of "cognitive mapping" and the "disalienation" of space (fundamentally for Jameson an *urban* space). This form of representation rejects direct mimesis and works instead to "enable a situational representation on the part of the individual subject to that vaster and properly unrepresentable totality which is the ensemble of society's structures as a whole." Jameson uses the metaphor of European navigators off the African coast to explain how "cognitive mapping in the broader sense comes to require the coordination of existential data (the empirical position of the subject) with unlived, abstract conceptions of the geographic totality." Jameson then extends the metaphor of "geographic totality" to the homologous metaphor of "social totality," a gain for his Marxist theory but a catastrophic loss from an ecological perspective. The implicit claim of postmodernism, even and especially "left" postmodernism, is that the social totality is both more significant and more complex than the absolute totality that is life on earth.

We can then see that it will not be the task of avant-pastoral to attempt to present the aura of nature through mimesis; nor will it merely reduce nature to one more mode, and hardly the most important mode, of the volatilized totality discourse. Instead, the avant-pastoralist must attempt a more difficult and complex form of representation, one which situates the human subject in relation to a socio-ecological totality that cannot be presented solely through images (whether sincere or ironic) of shepherds, birds, beasts, and flowers. Ecological processes and the natural history of biomes will be crucial to avant-pastoral, as they are not to its ironic postmodern cousin; at the same time, the social cannot be separated from the ecological, especially under postmodern conditions, and it too must be taken into account. The middle landscape of pastoral becomes not a landscape to be mimetically represented but a form of textual distantiation whose ultimate goal is to present the reader with his or her real relations to a totality that can otherwise only appear as fragments: of natural imagery, of social life, of capitalist structures of accumulation. The presentation of such "reality fragments" in the context of eco-totality adapts the avant-garde technique of montage and the non-organic to the most vital remaining task of pastoral: not nostalgia for old orders and old metaphysics, but the critical rediscovery of the human relationship to the structures of a totality in crisis.

The work of Charles Olson presents us with some ideas as to what avant-pastoral might be capable of. To understand Olson's version of pastoral, it will be helpful to briefly examine that of his mentor, Ezra Pound. In the *Cantos* written before 1945 (from "A Draft of XXX Cantos" to the infamous "Italian Cantos" that immediately preceded the poet's capture by anti-Fascist Italian partisans), natural images are inseparable from the tendentiously assembled fragments of myth in which they are embedded: drawn from Greek mythology, Chinese philosophy, and Pound's own myth of the Italian Renaissance as the time of fullest human flowering. From their initial ideogrammic and isolated resonances, these fragments of natural imagery are eventually used in the construction of Pound's ultimate myth: Mussolini as *artifex,* the statesman-artist who drained the Pontine marshes and who will build the utopian "city of Dioce, whose terraces are the color of stars." Pound's poem technologizes the fragments of nature and reassembles them in service to his new myth, a massive pastoral ideogram that binds positive values to nature and rejects everything else as "Usura," "CONTRA NATURAM." Of course this project fails when Mussolini does and Pound is imprisoned as a traitor in the "death cells" of the U.S. Army's Disciplinary Training Center at Pisa. Pound's return to pastoral comes in the form of the *The Pisan Cantos* and "the dream in the peasant's bent shoulders" that is now beyond political reach. It is at this point in Pound's epic that his natural images start to take on the ironic resonance, the confrontation with negativity, that avant-pastoral demands:

>   Le paradis n'est pas artificiel
>   but spezzato apparently
> it exists only in fragments unexpected excellent sausage,
>   the smell of mint, for example

Pound's paradise is at its most authentic and least "artificiel" when it is only partially realized, subjected to the "spezzato" law of the fragment inherent in avant-garde collagist technique. The path of the fragment of nature, necessarily compromised, is the path of sanity: "When the mind swings by a grass-blade / an ant's forefoot shall save you / the clover leaf smells and tastes as its flower." A new humility, assisted in part by detailed observation of minute natural phenomena, helps Pound to grasp his situation as a tiny node in an immense totality—the operations of the government, of the Army, of the war. It also helps him to situate that totality as itself contained and dwarfed by something even larger:

> The ant's a centaur in his dragon world.
> Pull down thy vanity, it is not man
> Made courage, or made order, or made grace,
>   Pull down thy vanity, I say pull down.
> Learn of the green world what can be thy place
> In scaled invention or true artistry,
> Pull down thy vanity,
>   Paquin pull down!
> The green casque has outdone your elegance.

It is only in *The Pisan Cantos* that we find Pound taking up the practice of composition by field in the avant-pastoral sense. That is, the field of the poem, and of the page, manifests a resistance to the will toward organic form that the earlier Cantos sought and strained after, for Pound had hoped his new Fascist myth would be able to contain and therefore organicize his collage. What many have taken as Pound's lament about the failure of his poem—"I cannot make it cohere"—results from its incorporation of fragments of reality that cannot be made to conform to a singular vision of paradise (or to any "grand narrative," to invoke Lyotard). The field of the page admits fragments of nature—ants, mint, the aching bodies of Pound and his fellow prisoners—and, as Reed Way Dasenbrock suggests, such details resist assimilation into any single ideogrammic generality: "what generalities can be born from particulars like the excellence of sausage and the smell of mint? In Pisa paradise exists in fragments, and these fragments are neither obviously nor directly part of any larger definition, any abstract entity." Only after the destruction of the historical possibility of Pound's paradise can it be "now in the mind indestructible"—no longer subject to representation as an image of fascination and anxiety, but a negative space around which the elements of Pound's poem coalesce so as to orient and represent him in his new, more difficult, but less delusional relationship to reality: helpless in the grip of the "vanity" of American military power and vulnerable to the elements ("If the hoar frost grip thy tent / Thou wilt give thanks when night is spent"). The field of *The Pisan Cantos* abandons the naive mimesis of Imagism and the rhetorical, mythologizing push of the earlier *Cantos* and instead becomes an active space, co-author, participant in the literary mediation between a brutal, technologized culture and the nature that that culture strains to dominate.

Outraged by Pound's politics yet seduced by his poetry, Charles Olson sought to adapt Pound's technique to create a discursive structure capable of containing contradictory impulses and vectors that would collectively add up to a cognitive map of the postwar American space in which he finds himself: "I am making a mappemunde. It is to include my being." Incorporating huge swaths of the human and natural history of Gloucester, Massachusetts, Olson's adopted home, *The Maximus Poems* represents Olson's attempt to create a "mappemunde" guided by the principle of history or rather its Greek root *'istorin*, defined as "looking / for oneself for the evidence of / what is said." In so doing, Olson risked turning Pound's technique— and Olson himself, as "Maximus"—into a new myth as tendentious in its will toward the organic as Pound's Fascism. But *Maximus* at its best shows a way forward for an avant-pastoral capable of providing a cognitive map of a reality that is both fully postmodern—that is, a discursive totality being rewritten by capitalism—and fully implicated in the fate of nature as a presence both discursive and the horizon for all discursivity.

In his prose, Olson struggles to articulate the values of a "human universe," opposed to the modern "UNIVERSE of discourse" that he believes has alienated human beings from reality; as he puts it in his 1959 "Letter to Elaine Feinstein," "I find the contemporary substitution of society for the cosmos captive and deathly." For him, this project begins with re-orienting discourse on and in nature, particular that nature with which we are most intimate, our own bodies:

> [T]he use of a man, by himself and thus by others, lies in how he conceives his relation to nature, that force to which he owes his somewhat small existence. If he sprawl, he shall find little to sing but himself, and shall sing, nature has such paradoxical ways, by way of artificial forms outside himself. But if he stays inside himself, if he is contained within his nature as he is participant in the larger force, he will be able to listen, and his hearing through himself will give him secrets objects share.... For a man's problem, the moment he takes speech up in all its fullness, is to give his work his seriousness, a seriousness sufficient to cause the thing he makes to try to take its place alongside the things of nature.

In this excerpt from "Projective Verse," Olson articulates a relationship between nature and the "non-organic" technique of the avant-garde. The "artificial forms outside himself" that he refers to are really Bürger's "organic forms," insofar as they subordinate their components to a single, "closed" design. But the poet that "is contained within his nature," who makes his speech and therefore his body a principle of composition, will be able to achieve a poetry that is "non-organic" in Bürger's sense. The body becomes the chief principle of composition through Olson's formulation, "the HEAD, by way of the EAR, to the SYLLABLE / the HEART, by way of the BREATH, to the LINE." It becomes one of the "fragments of reality" that for Olson is necessary to oppose the impoverished consensual reality of the culture industry—"that p. poor crawling actuarial 'real'—good enough to keep banks and insurance companies, plus mediocre governments etc." The poet is part of the field of his composition, part of Olson's "objectism": "Objectisim is the getting rid of the lyrical interference of the individual as ego, of the 'subject' and his soul, that peculiar presumption by which western man has interposed himself between what he is as a creature of nature (with certain instructions to carry out) and those other creations of nature which we may, with no derogation, call objects. For man is himself an object...." Olson's

"FIELD COMPOSITION" technique is meant to break up a false, naively mimetic organicism in favor of a performative non-organicism that is more true to human existence as a node in "the larger force" of nature.

By centering language so firmly on the body, Olson introduces into language a doubleness capable of grasping both discursive and nondiscursive realities—or as he puts it in "Human Universe," "we are ourselves both the instrument of discovery and the instrument of definition." He goes on: "I mean language exactly in its double sense of discrimination (logos) and of shout (tongue)." The body is the site of what Olson calls *muthologos,* an attempted suturing of what the progress of Western civilization has dissociated: mythic-holistic and scientific-discursive ways of grasping the world. Open, non-organic, projective verse is intended to restore language's doubleness as discourse and what he calls in an essay on Melville, "the continuous," writing that man in the nineteenth century "was suddenly possessed or repossessed of a character of being, a thing among things, which I shall call his physicality. It made a re-entry of or to the universe. Reality was without interruption, and we are still in the business of finding out how all action, and thought, have to be refounded." It's crucial to understanding Olson that he does not disparage or discard "the discrete" so much as that he wants to bring the two major modes of understanding back into dialogue with each other. He attributes such a balancing act to Melville: "Melville couldn't abuse object as symbol does by depreciating it in favor of subject. Or let image lose its relational force by transferring its occurrence as allegory does. He was already aware of the complementarity of each of two pairs of how we know and present the real—image & object, and action & subject—both of which have paid off so decisively since." This closely parallels the problem Jameson poses of the gap between the experiential image and the conceptualized totality. Discursive, quantitative, theoretical knowledge does not translate into a real and immediate sense of one's place in either social totality (as the object or subject of history) or eco-totality (statistics about global warming don't lead one to *feel* global warming); in Olson's terms, such knowledge is always metaphorical and distancing because objects are made to stand for meanings other than themselves. But to sacrifice *logos,* to live entirely within "allegory," outside any sense of "relational force"—to live, in short, within the immanence of metonymic relationships between one object to the next—is to cut oneself off from critical understanding of one's situation, which is the only possibility for altering it. Only the balance can provide real knowledge and, perhaps, a counter to another idea that Olson attributes to Melville, this time in *Call Me Ishmael*: "To Melville it was not the will to be free but the will to overwhelm nature that lies at the bottom of us as individuals and a people."

The body is a pastoral site in Olson's poetry, not just as the locus of double knowledge but also as a site of resistance to the cultural formations of the emerging consumer society of the 1950s. The image of the poet's own body, often naked or otherwise vulnerable and exposed, recurs continually in *The Maximus Poems*; as Stephen Fredman writes, the poet's body "represents the naked, heroic power of recognition resident in each individual … a power that projective verse summons forth." Olson wagers that his own physicality in the poem may serve as a marker for his acceptance of the "difficulties" of embodiment, of living in and as nature:

>   Holes
> in my shoes, that's all right, my fly
> gaping, me out
> at the elbows, the blessing
>
> > that difficulties are once more

In this excerpt from "Song 3," Olson celebrates the awkward and ungainly presence of his enormous (6'7", 280-pound) body while signaling his resistance to normative American standards of consumption. In a 1951 letter to Robert Creeley quoted by George Butterick, Olson writes "Work with how it comes, don't fix—or rather DON'T BUY…. Keep dough for for wine. Movement. Beat em. Beat em by not needing them. The WAY" And in a related letter from Olson's time in Yucatan: "like I tried to say, about, *leaving* the difficulties, not removing them, by buying the improvements so readily available at the corner. You buy something all right, but what gets forgotten is, that you sell, in that moment of *buying*—you sell a whole disposition of self." Olson's "difficulties" are transformed into "blessing" because they represent a casting-off of the commodification and reification that has already, by the early 1950s, become part of the official American ideology.

The town of Gloucester serves as a similar point of reference and site of resistance. A working-class town dominated by the fishing industry, on the margins of an increasingly urbanized society, it formed the model for Olson's ideal city or "polis," even as he saw it under threat from the forces of postwar capitalism and "pejorocracy." Gloucester has the peculiar double status suggested by Olson's self-description as "an archaeologist of morning," a term redolent of his methodology, which combines a preoccupation with the deep history of the West "from Homer back" with the "projective" work of writers like Melville and D.H. Lawrence who in his view "put men forward into the post-modern." Gloucester too is both a complex historical site to be unearthed and a utopian space to be imagined and struggled for, against the tide of American postwar history in which it is all too much caught up. He portrays it as a middle landscape, flowing imperceptibly into and out of the natural world:

> And all such colors as spring is, plus
> the colors men's buildings are, the differences
> his whitenesses are,
> the tidinesses
> he uses greens for, the bricks
> he lights his city up with

Olson goes on to imagine himself, and Gloucester, as outside of the violent human history he represents in the form of Alfred the Great, "a wild boar":

> versus
> my own wrists and all my joints, versus speech's connectives,
> versus the tasks

Joshua Corey

> I obey to,
> not to a nation's,
> or at all to history,
> or to building
>
>   Flowers, like I say
>
>   And I feel that way,
>   that the likeness is to nature's
>   not to these tempestuous
>   events,
>
> that those self-acts which have no end more than their own
> are more as plums are
> than they are as Alfreds
> who so advance
> men's affairs

Here again we see Olson's body, literally articulate given the metonymical relationship he establishes between "all my joints" and "speech's connectives," committed to a task that is neither building (the task of production and labor, which he honors in the fishermen he idolizes but nevertheless stands apart from) nor political in the sense of "advanc[ing] / men's affairs." Olson's poetic "self-acts" imitate nature's presencing—Heideggerian moments of *physis*, of *Gelassenheit* in the face of the nightmare of history from which Gloucester offers provisional refuge.

For Olson, nature and natural facts are never solely metaphors to be processed, as in traditional pastoral; Olson's "flowers" bear the mark of a human history that can be traced. One of the sites of Gloucester's resistance to the globalizing energies of capital is marked for Olson by the presence of a weed, the tansy flower:

> Tansy buttons, tansy
> for my city
> Tansy for their noses

> Tansy for them,
> tansy for Gloucester to take the smell
> of all owners,
> the smell
>
> Tansy for all of us

In a note to Donald Allen, Olson writes of the herb that it had been imported inadvertantly by traders from England and Wales, and describes it stubbornly unlovely terms: "It is strong (like goldenrod) and smells almost offensive with a pineapple odor. It doesn't grow anymore at the same place but that is due to more efficient mowers, and the desire (like blacktop) to have anything smooth and of one sort or character. We therefore celebrate TANSY MORE THAN BEFORE." A kind of bastard plant, then, non-native to these shores, an immigrant like Olson's parents, a kind of anti-commodity ("tansy for Gloucester to take the smell / of all owners"), and a signifier of otherness nonetheless "natural" to Gloucester. Like nasturtium, hyssop and the other herbs and weeds prominent in *The Maximus Poems,* tansy stands at the intersection of nature and culture, just as the human body does, a natural fact that, when brought to presence, interrupts the totalizing and territorializing discourse of American capitalism. In a later poem, "Maximus, at Tyre and at Boston," Olson speaks of "we who throw down hierarchy, who say the history of weeds / is a history of man." Weedy nature infiltrates the city, a far cry from a vision of the city as a merely beautiful garden to be tilled. Instead, it suggests a space pregnant with the possibilities of pastoral negativity and reformation.

In "Letter 3," Olson apostrophizes "this rare place": "o tansy city, root city / let them not make you / as the nation is." Gloucester is a tansy city insofar as it is marked by otherness and resistance to imperial "smoothing," but it is also the "root city," the site of anchoring: it thus occupies a liminal as well as a littoral space: not only between sea and land, Old World and New World, but between nature and culture. But Olson does not choose between these opposed signifieds:

the "tansy city, root city" is an uneasy sort of middle landscape, a provisional gesture toward autonomy rather than its incarnation: "As the people of the earth are now, Gloucester / is heterogeneous, and so can know polis / not as localism, not that mu-sick." Olson may share the nostalgia typical of the fascist pastoral's longing for a homogenous center when he writes that "I am of the heterogeneous present and not of the old homogeneity of the Founders, and the West." But there is also in this statement a sober recognition of his modern situation, and perhaps even an affirmation of it.

He insists that the diverse citizens of his tansy city must not be browbeaten into any provincial "localism," even as elsewhere he celebrates Gloucester's cultural and geographical peculiarities. At the same time the citizens of Gloucester are called upon to resist "mu-sick," Olson's trope for mass culture and its embedment in monopoly capitalism: "the trick / of corporations, newspapers, slick magazines, movie houses, / the ships, even the wharves, absentee-owned." What remains is something too fragile to go by the name of polis, or citizenry: there are only "isolated person[s]," "you islands / of men and girls," temporarily unified by the poet's address to them: "I speak to any of you, not to you all, to no group, not to you as citizens / as my Tyrian might have. Polis now / is a few, is a coherence not even yet new (the island of this city / is a mainland now of who?

Gloucester is not, then, a polis in the classical sense of the word; that notion of sociality has been rendered impossible by the modern conditions of globalization already well underway by the early 1950s. "What is our polis?" Olson asks, and answers, "'the very whole world,' not 'a bit smaller than the whole damn thing'; it is 'the State,' 'The System,' the 'totality,' adding, that it is necessary 'to invert totality—to oppose it—by discovering the totality of any—every—single one of us.'" Olson's polis is a process in which separate totalities—the totality of individual experience, the totality of human life, and the totality of nature—contest and conflict with each other, without easy or false resolutions. This force field of conflicts can only be maintained without collapsing into one totality or another by the vigilance of individual perception, as rendered in perhaps the most famous phrase from Olson's epic: "polis is / eyes." He goes on to lament that "so few / have the polis / in their eye" but this is not to argue, Pound-like, for an elite and undemocratic leadership (one is reminded of Pound's description of Hitler as being "furious with perception"). He insists, "There are no hierarchies, no infinite, no such many as mass, there are only / eyes in all heads, / to be looked out of."

The fragility of Olson's polis, "no such many as mass," "a coherence not even yet new," speaks to the provisionality and fragmentation characteristic of the avant-pastoral. The Gloucester addressed by Olson is an Arcadia populated by heterogenous individuals ("my Nova Scotians, / Newfoundlanders, / Sicilianos, / Isolatos") whose capacity for resisting the "smoothness" of capitalism depends on their intimate relation with nature (the "fishermans ffield" [sic]) but even more so on their own capacities for investigation and articulation, for the recreation of *muthologos* through the practice of *'istorin*—looking for onself, a process akin to Pound's notion of the periplum. The resistance of Olson's "Isolatos" to the territorializing forces of modernity depends in large part on their own continuing deterritorialization as "islands / of men and girls." Their labor is joined to their perception: "This town / works at / dawn because / fishermen do—it makes therefore a // very different / City, a hippocampus of a / City." The hippocampus is that part of the brain devoted to spatial memory and navigation; its fishermen are what make Gloucester the privileged site of orientation, the place from which Olson can construct his mappemunde.

Olson does not entirely avoid the naive idealization of nature and simple people that characterizes pastoral; and his fetishization of the figure of the fisherman can lead him into some troubling ecological blind spots. Nor, arguably, is his intention to construct as partial a pastoral vision as he has: a will toward homogeneity and "the center" recurs again and again in both Maximus and the prose. He seeks to restore the polis as a primeval, Arcadian space populated by a few active, thinking citizens—shepherds of Being, fishers of themselves—himself chief among them. I would agree, however, with Ralph Maud, that Olson's leftist political orientation counts for something—that "socialism" is the right word for the utopia that he imagines Sumeria to have been: "a city was a coherence which, for the first time since the ice, gave man the chance to join knowledge to culture, and, with this weapon, shape dignities of economics and value sufficient to make daily life itself a dignity and a sufficiency." The desire to articulate and recover some notion of the dignity and sufficiency of daily life is at the core of Olson's utopian vision. But this impulse can and must be incompletely fulfilled by collaging a cognitive map of one's local reality while maintaining a pastoral consciousness of the limits put on that reality when it is constructed in purely social terms.

The Poetic Thing: The Challenge of Francis Ponge

Man is a curious body whose center of gravity is not in himself.
   —Francis Ponge

An oyster, a cigarette, a pebble. What do these objects have in common? Their triviality? Their discardability?

Near the beginning of her book *Vibrant Matter: A Political Ecology of Things,* Jane Bennett provides a list of the objects she discovered in a storm grate in Baltimore: a black plastic work glove, a "dense mat of oak pollen," a stick, a bottlecap, and "one unblemished dead rat." "As I encountered these items," she writes, "they shimmied back and forth between debris and thing—between, on the one hand, stuff to ignore, except insofar as it betokened human activity (the workman's efforts, the litterer's toss, the rat-poisoner's success), and, on the other hand, stuff that commanded attention in its own right, as existents in excess of their association with human meanings, habits, or projects." Bennett's book represents a serious attempt to come to grip with the excess of the existents, seemingly trivial objects that represent, from a topsy-turvy angle, the "thing-power" of particulars to move and disquiet us.

So: why Ponge, now? And why, again, *Le parti pris des choses,* which has already been translated into English by many writers and in many forms?

One answer may lie in the polyvalence of Ponge's title, which cannot be translated into English in a form that captures all of its possibilities. *Taking the Side of Things* may come closer to the literal meaning of the French, but leaves open or blank the nature of the controversy or struggle that requires side-taking in the first place. *The Nature of Things* signals Ponge's self-conscious Lucretianism ("I would like to write a kind of *De rerum natura,*" he once remarked), but does not capture the *bias* toward things, the poetic *action* on their behalf, suggested by the French title. Such an action requires an actor: though Ponge's title suggests a desire to redress the poetic balance by giving pride of place to the object rather than the subject, only a subjective actor could conceive of and execute such a project. Ponge does in fact discover a subversive and quietly Ovidian subjectivity in ordinary things, man-made (a crate, a cigarette) and otherwise (trees, a pebble)—a subjectivity matched by the perversity and willfulness of words themselves. This is a poet who has recounted his discovery of his father's *Littré*, a French dictionary of etymology, as a kind of personal creation myth, and who in his essay "My Creative Method" stresses that in his poetics that taking the side of things is "equal" (*égale*) if not equivalent to "accounting for words" (*compte tenu des mots*). I have chosen the title *Partisan of Things* as being most suggestive of the war that Ponge tries to wage against the overwhelming subjectivism of language, while echoing Ponge's wartime activity in the year of the book's publication, 1942, when he first became active in the Resistance to the German occupation of France—a resistance, arguably, to the thingification of human beings central to Nazi ideology.

The prose poems of *Le parti pris des choses* were written over the fifteen-year span leading up to World War II; the book was published in the darkest days of that conflict, when Ponge's choice to join the Resistance was a gesture of unwavering courage but also, arguably, a forlorn hope. That historical experience is inscribed in the unconscious of the book, underwriting a darkly witty new materialism offered in resistance to totalitarian ideologies, and unexpectedly relevant to our own day. Once we might have interpreted Ponge's turn to things (and his turn away from the synthesis of Freud and Marx attempted by his one-time comrades the Surrealists), as a quietist retreat from the shadows of economic collapse and the rise of Fascism. But I believe it is more accurate, and more urgent, to discover how Ponge's *petits poèmes en prose* might open readers to the possibility of a subjectivity to come, a subjectivity of the commons, that accounts for the profoundly subtle network of interaction between humans and nonhuman agents. This in turn suggests an ethics, and perhaps even a politics, centered on surrendering the notion that matter, like history, is an object inert and lifeless, simply "there" to be shaped and dominated. Still, it would be a mistake to abstract a new ideology or even a new politics from Ponge's work. Its resistance to such readings, like the resistance offered by the commonplace objects Ponge studies, is an essential part of its charm and value.

As Ponge's friend and biographer the poet Jean-Marie Gleize has observed, Ponge is always one step ahead of whatever poetic or intellectual movement seeks to claim him. In the 1930s, when most of the poems from *Le parti pris des choses* were being written, he was writing in relation to and in reaction against Surrealism, the dominant avant-garde movement of that time—the aesthetic of which is notably attentive to the automatism of people and the uncanny liveliness of things. In the 1940s and 1950s, after the publication of Jean-Paul Sartre's influential 1944 essay "Man and Things," Ponge was read as an existentialist and an absurdist in the style of Camus (with whom Ponge had a rich correspondence). In the Sixties Ponge's work was taken up as a major precedent for the object-oriented fiction of Alain Robbe-Grillet and other practitioners of the *nouveau roman*. In the Seventies and Eighties an ecological or environmental interpretation became dominant, and this is how Ponge is still read today, particularly by Americans. Only the richest and most enigmatic literary texts lend themselves so readily to such constant re-interpretation and continual re-application to contingent circumstances. This is the "news" that, as William Carlos Williams observed, is so difficult, and yet so necessary, to get from poems.

The great help, and great obstacle, in reading *Le parti pris des choses* remains Sartre. Published two years after the first appearance of Ponge's book, Sartre's essay "Man and Things" set the terms for Ponge's reception and, ultimately, his canonicity for French readers. Sartre reads Ponge as an unwitting phenemenologist, a pantheist, ultimately a humanist. Ponge's major innovation, in Sartre's view, is to treat things as if they were people and people as if they were things. "Far from there being a humanization of the pebble here," Sartre writes, "there is a de-humanization of man, reaching even as far as his feelings." But what if Sartre has it backward? Ponge's work does not de-humanize so much as it redistributes subjectivity, transferring the valence of lyricism to the thing he writes while the speaking self adopts a cool, analytic, but nevertheless *active* tone. "His contemplation is active because it dashes from things the social order that is reflected in them ... its ultimate goal is the substitution of a true human order for the social order it dismantles."

Sartre's existentialist humanism does not permit him to follow Ponge to the most radical implication of his poetics: the possibility of a new social order that includes the more-than-human. This is understandable given Sartre's sense that Ponge's central technique is the Surrealist trick of reversal, in which objects act like people and people like objects, as in the book's most overtly satirical poems: "Gymnast," "Young Mother," etc. For Ponge, "things" offer the most fundamental manifestation of otherness, and he calls upon readers to submit themselves, if only for a few moments, to their strangeness and their laws. In his 1968 book *The Truth of Poetry* Michael Hamburger claims that the speaker of Ponge's poems is no speaker at all: "The ego that carries them is fictitious, a mere carrier of language." No less, and no more fictitious, is the subjectivity that this speaker discovers in the objects he handles: it is a fiction as necessary as the supreme fiction of a Wallace Stevens, subtracting the grandiosity. What may render Ponge's 1942 collection as permanently relevant as it is permanently radical is its appeal to a subjectivity that is not restricted to human beings, but which only reveals itself through human action: our willingness to get down and dirty with the things. Or as the "Objectivist" poet Louis Zukofsky—perhaps the closest in spirit to Ponge of any American writer—once put it, a focus on "the detail, not mirage, of seeing, of thinking with the things as they exist."

In the age of global climate disruption and the lapse of our ability to separate human history from natural history—in the epoch of the Anthropocene, a term that acknowledges the human arrival on a geological scale of affairs—Ponge's text has or ought to have a new urgency and a new English-language readership. *Anthropocene* signifies the recognition that humanity has become a force with the power to radically transform (for good or, far more likely, for ill) the climate and the destiny of all living things. At such a moment it seems more necessary than ever to take the side of things, recognizing, affirming, and reckoning with the multiplicitous agencies of the nonhuman, doing all we can to shed what Ponge refers to as our "nostalgie de l'*un*" (my emphasis), a nostalgia for a singularity of meaning that occludes our vision of what another "Objectivist" poet, George Oppen, called "the meaning / Of being numerous" risking instead the vulnerability of what in another poem he calls "rising // Into what is there."

The emerging disciplines of ecopoetics and ecocriticism transform our understanding of nature writing by critiquing the pastoral Romanticism of poets such as Wordsworth, whose poems tend to reinforce a vision of nature as *for* the human, a kind of sublime vacancy to be filled by his imagination. It is instructive to compare, as other scholars have done, the difference between William Wordsworth's famous ode to the daffodils, "I Wandered Lonely as a Cloud" with his sister Dorothy's journal entry on the same subject. Whereas William's speaker is a solitary, almost-transparent eyeball that "floats on high," Dorothy's prose speaks pragmatically to the eco-social *community* in which the daffodils are located, in which they are participants and actors:

> When we were in the woods beyond Gowbarrow park we saw a few daffodils close to the water side. We fancied that the lake had floated the seeds ashore and that the little colony had so sprung up. But as we went along there were more and yet more and at last under the boughs of the trees, we saw that there was a long belt of them along the shore, about the breadth of a country turnpike road. I never saw daffodils so beautiful they grew among the mossy stones about and about them, some rested their heads upon these stones as on a pillow for weariness and the rest tossed and reeled and danced and seemed as if they verily laughed with the wind that blew upon them over the lake, they looked so gay ever glancing ever changing. This wind blew directly over the lake to them. There was here and there a little knot and a few stragglers a few yards higher up but they were so few as not to disturb the simplicity and unity and life of that one busy highway.

Both Dorothy's and William's daffodils "dance," but Dorothy's are *in situ,* distinguished from each other by differing forms of anthropomorphization: some daffodils rest "their heads upon … stones as on a pillow for weariness" while a few others are "stragglers." Dorothy encounters the daffodils actively, as part of an intervening we, whereas the speaker of William's poem is alone both in the moment of discovery and later, indoors, lying on his couch "In vacant or in pensive mood / They flash upon that inward eye / Which is the bliss of solitude." William takes things in with a contemplative eye; Dorothy's on the other hand, searches out not only the sublimity of the flowers but the practical circumstances around going to see them. Her active mode of observation scrupulously includes observations of the observer:

> Rain came on—we were wet when we reached Luffs but we called in. Luckily all was chearless and gloomy so we faced the storm—we *must* have been wet if we had waited—put on dry clothes at Dobson's. I was very kindly treated by a young woman, the Landlady looked sour but it is her way. She gave us a goodish supper. Excellent ham and potatoes. We paid 7/ when we came away. William was sitting by a bright fire when I came downstairs. He soon made his way to the Library piled up in a corner of the window. He brought out a volume of Enfield's Speaker, another miscellany, and an odd volume of Congreve's plays. We had a glass of warm rum and water. We enjoyed ourselves and wished for Mary. It rained and blew when we went to bed. N.B. Deer in Gowbarrow park like skeletons.

It is left to Dorothy's prose to account for the Wordsworthian poetical economy, noting not only the seven shillings spent on the siblings' supper but the starvation of the local deer population, a sinister and deathly correction to the daffodils' seemingly lighthearted promises of a spring that has not yet come.

Contemporary American poets preoccupied by ecology and the more-than-human world have deconstructed the nature poem even further, as my experience editing *The Arcadia Project* alongside G.C. Waldrep taught me. Some of the poets in that anthology engage and resuscitate the Romantic, Transcendentalist approach of Thoreau, Whitman, and Dickinson in a critical, self-consciously untimely manner. Some explore the "textual ecologies" that arise when modernist techniques such as collage are applied to nature writing. Others bring empirical, scientific, and political attention and terminology to specific local conditions such as a disused Montana mill or an Illinois brownfield. The last group, perhaps most radically, pursues the negative Romanticism of a "necropastoral" that shuns the elegiac tone of most contemporary nature poetry and instead embraces a corrupted, all-too-human landscape striated by social tensions and forbidden desires.

As the anthology's subtitle indicates, all of this writing falls in some fashion under the banner of *pastoral,* which I define as a fundamentally ideological, ironic, and humanist approach to the natural world. Ponge is positioned to intervene powerfully and disruptively into this pastoral context: his writing suggests a way forward, not so much through his implicit posthumanism or decentering of the human as through the complex affective framework that his poems weave between human observer (who in his pose of scientific detachment can seem weirdly thinglike) and nonhuman object (which can appear by turns playful, sorrowful, reflective, or embedded in a history that seems somehow below or beyond the human, yet not unaffected by it). Put Dorothy Wordsworth in a lab coat, add a dose of (truly French) sympathetic irony, and we begin to approach the Pongeian sensibility, in which poet, poem, and object begin to mutually create and question one another.

Consider for example a short poem of Ponge's, *Le Feu* or "Fire," in which we are told *Le feu fait un classement*: "Fire classifies. " In this poem the nonhuman object or process of fire is rendered in all its beautiful indeterminacy: fire is depicted as following its own logic, which is human and Aristotlean ("Fire classifies") yet inhuman and animal-like in its movements. The poem never loses sight of its own agency (that of *L'on* or the "We," evocative perhaps of Heidegger's *das Man,* "the They"), but this agency is limited: it can only metaphorically "compare" (*comparer*) fire's progress or "march" (cognate of the French verb *marcher*) to the movement of two comically dissimilar animals:

an amoeba and a giraffe. Fire has its own *méthode*: it does not matter whether a human laid sticks for the fire or if drought conditions have led to a forest's being ignited by lightning: either way *les masses* (with its echo of proletarian "masses") are predisposed to collapse, giving rise to the final image that renders with stunning metaphorical accuracy the animate apex of the flames: "the escaping gases light a path for a solitary rabble of butterflies." *Language* in Ponge's poetry has an uncanny agency that exceeds the human, as do the mostly ordinary objects with which that poetry preoccupies itself. Language, like the translator himself, never contemplates: it intervenes and alters its object, bringing thing and reader into a new, surprising relation.

In his care for objects Ponge anticipates the post-Heideggerian thinking of object-oriented philosophers like Graham Harman, for whom all objects have a kind of potentiality or agency through "withdrawal": no object ever presents itself in such a way that exhausts all of its possibilities, just as Ponge's fire is never simply a human artifact but has a mysterious agenda all its own. Further, there is an apocalyptic dimension to "Fire," most visible in "the methodically contaminated masses" and the beautiful but disturbing remnant-like "rabble of butterflies." Ponge's covert apocalypticism suggests that we might find what Timothy Morton calls a "hyperobject" inside every Pongean object. A hyperobject, for Morton, is an object so massively distributed in time and space that it cannot be perceived or located as ordinary objects can: his chief examples are Styrofoam, plutonium, and global climate change. Ponge's objects are rarely massive, but they are "distributed" in uncanny ways that unsettle the ordinary distinction between subject and object; they are, as Morton describes hyperobjects, "viscous" in their entanglement with the other objects, human and nonhuman, that accompany them through a reading of Ponge's work.

Bridging or transcending the gap between Harman and Morton would be the French sociologist Bruno Latour, whose actor-network theory has given rise to what he calls (with a term that has influenced Morton's "hyperobject") "quasi-objects," things neither fully natural nor fully constructed which come to occupy a hybridic and ambivalent relation between nonhuman and human, object and text. As a political theorist, Latour has proposed the concept of a "new constitution," unwriting the modern division between nature and culture, human and object, that would lead to the creation of "the parliament of things," by which the non-human attains a form of political representation (in the sense that we must consider the agency of, for example, carbon in determining the use and effects of fossil fuels). Ponge's poetry, which in its cunning literalness is founded on a desire to bring textuality closer to objectivity (but also vice-versa), has much to offer the imaginative orientation of the readers of Morton and Latour as they negotiate the latest cry to go back to the things themselves.

Yet how can we return to that with which we are always already entangled? As physicist-theorist Karen Barad writes, ours is a universe of "intra-action," a neologism that "*signifies the mutual constitution of entangled agencies.* That is, in contrast to the usual 'interaction,' which assumes that there are separate agencies that precede their interaction, the notion of intra-action recognizes that distinct agencies do not precede, but rather emerge through, their intra-action" (emphasis in original). The networks and hyperobjects that we condition in turn condition us. Ponge's poetry is alert to that possibility. He welcomes the always-already entanglement of the poet with his object and invites us to participate, since we are ourselves always already enmeshed. His longest poem in the book, "The Pebble," concludes with a wry reflection on the subjective-objective entanglement of poet and object: "Trying to write a description of stone, he became entangled and turned into a stone himself."

To be turned to stone for Ponge might not be such a terrible fate. In an interview with Serge Gavronsky, Ponge remarks that "If you try to write with the qualities of the object in mind, somewhat like a scholar, at least, with simplicity … you conceive of it as a sort of character in a novel, like the hero in a novel, and henceforward, perhaps both tough and fragile"—qualities that Ponge, in the same interview and nearly in the same breath, attributes to poetry itself. To take the side of things is to take the side of *existence*—as Ponge remarks in "Snails," "They are heroes, that is to say beings whose existence alone is a work of art—not artists who merely make masterpieces." In a sense, Ponge seeks to extract heroism from humanism. The heroism and nobility inherent in mere existence is one of Ponge's great themes; there is for him no greater honorific than *hero*, a word that this lover of dictionaries undoubtedly recalled has its roots in the Greek concept of the demigod. Ponge's Hercules or Odysseus is the earth itself, "the ancient hero that was once the real world" as he writes in what is probably the thesis text of *Partisan of Things*, "The Pebble." "Nowadays," he remarks with characteristic irony, "the dead hero is confused with the chaos of the earth." The stony earth is far from timeless, it is *time-full*: "all the forms of stone, each of which represents some state of its evolution, exist simultaneously in the world." The seeming stillness of the stone is what put us in contact with the Heraclitean constant summarized so memorably at the opening of Charles Olson's poem "The Kingfishers": "What does not change / is the will to change."

To exist in this world is to be fragile, subject to constant change; to find acceptance of that fact is an act of heroism (and a form of toughness). But this acceptance is not and can never be merely passive, merely contemplative. For Ponge, the world is something that must be made, and this happens when we give *le monde muet*, the silent world, a *voice*. As he puts it in his 1965 book *Pour un Malherbe*:

> We have to flourish, develop, produce the world around us—bathed and immersed in the silent world—that is our natural environment, our only true home; around us, through us, feeding us; we are part of it, knotted up with it … we need it as it needs us; we breathe for it as it breathes for us.

Or as he writes in "My Creative Method," poetry's function "is to nourish the spirit of man by giving him the cosmos to suckle. We have only to lower our standard of dominating nature and to raise our standard of participating in it in order to make the reconciliation take place." If our civilization, let alone individuals, truly came to understand the time-fullness of the earth and the endlessness of the ramifications of our own actions, perhaps we would charge those actions with the wisdom, the nobility, and above all the patience of the pebble.

Lucretius's phenomenological epic famously begins with an invocation to Venus, only to discard her and the other gods as nothing more than myths and metaphors that conceal the material reality of a world composed by a self-organizing cascade of atoms. Ponge's book begins with the speaker's seemingly prosaic encounter with rain falling in the backyard. Venus does not appear; and yet the phenomenon of falling rain suggests by its appearance an uncanny allusion to the "motions mixed" of Lucretius' atoms:

> The rain, in the backyard where I watch it fall, comes down at different rates. In the center a fine discontinuous curtain—or network—falls implacably and yet gently in drops that are probably quite light; a strengthless sempiternal precipitation, an intense fraction of the atmosphere at its purest. A little distance from the walls to the right and left plunk heavier drops, one by one. Here they seem about the size of grains of wheat, there the size of a pea, while elsewhere they are big as marbles.

In Ponge's French the rain is compared first to a curtain (*rideau*) and then a network (*réseau*), both of which contain the word *eau*, or water, linking them on a semantic level as well as musically; this is a move entirely typical of Ponge, whose fascination with etymologies both false and actual led him to treat French as a mobile army of metonyms, each individual word, phoneme, and letter liable at any moment to suggest lateral relations. Ponge's language is in other words always already networked, fundamentally similar to the atoms that Lucretius describes as falling through the "intense inane" of the universal void, swerving and striking one another, accumulating into new patterns of self-perceiving matter, as like recognizes like. That swerve of perception is what Lucretius names the *clinamen* or swerve:

> For were it not their wont
> Thuswise to swerve, down would they fall, each one,
> Like drops of rain, through the unbottomed void;
> And then collisions ne'er could be no blows

> Among the primal elements; and thus
> Nature would never have created aught.

For Lucretius, the spontaneous swerve of the clinamen is nature's agency, the actuality for which Venus the goddess of love is only a metaphor. The swerve brings the atoms into contact with each other, accumulating and sticking together in spontaneous acts of prehension; the clinamen is *contact*, the material analog to the love of Alma Venus "for all of living things / Through thee alone are evermore conceived." For Ponge, the image of rain as network is part of its presentation as a "brilliant apparatus" whose mechanism evokes innumerable droplike shapes—"grains of wheat," "peas," "marbles," "individually wrapped candies," "brilliant needles." "Each of its forms," Ponge writes, "has its particular allure and corresponds to a particular patter" or noise; the word *bruit*, which we have translated as "patter," can mean simply "sound" but is especially evocative of agitation, rattle, and rumor.

Rain, for Ponge, has a Lucretian capacity to manifest form out of its thinghood: this will become the throughline for most of the poems in the book, in which again and again we are presented with natural and manmade things with a will toward form. More often than not that will is expressed in terms of language; though language alone, for Ponge, does express liberatory, agential capacities. The trees of "Changing Seasons," for example, seem trapped by their own "foliation"; their leaves are presented to the reader as "words" (*paroles*), yet the trees can only say one thing; again and again they "repeat the word 'trees.'" Only the passage of time, the change of seasons itself, offers "this riposte: 'There is no escape from trees by means of trees.'" The climactic intervention of "the old taciturnity, the plundering, *Fall*" brings an end, for now, to the self-declaration of the trees; only the cyclical passage of time can facilitate an "escape" from the thingly axiom at the poem's heart.

What is it, exactly, that the trees have escaped—from what have they been liberated? It may be that Ponge seeks to demonstrate the possibilities of human language against the backdrop of what Walter Benjamin, in his 1916 essay "On Language as Such and the Language of Man," calls "thing-languages." "We are concerned here," Benjamin writes, "with nameless, nonacoustic languages, languages issuing from matter; here we should recall the material community of things in their communication." For Benjamin, "Language communicates the linguistic being of things.... The language of this lamp, for example, communicates not the lamp (for the mental being of the lamp, insofar as it is *communicable*, is by no means the lamp itself) but the language-lamp, the lamp in communication, the lamp in expression." The human being, on the other hand, speaks with words, and therefore "communicates his own mental being (insofar as it is communicable) by *naming* all other things." To hastily summarize Benjamin's complex and para-theological argument, it is the task of human language to "translate" the mute language of things, since "It is a metaphysical truth that all nature would begin to lament if it were endowed with language." Yet our language cannot resolve nature's melancholy, since in human language, unlike the language of God, things are "overnamed," overdetermined by names that deny nonhuman objects their full expressive nature. The nonhuman world is thus caught between mourning for its muteness and melancholia at the "overprecision" of human language—a more pronounced version of "the overprecision that obtains in the tragic relationship between the languages of human speakers." (We must note here that Benjamin is writing from the midst of the Great War—a war that he saw from the beginning as an unmitigated catastrophe for European thought. The "tragic relationship between the languages" was surely for Benjamin a mark of the failure of the European project of a humanity uncircumscribed by a merely national identity.)

I said that Benjamin's argument was para-theological—it is in fact explicitly dependent on the account of language in Genesis and the primal scene of Adam giving names to the animals; so as to account, if only by implication, for an unfallen language of people and of things. But the fall in Ponge is not Edenic but Lucretian. For Lucretius, the gods are at best convenient metaphors, at worst ideological cudgels that lead to war and other forms of blindness and misery. For Ponge, ideology is a dangerous surplus of either subjectivity or objectivity—

of the all-too-human and the all-too-thingly. The fall in Ponge is a Lucretian fall of atoms that in their coalescence manifest the expressive possibilities of all things.

Consider for example "Snails," a witty and extended appreciation of the "immaculate clamminess," *sangfroid*, and "stretchiness" of the titular mollusk. Ponge celebrates the snail for the purity of its self-expression, in the generation of its shell and the silvery slime on which it glides—a slime that can be expressive, in Ponge's fanciful view, of both pride and anger. Its slime, of course, is ephemeral: "That's how it is with everyone who speaks in an entirely subjective way, in verses and lines only, without taking care to build their phrases into a solid dwelling with more than two dimensions. Something more durable than themselves." Ponge the prose poet implicitly tweaks the "entirely subjective" traditions of French poetry, reducing the proud alexandrine to *traces seulment,* mere tracks, marks, or streaks. But he then turns around and praises the snails for being "heroes, that is to say beings whose existence alone is a work of art—not artists who merely make masterpieces." Ponge's use of the word héros is never only ironic, though it is never not ironic either; he was surely aware that at its Greek roots, the word signifies someone born from the union of a mortal and a god—two surpluses, we might say, of mortality and immortality, thingliness and subjective energy. Ponge sounds a Satrean note in a different key: the existence of the snail precedes its essence as work of art, as that which secretes its own form. What seems to frustrate the trees of "Changing Seasons"—speaking, as "Snails" implies, "in an entirely subjective way, in verses and lines only" becomes the self-acceptance of the lowly snails. The poem concludes with the speaker urging human beings to emulate these saintly and heroic snails:

> How are they saints? Precisely by obedience to their nature. So: know yourself. And accept yourself for what you are. In agreement with your vices. In proportion with your measure.
>
> What is most appropriate to the human being? Words. Decency. Our humanism.

Taken too far, human thingliness becomes for Ponge a form of idiocy, as when he describes the gymnast who has tried to transform himself into a mere moving body as "the most perfect paragon of idiot humanity"; it is perhaps not too much of a leap from the mindless gyrations of Ponge's gymnast to the mass choreography of the *Wehrmacht*. Instead, the lure of the objective in Ponge can be found in his expression of a Lucretian ethics, which by taking the side of things seeks not to efface the human and subjective but to put them in dialogue with what he asserts is the fundamentally linguistic modality of material things.

"Snails" concludes with a place and date: "Paris, March 21, 1936." Two days prior, the League of Nations had condemned Nazi Germany for violating the Treaty of Versailles in its remilitarization of the Rhineland, an aggressive act that signaled the beginning of what would become the inevitable advance toward World War II. Given that fact we should not mistake Ponge's praise for the self-obedience of the snail as a form of political quietism. Rather by analogy he urges his readers to follow the nature of the human by expressing themselves through "words" and "decency," or as the French has it, *la parole et la morale,* which couples the melancholy foliate "word" of the trees in "Changing Seasons" with an implicitly objective morality, summarized in the poem's concluding words as "Our humanism" (*L'humanisme*). The "escape" from "purely subjective" language must be accompanied by a decency proper to the human being if it is to create "a solid dwelling with more than two dimensions." This is the dwelling of Ponge's prose, within which his exuberant wordplay scatters words like atoms in a heroic attempt to circumvent the "overprecision" of human language. Ponge keeps faith with things—he takes their side— by keeping faith with a translation of their thing-language that, in its mobility, values their communicativity over any instrumental use to which we might put them, as thing or word. For Ponge, decency in a time of absolute inhumanity requires the rediscovery of freedom in the nature of things.

Ponge takes the side of things, but he also takes them by surprise, revealing them as creatures of subjectivity and metaphor. As a poet he is perhaps less ecological than tektological. As McKenzie Wark has observed, the time of ecology—the ideology of a harmonious and homeostatic system that once governed the earth, and to which we might return—has been permanently disrupted by the onset of the Anthropocene, "a series of metabolic rifts, where one molecule after another is extracted by labor and technique to make things for humans, but the waste products don't return so that the cycle can renew itself. The soils deplete, the seas recede, the climate alters, the gyre widens: a world on fire." In place of ecology, which for Wark is always already a pastoral, ideological, indeed theological concept, Wark proposes, in a term borrowed from the Marxist thinker Alexander Bogdanov, *tektology*. Wark defines tektology as "a practice which generalizes the act of substitution by which one thing is understood metaphorically by another." In other words, it is an intrinsically metaphorical and thus poetic practice for producing knowledge, grounded in its confrontation of twinned modes of resistance, twinned materialities: "a resistant objective world and the resistant subjectivities of politics and culture."

Ponge's poetic anticipates and furthers such a tektology, as it plays with the subjectivity of objects and the objectivity of language through an always flexible and reversible stance toward personification and metaphor. The metaphors in *Partisan of Things* are complex, layered, sometimes self-undoing; the waste material that the crate in "Crate" is fated to become (a fate, the speaker notes ironically, "upon which we will not dwell for long") is inseparable from its location "[h]alfway between *crib* and *cage*" (*mi-chemin de la cage au cachot*) in Ponge's *Littré*. It is the space in which the commodity is sheltered like an infant and an emblem of the iron cage that Max Weber discovered in the spirit of capitalism. It is perishable and endlessly reproduced; perishable *because* it is endlessly reproduced. We produce, and are produced by, the silent world of things that compose, or discompose, the human world. In *Partisan of Things* things are given a voice, and implicitly return to us the responsibility of our subjectivity. As Italo Calvino puts it, Ponge fights "a battle to force language to become the language of *things*, starting from things and returning to us changed, with all the humanity that we have invested in things." Or as Susan Harrow claims, "it is here in these passionately 'objective' texts, in the movement of consciousness through material things and the fabric of language, that subjectivity affirms itself as process." His goal is "to nourish subjectivity in exteriority," and to accomplish this requires a Rimbauldian derangement, not of the senses but of the subject-object boundary: "it is not our task to fix things (ride the merry-go-round) but to be deranged by them."

There is much talk nowadays about technologies to come, such as the so-called "Internet of things," by which ordinary objects will be connected to the Internet and made into ever-more active participants in human life: houses that can sense when they are occupied, cars that drive themselves, razors that know when their blades need replacing, cattle that can report on their own health through implanted biochips, and so on, down to nanotech drones that can report on air quality. We are giving, it seems, more and more power and agency to our things. At what point does convenience cross over into derangement, or uncanniness into the ordinary? Do we ever get off the merry-go-round of command and consumption?

Tarry a while with the things, and with Ponge, who with gentle severity and compassionate wit shows how things express us, and it is just possible that we might, with the proper attention, come to grips with the reality and the resistances of the world we have made.

II
THREE FOR DUNCAN

The Dungeon Master: Robert Duncan

It is strange to have been drawn so deeply into the work of a poet that I once found all but illegible, except for a very few poems whose rhythmic or pellucid qualities overcame for me all the occultist mumbo-jumbo, those which seemed to embrace a more socially tangible reality rather than esoteric intimations of a Theosophical/Gnostic/neo-Platonic reality. I appreciated the anthology pieces—"A Poem Beginning with a Line by Pindar," "My Mother Would Be a Falconress," "Poetry, a Natural Thing," and most especially, "Often I Am Permitted to Return to a Meadow," which moved my wife-to-be and I so much that we incorporated into our wedding ceremony. But until comparatively recently I found Duncan's embrace of the mythic and vatic embarrassing where it wasn't incomprehensible; this in spite of the fact that in my personal life, for years and years, I was deeply involved in the kind of esoteric linguistic sociality that I now recognize as central to Duncan's life and work. I refer, as my title refers, to fantasy role-playing games like Dungeons & Dragons, which were in some ways my initiation into poetry—language made strange and tangible against the numinous background of quasi-medieval worlds overdetermined by narrative. A world, not least, in which words—"I cast *magic missile* at the troll!"—were indistinguishable from actions, and in which the Dungeon Master, the role I most often assumed, created a puzzle-like world which his players were meant to live in rather than to solve.

Yet when I became enamored of modernist poetry and poetics, I thought I was saying goodbye to all that. The rich intertextuality characteristic of Eliot and Pound, and to a lesser extent of Wallace Stevens and H.D., attracted me in spite of the remnant neo-Platonism—it was the intersection of eras and texts with a sensuous sensibility, plus the sheer cussed difficulty of the texts in question, that drew me. It is not much of an exaggeration to say that I pursued a PhD because of the opportunity it offered me to wrestle with the great modernist and late-modernist epics: Pound's *Cantos,* Zukofsky's

Joshua Corey

"A", Olson's *Maximus Poems,* and Ronald Johnson's *ARK.*

None of these poems is without mythic dimension, though the myth sometimes poses as something else, like the labyrinthine Marxism winding through the early sections of "A". That mythic dimension has always raised for me the question, Bug or feature? The analogy that came to mind was *Paradise Lost*: it was not necessary, or not very much so, to understand Milton's cracked Protestant theology to appreciate the poetry, even as I understood that the theology was the poetry's ground and not vice-versa. If Blake could persuasively say that Milton had been of the devil's party without knowing it, surely I could read *The Cantos* against their neo-Platonism, just as I read them against the grain of Pound's Fascism, anti-Semitism, and the sheer tediousness of his obsession with Major Douglas's Social Credit.

In a 1989 interview with John Tranter, Michael Davidson makes a very intelligent distinction between his generation of Language poets and the concern of Duncan and other late modernists with "the numinous"—that sense that true reality was something unavailable to the senses or conventional understandings of history:

> I guess the idea of the numinous was translated in my generation into the idea of the ideological. The ideological was also something that inhabits everything, and produces things. Ideology is something that emerges in the unconscious to create, in a sense, a kind of political unconscious. And so, while the gods may be dead, but the ideology is there, and that is an informing power in poetry. And you can play with that, and you can work with that. That's the difference, I think, between Duncan's generation and ours.

This transference, to use a psychoanlaytic term, from the numinous to the ideological takes on special resonance when processed through Louis Althusser's definition of ideology as that which "represents the imaginary relationship of individuals to their real conditions of existence." Instead of the innumerable deities (Greek, Celtic, Egyptian, and so on) that populate Duncan's poems, the Language generation turns capital, history, language, and other such theoretical-institutional entities into protagonists whose reality is determined by their access to the social imagination, rather than to some transcendent realm. (Though it may also be useful at times to consider the social itself as a realm transcendental to everyday life, its existence denied by those neoliberal atheists who claim, like Margaret Thatcher, that there is no such thing as society.)

Whatever names we give to the gods, the strategy of Language poets is, according to Davidson, fundamentally isomorphic with that of Duncan: both kinds of poet are "trying to establish relationships to an economy that you can have no control over, yet negotiate with it. But negotiation is another metaphor for a kind of field process poetry, it is your ability to deal with a power that is larger than yourself." And so when confronted with mythic figures in the work of Pound or Yeats or Stevens I've worked to translate their mythic figures (whether adapted from neo-Platonism, the Celtic Twilight, etc., or else invented by the poet, Blake-style—Stevens' ironic "Canon Aspirin" comes to mind) into nodes in a larger field of force that mapped or inscribed that poet's sense of a fundamentally social totality.

Duncan, however, won't play along with this strategy; the cost of translating his mythic gods into ideological entities is too high a price to pay—you lose the poem, just as you can't play Dungeons and Dragons without following its often byzantine structure of rules. At the same time, he's wilier than he's been taken for (by the likes of Charles Olson, for instance, whose essay "Against Wisdom as Such" accuses Duncan of drinking his own mythopoetic Kool-Aid) in terms of his own stance toward myth. He didn't come to the occult like most people do, because their given gods have failed them: he was born to it, having been adopted by Theosophical parents who chose him according to his astrological chart. He had, eventually, something of the same stance toward his parents' mythological worldview as Joyce came to have to Catholicism; that is, as a narrative, a force, whose power and significance operates almost independently of one's belief in it. If anything, from a sheerly rational perspective, it appears that the more outlandish a religion's tenets are, the more unshakable its adherents seem to be.

Joyce is not a bad point of comparison with Duncan: one can read *Ulysses* as an attempt to broaden and complicate the field of poetic action available to an early twentieth-century Irishman, not by "Hellenizing" Ireland as Stephen Dedalus' frenemy Buck Mulligan wishes to do, but by squeezing Thomas Aquinas, the Spinozan musings of Leopold Bloom, the Celtic Twilight, and Homer into the same Hibernian city-space to interact with and press upon each other, no one field of numinousness more authoritative than any other. It's a little bit like Bakhtin's idea of the dialogic novel, except it's the contention of mythic systems rather than persons that matters—or you could turn that around and say it's the person-ization of myth that gives Joyce's novel its matter.

The gods are real, then, for Duncan; no one of them, however, is THE God. As he writes in *The H.D. Book,* sounding remarkably like the protagonist of the 1960s British cult TV hit, *The Prisoner,* his submission to authority or initiation in any single order would be a betrayal of his poetics:

> I have written elsewhere that I am unbaptized, uninitiated, ungraduated, unanalyzed. I had in mind that my worship belonged to no church, that my mysteries belonged to no cult, that my learning belonged to no institution, that my imagination of my self belonged to no philosophic system. My thought must be without sanction.

That absence of sanction, and sanctity, reflects Duncan's Nietzschean feel for the eternal return that leads him to construct a notion of myth by which certain eternal forces recur throughout history under different names and with different valences. When Duncan uses a word like "Christendom" he seems to define it by its repression of primordial forces in Greek myth (Eros chief among them), forces which reincarnate in the transgressive "spirit of romance" of the troubadours and in heretical notions of Christ as Eros. Romance gets born again contra the Enlightenment in the late eighteenth century, and the flame burns on for Duncan in the twentieth century, transferred in a "rite of participation" to his hands from the nearly scriptural poetry of H.D.

I see now that it's this sense of the historical in Duncan, however eccentric or esoteric, that has opened the doorway to my being able to read him in truer sympathy than I could manage in more dogmatic days. It's also a question, in my case, of maturity: I am less embarrassed now by Duncan's indulgence in "magick" because I am less embarrassed by my own taste for high rhetoric, not to mention the kitschy pleasures of D&D (reading Duncan is a little like leafing through the old *Deities & Demigods*), prog rock, tarot cards, and the other emblems of an adolesence spent searching for alternatives to an oppressive reality that did not correspond to the truth of who and what I felt I was or could be.

Duncan's mythopoetics suggests rich and unexpected possibilities for a poetic ecology that his writing, in its radical inclusiveness and shrewd troubling of the immanent/transcendent distinction, may have to offer us. Something richer, and darker, is made available to modern poetry by Duncan's Freudianism, his nigh-Lacanian sense of the Real as something obscured from any single position or vantage point, his sense of disequilibrium and parallax. In his writing, particularly the great and troubling later poems, he comes close to what Timothy Morton calls "dark ecology," a greater intensity than what more literal notions of nature writing seem capable of bringing to bear.

But this is also personally important to me, a Rubicon in my own sense of poetics. Back of my infatuation with high modernism, Language poetry, and the Frankfurt School is this older sense of reality as something occulted, and the vocation and ultimate high of poetry-as-making: world-building, cosmological, crossing barriers of time and space. To the spirit of Romance—the spirit of the cosmopolitan and supra-national— "All ages are contemporaneous," as Ezra Pound said. In a time when poetry, and literacy itself, can seem a diminished thing, the figure of Duncan raises the stakes immeasurably.

Joshua Corey

Robert Duncan's Visionary Ecology

"The drama of our time is the coming of all men into one fate, 'the dream of everyone, everywhere.' The fate or dream is the fate of more than mankind." The opening of Duncan's essay "Rites of Participation," first published in 1967–68 and eventually incorporated into his herculean project *The H.D. Book,* outlines a postmodern ecology in which "We have gone beyond the reality of the incomparable nation or race.... The incomparable species, in which identity might find its place and defend its boundaries against an alien kind" requires "the extension of our 'where' into a world ecology": " We go now to the bushman, the child or the ape, who were once considered primitive, not to read there what we once were but to read what we are." Duncan recognized that the reality of what we today call globalization requires "our identification with the process of design beyond our own figure": "To compose such a symposium of the whole, such a totality, all the old excluded orders must be included. The female, the lumpen-proletariat, the foreign; the animal and vegetative; the unconscious and the unknown; the criminal and failure—all that has been outcast and vagabond in our consideration of the figure of Man—must return to be admitted in the creation of what we are."

Duncan's fidelity to a "derivative" Romanticism in a supposedly postmodern age—his "fictive certainties," his "sense of the fabulous as an intuition of the real"—makes his contribution to an ecological poetics as untimely as it is necessary. His road to ecological consciousness demands the reader's participation in the discovery of Duncan's notion of *kosmos*: an open ontology or "ground work" that locates the *oikos* in a floating world of ramifying and endless difference. Duncan's implicitly pre-Socratic kosmos is one from which the Pythagorean self-ordering implicit in the Greek word has been subtracted; instead we have a Heraclitean flux only provisionally harmonized by the poet's incomplete and uncompleteable song, what Duncan calls "a dancing organization between personal and cosmic identity" that recognizes that "the principle of life lies in its evasion of equilibrium." Duncan pursues this principle through an idiosyncratic version of pastoral characterized by a sense of interrelatedness so open that it blurs subject and object, figure and ground, aesthetics and politics. It is a pastoral that darkens as his career progresses, from the optimistic flux of *The Opening of the Field* through the struggle to incorporate the contradictions imposed by the Vietnam War in "Passages." The late poems of his last illness bring the negativity of such blurriness into the foreground, producing a changed, charged pastoral of disease and death that brings a mortal ecology into the most intimate, wounding contact with the dissolving self.

Duncan's sense of ecology is thoroughly mediated by his challenging poetics. In a little-known essay, "Notes on Grossinger's *Solar Journal: Oecological Sections*," Duncan writes of "Darwin's poetic vision" as it centers on the infinite diversity produced by "the weaving of sexual selection—the falling in love and loving—and of natural selection—the alchemical process within the field of the Universe in which we, as thematic forms, either perish or survive."[1] By adopting the dual principles of selection as a basis for his poetics, Duncan sidesteps the normative ethics associated with nature and the natural, writing that Darwin's theory inaugurated awareness of "a poetics not of paradigms and models but of individual variations and survivals, of the mutual affinities of organic beings and the evolution of living forms, not of good and bad works but of seminal and germinal works cast abroad in the seas of the world that was a worker in the origin of species." It is what Duncan calls the "Heraklitean" openness of Darwinian evolutionary theory that appeals to him: Darwin joins Freud in Duncan's thought as a modern alchemist who succeeds in marrying science to myth. Darwin understood, if reluctantly, that evolution was an ongoing and continuous process with no goal, conclusion, or telos. That radical openness is what gives his theory what Duncan finds to be its fundamentally mythic power: "To inherit or to evolve is to enter mythic existence."

1 I am indebted to Ben Friedlander for bringing this essay to my attention and providing me with a copy of the essay, which originally appeared as a preface to Richard Grossinger's book *Solar Journal* (oecological sections), published by Black Sparrow Press in 1970.

Though not a friend of rationalism or instrumental thinking, Duncan does not separate scientific knowledge from mythic knowledge but claims it as myth's ally against dogmatic ideologies: "For the religious mind, all human experience and facts of the universe that do not conform to the strait truth are false experience, either ignorant of their own true nature or dishonest about that nature." Science, on the other hand, is "at work in the field of what it does not know, conserving all the facts of what it has come to know in the light of a picture of a total order that it may never come to know; the laws of science are creative pictures, then, imagined orders that have their truth posited in physical facts." The difference between myth and science for Duncan may only appear in the latter's insistence on "a total order"; for it is mythic knowledge, more than scientific knowledge, that is open to the possibility that all orders are "creative pictures."[2] The spirit of romance is unexpectedly compatible with ecology if we imagine the latter as a form of what Duncan calls "a gnosis of not-knowing," by which "[t]he truth we know is not of What Is, but of What Is Happening. Duncan's sense of ecology is Freudian, "haunted by some premonition of the uncertainty principle in physical measurements that our own science must face, of the uncertainty of self-knowledge in terms of our psychology and physiology, of the uncertainty of our role in life raised by information of evolution. A psyche that is not all to be lightened! a universe that is not all to be ours!" Duncan adapts the open structure of ecology and evolution to the construction of his poetics: "in the ecology of forms we begin to see, as we have held in faith, the fittingness, the tellingness of events—their truth—lies in their belonging to the evolution of forms. They cannot *not* belong.

---

2 There are obvious resonances here with the quarrel between Olson and Duncan crystallized in Olson's essay "Against Wisdom as Such," in which Olson warned Duncan against the temptations of myth and mysticism: "the poet cannot afford to traffick in any other 'sign' than his one, his self, the man or woman he is. Otherwise God does rush in. And art is washed away, turned into that second force, religion." Duncan's response was complex; in a way, the whole of his poetry in *The Opening of the Field* and after constitutes his justification of a poetic stance antithetical to Olson's faith in empirical knowledge of an ontologically coherent world—faith in "facts, to be dealt with, as the sea is."

Our responsibility as artists is to recognize as fully and deeply as we can what that belongingness consists of; to quicken our responses in what we are doing in the poem."

In the Grossinger essay, Duncan suggests that "ecology" represents for him the most comprehensive mode of knowledge available to a poet working in the Pound-Williams tradition. Citing Charles Olson's remark at the conclusion of *Mayan Letters* ("The trouble is, it is very difficult, to be both a poet and an historian"), Duncan writes of Grossinger that "he is not an historian but an oecologist, and the great house in which we dwell is to be known in more than is apparent." Ecology, for Duncan, reveals a "historicity" that supersedes both Ezra Pound's egoistic "poem that contained history" and Olson's sense that "the poetic was the primary knowledge from which the truth of history must spring." In that sense ecology as Duncan understands it aligns closely with a transformed sense of pastoral. In the American tradition of pastoral as developed by Thoreau and carried forward into the work of poets as diverse as Marianne Moore, Robinson Jeffers, Wendell Berry, and Gary Snyder, the natural world functions not as a retreat from human history but a transcendence of it that incorporates human activity into a larger ecological patterning. This American pastoral carries with it a strongly utopian dimension, going back at least to Thoreau's essay "Walking" which establishes a dialectic of sustainability between the human and nonhuman realms with its claim "that in Wildness is the preservation of the World." An ecological pastoral, properly conceived, is no nostalgic refuge but opens itself to a radical and dangerous "Wildness" that may not resemble what we ordinarily think of as "nature poetry." Duncan practices just such a version of pastoral and opens it further to the utopian powers of myth in and through his sense of "oecology."

Crucially for Duncan, Grossinger's version of ecology is rooted "in the resonances of chords and serial orders which he draws from 'Astronomy and Biology and Geology Depts." The scientific disciplines folded into "oecology" resonate with larger, older patterns of knowledge, so that "every study of the lore of the stars returns to the *common concrete* sensory knowledge of the stars, in every biological learning returns deep into the native sense of life and of living, that brings all of Geology into a Geo-Logos into an acknowledgment of the Earth."

Duncan does not want to mystify ecology, but to mythify it as "Geo-Logos" or what we might call *Oikos-Logos* ("household Word"), a mode of processal engagement compatible with and best addressed by an open poetics obedient to "what is happening in the composition itself." He is not concerned with natural phenomena per se; his focus is on language as neo-Platonic Logos, a transcendental incarnation of forces in the poem that poet and reader undergo without being able to fully grasp or control them: "The Word, as we refer to it, undoes all the bonds of semantics we would draw in its creative need to realize its true Self." Wendy MacIntyre writes that for Duncan, "The poem is thus not an Aristotelian *mimesis* or imitation of nature, but an autonomous life-form, developing its being through impulses, rhythms, and laws identical with that of the Cosmos: 'It is not that poetry imitates but that poetry enacts in its orders the order of first things.'"

"Nature," then, as it figures in Duncan's poetry is allegorical and textual, distancing it from the central trope if not the major concerns of most nature writing. That textual focus tends to lead to the blurring of figure and ground that Timothy Morton calls "ambient poetics": the "critical ecomimesis" of ambient artworks "open[s] up the rendered environment to the breeze of the cosmic, the historical, the political." This is somewhat reminiscent of Roland Barthes' well-known distinction between "readerly" and "writerly" texts: between the text as environment to be passively absorbed and the text that self-consciously enlists the reader in its own production: "the writerly text is ourselves writing, before the infinite play of the world is traversed, intersected, stopped, plasticized by some singular system (Ideology, Genus, Criticism) which reduces the plurality of entrances, the opening of networks, the infinity of languages." Against a simplistic pastoral ideology that forecloses "plurality" in the name of a singular authentic encounter with nature that effaces the role of language, Duncan's textual collage opens the poem not to a vision of "nature" but of "networks" inseparable from "the infinity of languages."

An ambient poetics, Morton claims, brings us into contact with "the ecological thought": a disturbed and disturbing field of fields, "a vast, sprawling mesh of interconnection without a definite center or edge. It is radical intimacy, coexistence with other beings, sentient and otherwise." Compare this with Philip Kuberski's description of the Deleuzean "chaosmos": "unitary and yet untotalized, a chiasmic concept of the world as a field of mutual and simultaneous interference and convergence, an interanimation of the subjective and objective, an endless realm of chance which nevertheless displays a persistent tendency toward pattern and order." Or as Duncan puts it in "Man's Fulfillment in Order and Strife," "I am fascinated by boundaries, by the fact that the real has just those boundaries we are willing to imagine.... a plurality of boundaries means a multiphasic image of what is."

Duncan's chosen method for achieving this anti-mimetic and multiphasic image is collage, a collage inclusive not only of the elements he selects but of the entire poetic tradition: "a poetry of all poetries, *grand collage,* I name It, having only the immediate event of words to speak for It" (italics in original). This ecological sense of collage is rather different from the conception of "organic form" with which Duncan is often associated. In a letter to Denise Levertov responding to a draft of her essay, "Some Notes on Organic Form," he resists that classification and instead describes himself as a "linguistic" poet, whose attentiveness to language as medium removes him from the preoccupation with the personal and local that he ascribes to "organic" poetry:

> "linguistic" form— the artist uses language to make forms, and in this he {is} in a creature/creator relation to a god who is also creature/creator of the whole. Where "organic" poetry refers to personal emotions and impressions—the concourse between organism and his world; the linguistic follows emotions and images that appear in the language itself as a third "world"; true to what is happening in the syntax as another man might be true to what he sees or feels.

This notion of language as "third 'world'" (resonating curiously with Duncan's response to the U.S. war in Vietnam), by renouncing or deferring "the concourse between organism and his world," marks the fundamental difference between Duncan's ecological poetics and nature poetry as such—even the most open and complex forms of American nature poetry enabled by poets like Gary Snyder and Charles Olson, sometimes grouped under the umbrella term *ecopoetics*.

Where a poet like Olson commits himself to a complex and intertextual version of ecomimesis ("objectism") that seeks to discover firm distinctions between individual and environment, figure and ground, Duncan's poetics, as Michael Davidson writes, tend to erase that distinction: "The consequences of this collapsing of subject and object is a poetry deeply conscious of its textuality." This ambient tendency in Duncan's writing is sustained by his sense of *oikos-Logos*: the environment or household is penetrated and opened by language, which—like habitat, species, and climate—comes to appear excessive, troubling, palimpsestic, blurred. To participate in such a poetics requires the reader to take on the difficult responsibility of an ecological vision decoupled from nostalgia for an idealized nature. As Nathaniel Mackey has noted, in Duncan, "[a] mingling of vertical and horizontal inclinations inflates the words *commune* and *household*." The Logos enters the Household—the transcendental penetrates the immanent, the exalted stands in what's most common—affirming the uncanniness and inescapability of ecological immanence. As adventure and event, a Duncan poem enacts a fragile relation between self and other, human and nonhuman: "the weaving of a figure unweaving." Such a structuring of reality has obvious roots in Emerson and Whitman, but Duncan's reading of Freud and Darwin renders him less optimistic than his forebears: "I read my Emerson dark."

Duncan's sense of textuality and eco-Logos inoculates his poetry from a more traditional pastoral's desire for purification, its "ecomimetic" tendency to police the boundary between humans and nature in the name of its vision of reconciliation between them. The dialectic of purification and translation is central to what the philosopher and anthropologist of science Bruno Latour calls "the modern Constitution": the ontological-political contract by which the social and natural worlds are separated, but which is also productive of an endless series of social-natural hybrids or "quasi-objects." Latour argues that the modern worldview since at least the seventeenth century is structured around a paradoxical relation between the realms of nature and the social: nature "is not our construction; [it is] transcendent and surpasses us infinitely" while "Society is our free construction; it is immanent to our action." Yet at other moments, these positions are chiasmically reversed: "Nature is our artificial construction in the laboratory; it is immanent"; "Society is not our construction, it is transcendent and surpasses us infinitely." This mobile and paradoxical configuration, capable of transforming objects into subjects and back again, can be understood in terms of figure and ground. In the first moment, society, and any given subject position, stands in the foreground while nature lurks in the background as transcendental guarantor of the "really real" (in the postmodern dispensation, this natural background is barred from consideration altogether; in the notorious formulation of Jacques Derrida, "there is nothing outside of the text"). Whenever convenient, we can flip our stance and see nature as the mutable, changeable, and created thing, while the social stands immobile in the background (the point of view of technocratic neoliberalism.) Thinking both fields in motion, equally constructed and yet equally real, is a possibility that eludes and is in fact forbidden by the "Constitution" that circumscribes modernity, which can only regard "primitive" societies in such an anthropological light.

Duncan's poetics can function as a form of translation, mediating between the zones of human and nonhuman life as it mediates between the quotidian and the mythic. Whereas "ecomimesis"—the naive description of nonhuman phenomena—conceals the ecological "mesh" by enforcing the stability of figure and ground and the separation of subject and object, an ambient poetics casts its readers into the mesh by blurring the bounds between figure and ground, human and nonhuman. It fosters hybridity and the production of poetic objects neither fully transcendental (i.e., beyond individual or social control) or fully immanent. The landscape of a Duncan poem, which is inseparable from the poem itself, functions as such a "quasi-object." It brings its readers into the mesh, often uncomfortably so.

A paradigmatic such quasi-object in Duncan's corpus is the titular meadow of "Often I Am Permitted to Return to a Meadow." As Devin Johnston writes, "Rather than exclusively psychological or physical, the meadow is presented as a hybrid, perhaps ideological in nature." The poem is presided over by an ontologically open "as if," distinct from the epistemologically closed "as I write" of ecomimesis: the meadow is "vertiginous," betwixt and between self and other, the "made-up" and the natural. The meadow is a *locus amoenus,* an "eternal pasture folded in all thought" and "place of first permission," but it is also a site of meshed experience, even of terror.:

OFTEN I AM PERMITTED TO RETURN TO A MEADOW

as if it were a scene made-up by the mind,
that is not mine, but is a made place,

that is mine, it is so near to the heart,
an eternal pasture folded in all thought
so that there is a hall therein

The palimpsestic and rhetorical qualities of Duncan's poem are what give the reader the uncanny feeling of encounter with a meadow, a reality, that is both made and given, transcendent yet immanent: "the image becomes informed, from above or below, and takes over as an entity in itself, a messenger from a higher real." The meadow is the "made" and yet given field of the poem, a place in which the act of writing or inscription (not description, for the poem is almost devoid of descriptive images, necessary for its shedding of actuality) sets up what Duncan calls "a constant disequilibrium." The mythic "Lady" who presides over the poem holds sway through her army or "hosts" that "are a disturbance of words within words": like a Russian doll, the military definition of "hosts" is made to contain its nearly opposite definition of hospitality. The reverberations of these opposed meanings of the same word suggest hybridity, turning it into a node of the poem-meadow's mesh, which hosts the reader but also threatens and disturbs her.

Johnston argues that, "the explicitly natural connotations of 'meadow' remove it from any directly social context"; this is the pastoral or Orphic dimension of "first permission," which implies that the "return" to the meadow is an Adamic if not Edenic return to the beginnings of language, before words were weighted with what Duncan elsewhere calls "adverse meanings." At the same time, the syntax of the closing lines marks the meadow as "everlasting omen of what is." As nature or "given property of the mind," the meadow is eternal, outside of history; as "scene made-up by the mind," it is fully social and historical. The meadow, as myth, is quasi-objective; for Duncan, the mythic is not confined to supernatural allusions but arises through "the music of the poem—a music of sounds and of meanings—[that] awakens the mythological reality in the actual." This "music" corresponds with both melopoeia and with logopoeia, to use Pound's terms, and suggests the inseparability of the two varieties of linguistic play; the double- and triple-jointed syntax of "Often I Am Permitted to Return to a Meadow" produces the meadow's "mythological reality" as surely as the relatively inobtrusive and veiled figure of "the Lady" does. Pellucid and dreamlike, the poem is open to the possibility of a nearly self-contradictory pastoral of excess, open in a way that pastoral rarely is to the blurring of figure and ground, subject and object, actual and real.

This opening through blurring is, of course, the larger project of *The Opening of The Field*. "I will not take the actual world for granted," Duncan writes in "The Structure of Rime I," and "a woman who resembles the sentence"—that is, the Law of linguistic form—responds:

> *Why not?* she replied.
> *Do I not withhold the song of birds from you?*
> *Do I not withhold the penetrations of red from you?*
> *Do I not withhold the weight of mountains from you?*
> *Do I not withhold the hearts of men from you?*

Joshua Corey

> *I alone long for your demand.*
> *I alone measure your desire.*

A difficult dialectic is established between "the actual world" disclosed by images (that is, ecomimesis: the song of birds, the weight of mountains) and the language that, like the Freudian unconscious, "alone" responds to poetry; the poet is "*a fierce destroyer of images*" and this destruction forces language into contention with itself, "*vomiting images into the place of the Law!*" (13, italics in original). The eco-Logos of this poetry manifests in Duncan's remaining "true to what is happening in the syntax as another man might be true to what he sees or feels"; it is not fidelity to the actual but what Duncan calls "THE SENDING OUT" that matters: "*I see the tree. It changes. Mineral / vegetable   animal.   Of generations. / It exceeds me.*" Duncan is a "polysemous" poet for whom even individual words are hybrids, like hard-to-classify species: "the artist of abundancies delites in puns, interlocking and separating figures, plays of things missing or things appear 'out of order' that remind us that all orders have their justification finally in an order of orders only our faith as we work addresses." Let us dwell, he says, in the moment of translation or mediation between nature and culture, self and history, without being too hasty to pass on to one zone or the other; for poet and world emerge in the flux between them as mediated by language: "I name myself your master, who come to / serve. / Writing is first a search in obedience."

Duncan's poem "Returning to the Rhetoric of an Early Mode" celebrates his embrace of "rhapsodic excess in a time / despising the rush, the being carried away." Many of the poems collected in *The Opening of the Field* and *Roots and Branches* develop a pastoral of "abundance, / the verdant rhetorical," that supplements the "actual": "There were actual orchards. There were actual men," he writes, but "these were not the trees, this was not the ground, the primordial / dirt and seed / where the form of my tree slept." "This divine image coming forth": the *divine* image of Duncan's poetry is figured through the excesses of language with which he keeps faith—signaling that

Duncan's idealized landscapes are not classically balanced but participate the sublime openness of a poetic ecology.

Linguistic form as "a gnosis of not-knowing" means operating unconstrained by neither normative social conventions nor by merely personal perceptions and intuitions, but through obeying language's Law of radical inclusion. This is the anti-Linnaean ecological knowledge that Duncan demands of poetry, as suggested by a quotation from Ernst Cassirer that he includes in his essay, "Ideas of the Meaning of Form":

> We must apply the principle of connection rather than that of analytical differentiation; instead of assigning living creatures to sharply distinguished species, we must study them in relation to their kinship, their transition from one type to another, their evolution and transformations. For these are the things which constitute life as we find it in nature.

Poets must, as Duncan writes in a letter to Levertov, "become biologists not moralists, fascinated finally by facts and forms of how life goes on, beyond judgments." Duncan's is a "fascinated" pastoral of propositions rather than judgments; he views literary tradition as "the open-ended series of variations on a corrupt and corruptible text" and it is fair to say that the actual world as it appears in his poems is equally textual and equally corruptible. The interpenetration of the textual and the actual: this is how the ecological mesh makes itself felt in Duncan's work.

The most immediate and unsettling manifestation of the mesh in Duncan's time was the Vietnam War, which is not, the use of Agent Orange notwithstanding, usually understood as an ecological crisis. But the highly mediated Vietnam War did form a kind of inescapable and violent climate that seemed to capture and entangle everything, bringing ordinary Americans into queasily intimate contact with the consequences of their foreign policy, summarized by the terrible logic, as quoted by Duncan, of "the American general's '*It became necessary to destroy the town to save it.*'" The Vietnam War formed, for its time, the horizon of all quasi-objects, something made by us and yet strangely impervious to alteration. "But where are we to classify the ozone hole story, or global warming or deforestation?" wonders Bruno Latour. "Where are we to put these hybrids? Are they human? Human because they are our work. Are they natural? Natural because they are not our doing. Are they local or global? Both.... The destiny of the starving multitudes and the fate of our poor planet are connected by the same Gordian knot that no Alexander will ever again manage to sever." The difficulties of Duncan's poetic and ethical stance toward that war foreshadows the difficulties twenty-first century poets experience contending with the proliferating hybrids of the twenty-first century.

One of the challenges of Duncan's Vietnam War poems, as many critics have observed, is that it they are in fact war poems, not anti-war poems. Duncan is intent on a kind of war pastoral, bringing the mediatized war's hybridity, and the hybrids that it produces between self and other, America and Vietnam, poet and poem, into focus. As Duncan wrote in a now notorious letter to Levertov, "The poet's role is not to oppose evil, but to imagine it." By now the story of Duncan's conflict with Levertov over their differing poetic-political stances is quite well known. Rather than rehearsing it, I want to focus on the appearance of pastoral gestures in their war poems and the ways in which they adapt pastoral to fundamentally different ends. Specifically, I want to examine how Levertov's activism led her to pursue a largely ecomimetic pastoral of purification, whereas Duncan tried, in increasingly agonized ways, to keep faith with translation and, as Robert Kaufman has written, his commitment "to the nothing that is in fact the yet-to-be-determined: the poem's commitment to the space of illusion or semblance that keeps determination and ethical possibility open for exploration, over against the delusion that the poem itself is already an ethical or political act."

The hybrids that modernity produces through the work of translation are swept under the carpet, ideologically and ontologically homeless. Levertov's encounter with the war reveals a similar constitution on her part, through which evil and good, war and peace, get mapped onto the zones of culture and nature, with the one deprecated and the other celebrated. In her poem "Life at War," Vietnam is an inexplicable malignance that invades the peaceful realm of "delicate Man"; she responds to it by attributing a vast unnaturalness to the war, a kind of infection in the atmosphere and in the lungs. In a passage evocative of Hamlet's "What a piece of work is a man" speech, human beings are described in hyper-idyllic terms, brought close to a nature that they "excel":

> delicate Man, whose flesh
> responds to a caress, whose eyes
> are flowers that perceive the stars,
>
> whose music excels the music of birds,
> whose laughter matches the laughter of dogs,
> whose understanding manifests designs
> fairer than the spider's most intricate web

The poem's "ecorhapsody"[3] is succeeded by a grisly catalog of the war's horrors and the hideous, unnatural stink it has created: "burned human flesh / is smelling in Vietnam as I write." The *as I write* trope is a marker of ecomimesis, albeit in a condemnatory mode; the phrase conveys the poet's sense of dissonance in writing as flesh is burning, and this dissonance is intended to have a primarily ethical rather than an aesthetic effect. The smell of burned flesh transcends geographical distance, forming an intensely negative, unnatural, and encompassing climate that the speaker wishes to escape:

> our nerve filaments twitch with its presence
> day and night,
> nothing we say has not the husky phlegm of it in the saying,
> nothing we do has the quickness, the sureness,
> the deep intelligence living at peace would have.

---

3 The term is Timothy Morton's, from *Ecology Without Nature*: "*Ecorhapsody* is a mode of ecomimesis. The environment in general manifests in some specific element, as if it were magnetically charged.... The general enters the realm of the particular. An abstraction passes into an empirical domain."

Levertov's poem presents us with two forms of "intelligence" or knowledge: the idyllic, supra-natural "understanding" of man at peace and the dark knowledge of war, "the knowledge that jostles for space / in our bodies along with all we / go on knowing of joy, of love." Though she locates the two forms of knowledge "in our bodies," the poem affirms their incommensurability, for one has polluted the other: "the mucous membranes of our dreams / coated with it, the imagination / filmed over with the gray filth of it." Another poem in the same volume, "Second Didactic Poem," allegorizes the pastoral purification that Levertov demands: "Nectar, / the makings of the / incorruptible, / is carried upon the / corrupt tongues of / mortal insects." "The honey of man" is produced through an excremental process: "Beespittle, droppings, hairs / of beefur: all become honey. / Virulent micro-organisms cannot / survive in honey." The desired consummation is for the impure to become pure.

Duncan's response to the war is focused on the corrupt and corruptible zone between war and peace, soldier and protester—the hybrid ground of "common speech" or translation which for Duncan is also always uncommon and uncanny. The instability of the "we" suggested by Levertov's poem is at the center of his meditations in the introduction to *Bending the Bow*, which in its first pages takes the form of an oblique narrative of his own experience as a war protester. Like Levertov, he engages in a generalized form of ecomimesis of the war: "Cities laid waste, villages destroyd, men, women and children hunted down in their fields, forests poisond, herds of elephants screaming under our fire—it is all so distant from us we hear only what we imagine, making up what we surely are doing." This catalog gives nearly as much emphasis to the devastation done to the nonhuman world as the human. But Duncan's prose is less confident in the value of mimesis than Levertov's poem: instead of an "as I write" intended to close the distance between the poet and what the poet describes, Duncan self-consciously increases that distance, inviting mimesis' failure. Imaginative language is the inescapable mediator between the reality of Vietnam and the reality of an American civilian: to write about the war requires "making [it] up."

This familiar crisis of representation is resolved, or rather ventured, by Duncan's Logos-centrism, his understanding that any war takes place in language itself and, like language, produces innumerable hybrids. The inarticulate "desolate bellowing of some ox in a ditch" refuses to stay put in the realm of the nonhuman: "The pulse of this sentence beats before and beyond all proper bounds and we no longer inhabit what we thought properly our own." In the face of such dispossession, both the poet and a "boy raised in Iowa," now a soldier confronting war protesters, must each resign himself to having "Only this terrible wounded area in which to have his soul-life." And the pressure that the war puts on these men, and on language, forces a new, recognizably ecological awareness: "All my common animal being comes to the ox in his panic and, driven by this speech, we imagine only man, *homo faber*, has, comes into a speech words mean to come so deep that the amoeba is my brother poet." In "Life at War," Levertov is shocked that "men who can make; / whose language imagines *mercy, / lovingkindness*" nevertheless "do these acts" for "these acts are done / to our own flesh." This "knowledge that jostles for space / in our bodies" forms a foreign body, a source of contagion. Duncan pursues instead the logic of hybridity: for him, the war forces recognition of kinship with the animal on the level of bare life: ox, amoeba, Iowan, poet, all move into "this poetry, the ever forming of bodies in language in which breath moves, [that] is a field of ensouling." Levertov's poem in effect unwrites the powerful brooding commonality created by the war—the "our" and "we" infected and inflected by the war-smoke—calling instead for quickness, sureness, and purity, so that the poem's ambience manifests in spite of the rhetorical content of the speaker's speech. For Duncan, "the real 'we' is the company of the living, of all the forms Life Itself, the primal wave of it, writing itself out in evolution, proposes." Such a *we* is inherently unstable: "we meant to fulfill our humanity. But we were, in turn, members of a company of men, moving forward, violently, to overcome in themselves the little company of others kneeling and striving to speak to them, a refusal of all common speech that strove to maintain itself before us." The failure of speech brings protestors and soldiers together, as it unites poet and amoeba, in a field charged with violent potential, undoing the simplistic binary that Duncan ascribes to Levertov The impasse itself is Duncan's truth, the ground of "common speech" that produces disturbing and melancholy hybrids: soldier-protesters, amoeba-poets. He is already embarked on "ground work: *before* the war": standing on a pastoral "common ground" that is before the war (outside it, with a view of it, but conditioned by it as climate and prior to it as historical event). The "ground work" of war pastoral enters the truth of ecology, risks translating or "ensouling" the Other.

The poetic fulfillment of these claims comes in "The Fire (Passages 13)," which begins with a symmetrical cluster of words, arranged in a six by six grid, a kind of collage or concrete poem. The isolation of each word seems to demonstrate Duncan's claim that, "A word has the weight of an actual stone in [the poet's] hand"; they are presented as natural objects, a collection of what are for the most part Anglo-Saxon monosyllables: *jump, stone, hand, leaf, shadow*. As Anne Day Dewey writes, "the grids appear to contain and dissolve destructive historical order into a syntactical chaos with liberating potential" The words accumulate, asyntactically, into a kind of reduced vision of the wider landscape or view: "blood   disk / horizon   flame."

Peter O'Leary has written that the opening and closing grids represent "the poet's attempt to encapsulate horrible images with some form of peace." However, I would emphasize the contrast between the *images* that dominate the center of the poem—an extended ekphrasis of two Renaissance paintings—and the pastoral peace promised by bare words: *cool, green, waver, circle, fish, sun*. As O'Leary notes, the poem's first fourteen lines are "uncharacteristically laconic.... For a poet whose mode is nearly always intensely musical, this writing feels like a regression." The grids perform a subtle parody of the stripped-down ecomimesis Duncan associates with canonical Imagism, though they also undeniably function as a refuge from the horrors that they bracket.

The two paintings at the center of the poem are described in it as "Piero di Cosimo's great painting *A Forest Fire,* dated 1490–1500, preserved in the Ashmolean Museum at Oxford" and "Bosch's illumination: / Hell." The first painting, in spite of the conflagration at its thematic and visual center, is notable for its odd combination of whimsy and accuracy. The fire terrifies the animals in the picture but at the same time it unites them, in a sort of parody of the peaceable kingdom:

>   From the wood we thought burning
>   our animal spirits flee,   seeking refuge wherever,
>   as if in Eden,   in this   panic
>   lion and lamb lie down

The only human in the picture, a herdsman, urges his cattle toward a house but seems unconcerned by the fire. Two of the animals, notably, are literal hybrids: "the man-faced roe and his / gentle mate; the wild boar too / turns a human face." Instead of terror their faces display "a philosophic sorrow," a kind of tarrying with the negative—that is, their own human-nonhuman hybridity. Most emblematic is the ox in the foreground "fierce with terror, his thick tongue / slavers and sticks out panting / to make the gorgoneion face." *Gorgoneion* refers to a pendant with the Gorgon's petrifying visage on it, used to ward off evil. Duncan most likely knew of the gorgoneion from Jane Harrison's account of it in her book *Prolegomena to the Study of Greek Religion,* in which she claims that its object is not only to ward off the evil others might do, but one's own. "The function of such masks is permanently to 'make an ugly face' at you if you are doing wrong, breaking your word, robbing your neighbor, meeting him in battle; *for* you if you are doing right." The word in the poem then is another indication of Duncan's conception of evil or adversary as something internal, not "out there" in the Other. We should also remember the "ox in a ditch," whose bellowing challenges the poet to imagine a wider "field of ensouling."

The painter's technique of *sfumato* dissolves "certain bounds [held] against chaos" into translation: "there is a softening of outline,   his color fuses. / A glow at the old borders makes / magic." This painterly technique, which obstructs the clarity of mimesis, is akin to the music of poetry "in David's song ... music / Orpheus first playd, / chords and melodies of the spell that binds / the many in conflict in contrasts of one mind." This key to Duncan's eco-pastoral vision, which gives priority to imagining over opposing: "the many in conflict" are united in "one mind," though the word "contrasts" suggests an uneasy and provisional unity in analysis, in the weighing of opposites:

> Di Cosimo's   featherd, furrd, leafy
>
>   boundaries where   even the Furies are birds
>   and blur   in higher harmonies Eumenides;
> whose animals, entering a charmd field
> in the light of his vision, a stillness,
>   have their dreamy glades and pastures.

The floral and faunal "boundaries" of the painting blur imperceptibly into the transformation of the Furies into the Eumenides, or "kindly ones"; the savage yet hopeful narrative of the *Orestia* cycle, in which vengeance evolves into justice, is compressed into an aspect of Duncan's mythic ecology. In spite of the panic and terror of the scene, Di Cosimo's animals might well paraphrase Marlowe's Mephistopheles by saying, "Why this is pastoral, nor am I out of it." But such a statement, by blurring the bounds between Arcadia and Hell, suggests that we must contend with a larger and more fluid universe than either mythscape can present on its own.

"Hell breaks out   an opposing music" to the "dreamy glades and pastures" of Di Cosimo. Hell shines forth in "The faces of the deluded.... enthralld by fear,   avidly / following the daily news: the earthquakes, eruptions, / flaming automobiles, enraged lovers, wars against communism, / heroin addicts, police raids, race riots...." These are the human "faces of evil openly / over us, / bestial extrusions no true animal face knows." In the midst of this grotesquerie is an image of Christ: "The painter's *sfumato* gives His face / pastoral stillness amidst terror,   sorrow / that has an echo in the stag's face we saw before." The ambiguous terror of "the fire" that Di Cosimo placed in diverse animal, human, and human-animal faces is located by Bosch in the face of Christ, as much a hybrid in his way as the "man-faced roe." Here the blurring technique of *sfumato* is closely associated with the "pastoral" (one of the only uses of this word in Duncan's mature poetry) which is in turn associated with a seemingly impotent Savior: "Is His Kingdom / not of this world, but a dream of the Anima Mundi, / the World-Ensouling?" Again we have an echo of Duncan's Introduction and the Keatsian notion of the world as "The vale of Soul-making": "There may be intelligences or sparks of the divinity in millions—but they are not Souls till they acquire identities, till each one is personally itself."

In the context of the poem, Christ's dream can thus be identified with an ecological notion of ensouling, in the sense of recognition of a hugely diverse array of individual identities, located on a sliding scale between divine, human, and animal; as Duncan writes elsewhere, "the potentiality requires the multitude of individualities." Opposed to this is the "idiot" reductiveness of "Satan [who] looks forth form / men's faces." "His face multiplies" like an invasive species in an unprotected habitat, the hidden face of an ideologically diverse range of politicians and statesmen from Eisenhower and Nixon to "Roosevelt, Stalin, / Churchill, Hitler, Mussolini" as well as the nuclear scientists "Oppenheimer, Fermi, Teller, Vannevar Bush, // brooding the nightmare formulae— to win the war!" "My name is Legion   and in every nation   I multiply": the terror of the Biblical allusion lies in that multiplication which is also a form of purification. Such (anti-)pastoral purification would obliterate the ecological diversity that can *include* evil, in the name of a Satanic homogeneity that presents a direct threat to the "eternal pasture" crystallized in the figure of "Pan's land":

> They are burning the woods, the brushlands, the
>   grassy fields razed;   their
>   profitable suburbs spread.
> Pan's land, the pagan countryside, they'd
>   lay waste.

The poem concludes, as noted earlier, with a reconfiguration of the pastoral grid that began it, suggesting the temporary survival of "the pagan countryside [that they would] / lay waste." But the stakes are clear. The pastoral of purification that Levertov clings to can offer no resistance to evil as Duncan imagines it. Evil passes through his pastoral of translation into a larger vision that contrasts the "evil" of hybridity with the greater evil of a Satanic or Napoelonic monoculture that does not stand "before the war" but tries to *win* it, to achieve a victory that can only bring about annihilation: "Napoleon knew no language but the language of his ideal world, where he could know the bitterness of defeat, yes, but now news of deeper disorder that might reveal the duplicity of the ideal itself." The duplicity of the ideal: this is the darkness uncovered by a hybrid pastoral, an eco-Logos that does not oppose evil by polemic (a word that itself means *war*) but imagines a complex and unboundaried "ensouling" of the enemy, most especially of the enemy within.

Duncan's faith in translation and hybridity—his ethical insistence on blurring figure and ground—is arguably based on purification on a much vaster scale, for which "cosmos" is seen as immune to whatever might transpire on earth. From this point of view, the destruction of Vietnam, or the destruction of the entire biosphere, is not a significant event—this takes us to the heart of what Levertov and other critics have found so troubling about Duncan's relation to history as it is actually lived:

> The cosmos will not
>
> dissolve its orders at man's evil.
>
> "That which is corrupted is corrupted with reference to
> itself but not destroyd with reference to the universe;
>
> for it is either air or water"
>
> Chemistry having its equations
>
> beyond our range of inequation.

> There must be a power of an ambiguous nature
> and a dominion given to choice: "For the
>
> electing soul alone is transferrd
> to another and another order ... "

These lines from "Orders (Passages 24)" insert a cosmic gulf between the poet of eco-Logos and those of us who live on the "corrupted" earth; as Mackey notes, "The poem's cosmic insistences border on misanthropy, a kind of masochism at times." A similar distaste has been expressed by the critics of deep ecology, a movement in some ways close to Duncan which can assume misanthropic or *dis*anthropic tones, productive of post-human fantasies such as Alan Weisman's book *The World without Us*. Certainly Duncan can assume a distance from events, an insistence on the poet's freedom that smacks of quietism and irresponsibility. "Responsibility is to keep / the ability to respond": it is an ingenious and thought-provoking aphorism but does not stand up to purely logical scrutiny.

For Mackey, what is most ethical in Duncan emerges in the strain of this stance, its failure to wholly convince us: "We hear the pathos of an upward aspiration that we both identify with and are put off by, hearing the echo of our own resistance in Duncan's inability to keep the godly voice aloft." But I believe his ecological ethics boils down to the lines, "There must be a power of an ambiguous nature / and a dominion given to choice." In these lines, adapted from the commentaries of the Neoplatonist philosopher Proclus on Plato's *Timaeus*, Duncan does not capitalize "nature," so that it must be read as qualifying the ambiguous power of "choice." But the lines may also ask us to acknowledge that Nature's power is inseparable from its ambiguity, "having its equations / beyond our range of inequation." The gnosis of not knowing the limits of species, habitat, and ecology requires us to make choices about how we think of and interact with them, alive to the law of unintended consequences. Only "the / electing soul," the one who chooses, "is transferrd / to another and another order"; the multiplication of orders through choice is Duncan's greatest good.

But there is a dark side to hybridity for its own sake: the sleep of reason produceth monsters. Duncan at times seems to long for apocalypse; he is not without, as Mackey says, a masochistic as well as a misanthropic side. This comes to the fore most luridly in the poems of his last illness, in which Duncan's hybrid pastoral of translation turns into what Joyelle McSweeney calls "necropastoral." The term intends to invert the dream of purity that McSweeney locates in pastoral proper:

> The Pastoral, like the occult, has always been a fraud, a counterfeit, an invention, an anachronism. However, as with the occult, and as with Art itself, the fraudulence of the pastoral is in direct proportion to its uncanny powers. A double of the urban, but dressed in artful, nearly ceremental rags and pelts, the Pastoral is outside the temporal and geographical sureties of the court, the urbs, the imperium itself, but also, implicitly, adjacent to all of these, entailing an ambiguous degree of access, of cross-contamination.

For McSweeney, necropastoral "manifests the infectiousness, anxiety, and contagion occultly present in the hygienic borders of the classical pastoral—i.e., the most celebrity resident of Arcadia is Death—but also its activity, its networking, its paradoxical proliferation, its self-digestive activity, its eructations, its necroticness, its hunger and its hole making, which configures a burgeoning textual tissue defined by holes, a tissue thus as absent as it is present, and therefore not absent, not present—protoplasmic, spectral" ("Strange (Political) Meetings," n.p.). *Et in Arcadia ego*: death is present, even central to pastoral, as seen in "Often I Am Permitted to Return to a Meadow," a marker of the decay and melancholia of hybridity that the classical pastoral of purification labors to conceal. "The Fires (Passages 14)" locates death "before the war" that is for Levertov an infection she wishes to cure. Though "The Fire" is awash in hybridity, the war is still fundamentally separated from the experience of the poet (contained, as it were, by the grids of pastoral language), who must imagine the evil he refuses to oppose.

In the poems "In Blood's Domaine" and "After a Long Illness," on the other hand, death is a terrifyingly intimate presence: "the specter I have long / known as my Death is the / Lord of a Passage that unites us." To quote Michael Davidson again, Duncan sees literary tradition as "the open-ended series of variations on a corrupt and corruptible text"; in these late poems, that text is inseparable from Duncan's own corrupted body. As Duncan asserts a universal humanism in "The Homosexual in Society" and refuses the ground of identity politics, so he does not refuse the ground of death—no longer *before* the war, but *in* the dark—that unites individual human beings with other species, habitats, and life-worlds for which extinction is a possibility. Such a necropastoral represents the severest test of Duncan's ecological ethics. "As long as the battle is for real," Duncan writes, "where so much depends upon control of self or of environment, there is pathos and even terror in the reasonable man, for there is so much in man's nature and experiences that would never be within his authority." What does it mean to imagine, rather than oppose or control, the evil that is consuming your own body?

"In Blood's Domaine" is the fullest rendering of what Peter O'Leary calls Duncan's Gnostic contagion: the kidney disease that is killing him is likened to the syphilis that killed "Baudelaire, Nietzsche, Swift" and so cannot be separated from "the heart Eternal of what Poetry is / answer to the genius and science of the Abyss." The "ring a round of roses told" from "Often I Am Permitted to Return to a Meadow" returns in this poem in the form of "spirochete invasions that eat at the sublime envelope,   not alien, but familiars"; Rilke appears in his last illness bleeding from every orifice "news his whole body bears as its truth   of the septic rose." As O'Leary writes, "for Duncan, the experience of disease recreates the experience of language"; one is possessed by, obeys the logic of, the unfolding poem, as Duncan's body now obeys the inexorable logic of kidney failure. Diseases appear in the poem as angels—"The Angel Syphillis," "The Angel Cancer" —terrible like Rilke's angels, of which he asks, "What Angel,   what Gift of the Poem,   has brought into my body // this sickness of living?" The immanent life of the disease in Duncan's body transcends, defines, and limits that body. And that disease, like a pandemic, is a network that cannot be disavowed: "Link by link I can disown no link of this chain from my conscience." Duncan keeps faith with the terrible knowledge of "this sickness of living," invoking a "Jesus" who cries "I come not to heal but to tear the scab from the wound you wanted / to forget. / May the grass no longer spread out to covers the works of man in the ruin of / earth." Duncan's necropastoral dwells with and in that ruin—at the moment he might wish most intensely for purification, a higher dialysis, he affirms the need not to conceal "the works of man" in the pastoral grass.

Is this not the fullest melancholy, the work of mourning demanded by the ultimate hybridity of subject and object—the living and non-living? "Ecology is stuck between melancholy and mourning," Timothy Morton writes. "Nature language is like melancholy: holding on to a 'bad' object, a toxic mother whose distance and objectlike qualities are venerated. Environmentalism is a work of mourning for a mother we never had." Perhaps Duncan goes even beyond this in the depiction of his own mother in one of his most arresting poems, "My Mother Would Be a Falconress:"

> My mother would be a falconress,
> and she sends me as far as her will goes.
> She lets me ride to the end of her curb
> where I fall back in anguish.
> I dread that she will cast me away,
> for I fall, I mis-take, I fail in her mission.

O'Leary writes of this poem that it enacts "a full-blown, poetic, ritual destruction of the mother.... Duncan heals himself from his complex relationship with his mother by portraying that relationship as complexly as possible. He achieves complexity by the subtle reversals of mother and guide, violence experienced and violence done." A strong (mis)reading of this mother as Mother Nature turns the poem into a complex allegory of the violence that has been done in the past in her name, going "as far as her will goes," as well as the violence that we may yet do in the future to free ourselves from "the little hood with many bells" that is the pastoral of purification: "I would be a falcon and go free. / I tread her wrist and wear the hood, / talking to myself, and would draw blood." The plausible necropastoralization of this poem, encapsulating Duncan's melancholy fealty to translation, hybridity, and eco-Logos, offers a powerful alternative to a more conventional and ecomimetic nature poetry, an enmeshed reckoning with the nature we have destroyed and the "Nature" we must destroy.

Robert Duncan's Polysemous Turn

When I consider the role of the *volta* in poetry, my mind is immediately and perversely drawn to the work of Robert Duncan, which has preoccupied me incessantly for the past couple of years. I say perversely because of all the major American poets of the postwar period that occur to me—Frank O'Hara, Alice Notley, John Ashbery, to name one trinity—Duncan's poetics is possibly the least indebted to the qualities that I associate with the poetic turn, at least at first glance. Where a poet like Ashbery astonishes his reader constantly with his wit, practically line by line, Duncan seems to use no wit at all—if by *wit* we mean that capacity for joining unlike things in a flash of fire that only seems inevitable after the dazzle fades. Duncan, the "derivative" poet, arriving late to the party of High Modernism, is not at all metaphysical in T.S. Eliot's sense of the famous "dissociation of sensibility" that requires the poet, in Frank Kermode's words, to "become more and more comprehensive, more allusive, more indirect, in order to force, to dislocate if necessary, language into his meaning." This violent dislocation—call it the extreme volta—is indeed characteristic of modern and contemporary poems which, by their startling juxtaposition of unlike elements from wildly different discursive regimes, whipsaw the reader into admiration, or better, recognition: these poems, at their best, present readers with an uncanny experience of what postmodern life is really like, ready simulacra of the operations of distracted minds half-distressed and half-relieved by the tendency of such turns to pull down all hierarchies. The twists and turns taken by a figure like Popeye, in Ashbery's supremely witty sestina "Farm Implements and Rutabagas in a Landscape," are made to undercut the possibilities of Romantic resonance and heroism that the poem ironically invokes, and if there is melancholy in this there is also a certain giddy relief, a grounding in groundlessness: "'But what if no pleasant / Inspiration plunge us now to the stars? *For this is my country.*'"

For Duncan, "metaphysical" is not a derogatory epithet but a simple descriptor of the territory disclosed by poems: they discover as

Dante discovered "by the sweetness of his language ... the evocation of the supreme sweetness he knew to be the order of all orders in his universe." What fascinates me in Duncan is less the turn of his line than the turn of his poetry as a body away from the reductiveness of ideology critique and toward what Ezra Pound called the spirit of Romance, which for Duncan evokes "a sweetness and an ardor all but heretical in the poetics of our own day." To do this, Duncan risks what he calls "muddle and floaty vagaries" in writing esoteric poems that insist on the inseparability of the literal forms of words and the Word, the *Logos*: poems that perform experience rather than representing it. Duncan's turn, broadly, from mimesis toward a form of metaphysical rhetoric makes him strange, an outlier to the main stream of innovative poetry that seems in part to flow from him (i.e. Language poetry). But this strangeness is what makes him irresistible, a tonic, a pathway into and through the Modern toward poetry as high adventure, as physical as it is metaphysical.

That is why I want to say a few words about Duncan's "Sonnet 3 (From Dante's Sixth Sonnet)," part of a series of "sonnets" (claimed to be such primarily by their titles: "Sonnet 1," "Sonnet 2"), freely adapted from or inspired by Dante and published in Duncan's important mid-period book *Roots and Branches*. This particular sonnet is a very loose translation of Dante's "*Guido, i' vorrei che tu e Lapo ed io,*" an invitation to a voyage that brings two other poets, Duncan's close friends and rivals, inside the poem's charmed circle:

> Robin, it would be a great thing if you, me, and Jack Spicer
> Were taken up in a sorcery with our mortal heads so turnd
> That life dimmd in the light of that fairy ship
> *The Golden Vanity* or *The Revolving Lure,*
>
> Whose sails ride before music as if it were our will,
> Having no memory of ourselves but the poets we were
> In certain verses that had such a semblance or charm
> Our lusts and loves confused in one

> Lord or Magician of Amor's likeness.
> And that we might have ever at our call
> Those youths we have celebrated to play Eros
> And erased to lament in the passing of things.
>
> And to weave themes ever of Love.
> And that each might be glad
> To be so far abroad from what he was.

This poem enchants me, is in fact intended as an enchantment: an incantation that brings the inner circle of the San Francisco Renaissance aboard a "fairy ship" sailing on the breath of music, away from the ordinary heterosexist grind of "life dimmd" and from the history of contention among three strong egos (the three poets disagreed violently: Spicer could be vicious to those he loved most, and Duncan nearly broke with Blaser over the latter's translations of some poems by Gérard de Nerval). But even as the poem expresses its utopian aspiration for an ideal community of poets (as in the poem's other famous English translations, by Percy Bysshe Shelley and Dante Rossetti), it complicates and reflects back on such a wish. A poem that has been translated by such forebears, translated again, bears its own special reflexivity: the echoes of Rossetti and Shelley remind us of Duncan's quasi-Nietzschean belief in the eternal return of fundamental archetypes, "the order of all orders" made manifest by the magic of poetry, the sorcery that *turns* "our mortal heads" away from ordinary concerns: "life dimmd in the light of that fairy ship." In that sense the poem's turn comes, explicitly, right there in the second line; the rest of the sonnet is devoted to exploring the consequences of the "great thing" that the poem imagines. The volta of this sonnet comes not at the sestet, as in the original: in Dante's poem the female beloveds of the poets are introduced at this point, but Duncan, Blaser, and Spicer are gay men, and their beloveds appear abstractly as "Those youths we have celebrated to play Eros / And erased to lament in the passing of things." The possibility of a turn on the sestet is further obscured by the fact that it is actually a septet, and by the enjambment of the second strophe that hides Dante's turning point, "And" in the third strophe. The only other possibility of a turn, then, comes in the final three-line strophe, which itself represents a partial turn back to the literal sense of Dante's poem:

> *e quivi ragionar sempre d'amore,*
> *e ciascuna di lor fosse contenta,*
> *sì come i' credo che saremmo noi.*
>
> and there discourse always of love,
> and each of them happy,
> as I imagine we too should be. (my translation)

The first two lines of Duncan's final strophe are very close to Dante's; only the last line returns us to Duncan's theme of transport, not into the ideal but away from "what he was": the false self from which each poet has been lured by what Rossetti called "the boat of love." Duncan's "fairy ship," with its competing, complementary names (that do not reference love but rather deception and vanity) functions as a sort of alluring trap—the glamor of the poetic image, perhaps, driven by "music as if it were our will." That "as if," however, places the music of poetry outside of and beyond willing, just as the poets who sail with Duncan shed all "memory of ourselves" in favor of "the poets we were / In certain verses," verses that confused the ground of "lusts and loves" the face of an archetypal "Lord or Magician of Amor's likeness." Amor, the terrifying god of Dante Alghieri's *La vita nuova,* who commands the beloved to eat the poet's heart, is conflated here with the magician or wizard, "*il buono incantatore,*" of Dante's original poem (the word *incantatore* set to rhyme with *amore* and including of course *canto* or song). Duncan's sonnet is slippery then with turns or half turns, turns among its varying translations and between the enchantments of a wizardly Love that can scarcely be trusted for the poem's brief duration. Duncan characteristically withholds from the reader any single "aha!" moment of surprise: the poem, hardly one of his most complex, layers sinuously upon itself, presenting its fantasy as fantasy, a paradoxical wish-poem that charms by virtue of its velleity.

In a 1974 letter to John Felstiner, Duncan wrote "The sonnet 'form' i.e. the shape of the sonnet conveys as such the classical mode of stillness—we read it as such." Felstiner had sought Duncan's commentary on a translation he was at the time embarked on of Rilke's sonnet *Archaïscher Torso Apollos,* which concludes with perhaps the most famous and most imitated turn in modern poetry: *Du musst dein Leben ändern* ("You must change your life"). Duncan characterizes this moment in the poem as a "sign": "the music of the poem projects a vision in being seen, a lure of the god, that is a counterpart of a visionary and oracular dream." The "stillness" of the sonnet, like that of the Greek torso, is paradoxically animated by "the music of the poem," like the music that drives Duncan's "fairy ship" into vision: "Whose sails ride before music as if it were our will." The curious syntax of that line may represent the most mysterious Duncanian turn of all, the turn from the music of words toward the image, for it seems to show how the music of a line of poetry is prior and primordial to the things it mimetically presents to the eye. Music opens the poem, and makes "our mortal heads" each glad instead of fearful "To be so far abroad from what he was." As Felstiner notes, "In *Archaïscher Torso Apollos* we do not look in order to see. Instead, our look opens us to the gaze of another."

The excessiveness of the lack marking the torso in Rilke's poem, that eyeless transfixing Other, is transformed by Duncan into an object of desire in "Passages 18: The Torso": "For my Other is not a woman but a man." In "Sonnet 3 (from Dante's Sixth Sonnet)," however, desire is suspended in the time of loss. For the poem is at its most strained in the moment before the turn back toward Dante, in its penultimate sentence: "And that we might have ever at our call / Those youths we have celebrated to play Eros / And erased to lament in the passing of things." The wish-sonnet here tips toward elegy, acknowledging the impossibility of the fellowship it imagines, and of recapturing "Those youths" (the poets' own youths? Or young men, objects of desire? Both!). Elegy means consolation, and the consolation suggested here is a curious one: the flip side of Eros is "lament," a Rilkean word if we recall the "world of lament" created by Orpheus in his great poem "Orpheus. Eurydice. Hermes": a world "in which / all nature reappeared," terribly mirrored in the agony of the poet's love. And so the turn that comes in the final strophe of Duncan's sonnet is a real turn after all, staining the "themes ... of Love" with the darkness of terror and erotic loss, so that the fairy light of the poem, a golden vanity or revolving lure, leads the reader into a far more open and perilous experience than the poem's rather slight model would seem to promise.

The slippery proliferation of turns in "Sonnet 3 (from Dante's Sixth Sonnet)"—turns in translation, in tradition, in biography—marks it as a work of open form, an open sonnet: that is, as a poem intended to reflect and interact with experience rather than narrate or represent it. This is the turn of the *polysemous,* a term that Duncan closely associates with Dante's visionary qualities, and which stands near the heart of Duncan's poetics: "This satisfaction of right understanding is counter to the mode of Dante's poetry, which is not that of a romance about imaginary beings but of a testimony of visionary experience. The poem insists upon the primal reality of the angel Amor, of Beatrice, of Virgil; and all the polysemous meanings of these persons are also, if the poem be not trivial, polysemous meanings revealed in the poet's actual life." It is the polysemous turn in Duncan, anchored in music and in the fourfold levels of interpretation proposed by Dante (literal, allegorical, psychological, anagogical) that seems so strange, so "liberal, radical, pluralistic, multiphasic," so vital and untimely now.

III
The Poet in the Worlds

New American Writing and the New Establishment

New American Writing is a centerpiece of what might be called the postmodern establishment of American poetry, as long stewarded by Paul Hoover and Maxine Chernoff. Founded in 1986, their magazine has come to represent a sort of new establishment poetry, insofar as it palpably conserves the tradition of postmodern lyric that occupies, I think, the capacious middle ground between the austerities of Language poetry, the heterogenously "personal" poems of the New York School(s), and the more or less overtly mystical modes of Black Mountain and the San Francisco Renaissance. I associate this postmodern middle with the Bay Area, perhaps because that's where I first became aware of it in its various manifestations, both hard (or abstract, or minimalist: Michael Palmer, Elizabeth Robinson, Rae Armantrout) and soft (more narrative, expansive, "hooked": Robert Hass, Donald Revell, Jeff Clark). But I think it's now accurate to characterize such poetry as the new American mainstream (if not the New Americans gone mainstream), retaining whatever oppositional force it still possesses largely through institutional memory—though it still stands strongly enough as a bulwark against the laziness and anti-intellectualism of the genuine mainstream of American cultural life. Or as Brenda Hillman puts it in an essay from the 2007 issue, "On Song, Lyric, and Strings, "Current aesthetic quarrels and conversations between poets are real enough, and the aesthetically abstract or non-referential lyric poetry may have a different readership from poetry that announces its purposes in more narrative styles, but these issues should concern poets far less than keeping poetry alive in a culture of appalling greed, a culture that doesn't read much of anything, a culture that does business as usual in a time of Enron and retributionist wars."

That same issue, number 25, opens with new translations of some haunting sonnets of Borges, includes a poem by Cal Bedient (one of the most passionate advocates of a return to lyric modernism in contemporary poetry; now as editor of *Lana Turner* he tries to square that circle with an acute revival of Marxism), and centers, it seems on Hillman's essay. This seems fitting enough, as Brenda Hillman, one of the most activist and ecologically conscious poets writing today, comes so close to the center of the postmodern lyric assemblage (I hesitate to call it a "movement") as almost to embody it. Hillman makes a case for the lyric as exceeding and preceding whatever aesthetico-ideological program you want to assign to it:

> It's hard to know what *lyric* means for post-romantics, post-symbolists, post-modernists and post-postmodernists. Lyric is an element in poetry, not a type, rendering human emotion in language; attention to subjective experience in a songlike fashion seems to be key in all definitions of lyric, and when "lyric" has been pitted against "epic" and "dramatic" forms, it has mostly been thought of as short, though it isn't always. Once lyric meant unbroken music, but since the nineteenth century, it may be broken. It cries out in singular, dialogic or in polyphonic protest. There is the question of the individual "singer," not to mention the individual lyre or the famous problem of the solitary self—can't live with it and can't live without it. Since the twentieth century unseated all certainty, the lyric is rendered on torn, damaged or twisted strings. A lyric poet sings boldly and bluntly to the general populace or is visited quietly and obliquely by the distressed hero who needs an oracle.

You can hear a bit of Hillman's own post-romantic commitments in that last sentence; elsewhere in the essay she writes, "Robert Duncan uses the word 'romantic' to recall a process-oriented seeking of original song," and then goes on to discuss the quest for originary "poetization" found in modernist commentaries on Romantic poetry (Walter Benjamin on Hölderlin being the primary example). She shows her hand further, claiming "almost all lyric poets are beauty-mongers in some way," and I think of my own attachments to and discomfort with sheer beauty. Ultimately her essay takes a stand for the necessary messiness and fragmentation of postmodern beauty, which Hillman deliberately opposes to the newspeak of our time, wondering "how the outlaw poetic sentence can address itself to the meandering sentence of official bad faith, and so makes again the large claim that poetry, audibility, synesthesia, are weapons with which to oppose the culture that our politics produces, if not the politics themselves." It's a claim I subscribe to provided we detach it from grandness and rhetoric: I think poetry does constitute a form of resistance but only on a micro, cellular level, perhaps only on the most basic level by which life opposes death.

I find less beauty in the poetry in this or any issue of *New American Writing* than I do adrenaline, a jazzing and jangling of the nerves, pleasurable but also anxiety-inducing, like a coffee mug filled to the brim with espresso. I get the high of contact with reality as it's being processed through clever, linguistically attuned minds all seeking for it in idiosyncratic ways. Their language vibrates with a dual awareness of history—the history of the present, or what I think of as "nap-of-the-earth" historicizing, an aerial view necessarily and perilously close to the surface, under the radar of the large dumb arguments that constitute our everyday comportment. But there's also the palpable impact of history on that subjective kernel that each poet proudly or shamefacedly or matter-of-factly carries with him- or herself, the energetic and continual collision of the unconscious with our intolerable Real. Some poets, like Andrew Joron, make the collisions and elisions explicit in their play, as words transform themselves to translate their nervous seeking into the reader's own nerve network in these lines from "I Am the Door":

> I, my
> > being to begin, my die
> To decide my deicide, am
>
> Gone again to distance, & sand, & stand
> > by fear
> Entranced before the door.
>
> Or do I travel as travail of a veil?

Flarf is not outside the task of the lyric as Hillman broadly defines it, as demonstrated by the inclusion of two poems by Rodney Koeneke. "A Birthday Poem for Nada Gordon" praises the Bellydancing Queen of Flarf in ludicrously elevated yet utterly sincere terms for her work "water[ing] the meaty blossoms of excess," "generously spiking our brownies with hashish" and otherwise disordering our capital-confiscated senses:

> Pack animals drop from exhaustion daily
> in the snowy Himalayas of the everyday;
> businessmen enjoy their vinaigrette
> at busy restaurants where the unconscious scrunches uneasily in
>   booster chairs.
> Above them, cool in the mind's high court you sit
> invigilating specialness
> the non-fun want eclipsed.

These poets are resurrection men and women, raiding the graves of "romantics, symbolists, modernists and postmodernists" to assemble ungainly, self-parodying, occasionally gorgeous creatures with their organs on the outside, to remind at any rate this reader that he has a pulse, neurons, hormones, ears, and a tongue. And I'm not sure it's fair to ask more of poetry than that; though we do, of course, we ask the moon, we ask for some sensation, some friction, from what we're pleased to call "the self" rubbing up against "the world," hoping for sparks, or to discover there's no separation, or that there is. Consider the first stanza of Lisa Samuels' poem, "Open your eyes to the terrible sculpture of bedclothes," a poem and title representative of the impulses I've tried to describe here:

> Kenneth Koch held three oranges, waiting for the bus.
> The oranges were self-mesmerized: each was one side of his
> four-sided-self. He was taking the bus to present his ideas.
> He had to keep his sole awake (fourth side) awake.

So what might it mean to pursue avant-garde strategies in the wake of the collapse of any strong distinction between the "inside" and "outside" of American poetry? The powerful antagonism between an academic inside (master signifier: the AWP) and an anti-academic outside (the New Americans, the Langpos) collapsed almost entirely in the first ten years of my life as a publishing poet. Is the avant-garde still a term with any meaning, or is the "post-avant" merely a relic of poetry wars that signify less than the larger marginalization of literacy that we seem to be witnessing at the advance of the twenty-first century?

The post-avant—a term popularized by Ron Silliman—is often presented as a "third way" between avant-garde and mainstream, but just as often it seems merely to signify the period style of early-twenty-first-century American poetics, defanged and deracinated as the "legitimate dangers" of the eponymous anthology edited by Michael Dumanis and Cate Marvin or the mushy *American Hybrid* anthology edited by David St. John and Cole Swensen (published in 2006 and 2009, respectively). Ange Mlinko has argued that to be avant-garde is a political position before it is an aesthetic one: the avant-garde it assumes a negative, outsider's stance toward aesthetic establishments and institutions. If, as she claims, there is no longer any meaningful "outside" in American poetry, the avant-garde is emptied of its content and becomes at best a style, at worst a pose; one more chip to be played in the increasingly disorganized game of Texas hold 'em that is our boundaryless poetry present.

The notion of the post-avant as a "third way" is therefore subject to the same criticism that the political Third Way is open to: that it's really just the "first way" (i.e., hegemony) with an updated sales pitch, the School of Quietude with a human face. From my perspective, the post-avant predicament has less to do with the disappearance of the outside than it does with the disappearance of the inside. That is, literary culture (not just poetry!) no longer has a meaningful relation with our culture-in-general, which in itself no longer seems to serve the function of legitimizing political power, or even of legitimizing markets. Put in a more concrete way, many poets associated with the "post-avant" now have tenure-track academic jobs; but I would argue such positions no longer constitute a meaningful "inside" because neither American culture nor American poetry center on academia any more, and haven't for quite some time. An endowed chair at Harvard or Penn just ain't what it used to be: the cultural capital accruing to a Bob Perelman or a Jorie Graham is microscopic in comparison with the capital enjoyed by previous generations of poets and profs from Mark Van Doren to Lionel Trilling, or even to Perelman (still "outside") and Graham (very much "inside") as recently as the 1980s. The flip side of this is a tremendous democratization: it's harder than ever to write a book of poems that will make any sort of splash in the larger culture, but it's easier than ever for talented poets, academic and non-academic, to find *an* audience (if not *the* audience) via chapbooks, small presses, and the Web.

So it seems to me that poets of every aesthetic stripe save perhaps the most conservative (the ones approved of by Adam Kirsch, say, or the ranks of the poets laureate) are best described as post-mainstream, because the center of the cultural margin is still the margin. Almost any sort of poetry writing or life in poetry counts as countercultural in a manifestly postliterate society. But that doesn't mean we get to reclaim avant-garde status because a literary avant-garde has to attack the literary establishment, and the latter simply doesn't exist any more, at least not in the sense that "establishment" ought to have (i.e., bearing some intrinsic relation to power). This doesn't mean that poets have stopped competing for status and recognition; nor have I resolved, or adequately raised, the question of literary culture's relationship to the marketplace. But it seems clear that the game has changed, and more radically than we've realized, in just the past decade or so; and I'm not at all convinced that what will take the old culture's place will much resemble the field we're all still half-heartedly running up in down in, with the avant-garde guarding one goalpost and the reactionaries guarding the other (while proclaiming loudly that there is, in fact, no game taking place).

What we're left with is style: mere aesthetics. And that's not such a terrible thing, if only because of the enormous freedom it offers poets and readers; and because it throws us back upon what Ron Silliman recently said in his response to a Poetry Foundation questionnaire (the simple fact of having been asked for such suggests that the Foundation can't be what we once thought of as an establishment, nor can Ron be what we once thought of as avant-garde): "Whether you are a new formalist or a slam poet, a visual poet or a language writer, the absolute materiality of the signifier, the physicality of sound and of the graphic letter, is the one secret shared by all poets to which nonreaders of poetry seem literally clueless." Ours is a language art, and whatever else we are likely to become as a species, it seems unlikely that we'll become post-language. So there's room for the new—and perhaps, an outside—after all.

Joshua Corey

Phantasmagoria of Authorship

The crisis of confidence in literature has been building since at least the advent of the NEA's 2004 "Reading at Risk" report, supplemented by the perennial flood of think pieces on the death of poetry and the death of the novel, corresponding roughly with the "crisis in the humanities" that is a symptom of the larger crisis of privatization writ large, the enclosure of the everything, not least the imagination. But to stay local for the moment, consider one of those think pieces, Tom Chatfield's essay "Do Writers Need Paper?," published in the British magazine *Prospect*. It's an elegant bit of hand-wringing, notable for how archaic the laments of nominally successful writers quoted in it are; the novelist Lionel Shriver is quoted as saying she has "a conventional authorial life: I get advances sufficient to support me financially; I release my books through traditional publishing houses and write for established newspapers and magazines." She worries that should "electronic publishing takes off in a destructive manner ... the kind of fruitful professional life I lead could be consigned to the past." Am I crazy for thinking that sort of "professional life" is already in the past? How many literary writers—heck, how many writers of thrillers and potboilers—make any sort of living, let alone a comfortable one, from writing alone? The notion of literary writing as a "profession" seems positively quaint, worlds away from the idea of *vocation* (with its accompanying whiff of monklike devotion to chastity [originality], obedience [aesthetics], and poverty [poverty]) that functions for me as the necessary veil between *writing* and the grim progress of ever-increasing specialization that alienates every function of life from every other function.

    I digress. As many have observed, the old model of authorship is crumbling, and success is no longer measured in sales but in the size and vibrancy of the networks writers and readers are building together, connections counted in terms of page views, Facebook friends, and the size of one's Google (to use the awkward, vaguely phallic noun-phrase adapted by Keith Gessen in his appropriately titled novel *All the Sad Young Literary Men*). And as Chatfield observes, the waning of literature as we've known it has hardly meant an end to narrative and storytelling; it's just *authorship* as we've known it that is dying: "Today, in an age of collaborative media, most of our grandest, most popular narratives are the products of team efforts: from sprawling television dramas like *The Sopranos* to the latest Hollywood movies or hit videogames." Increasingly, according to Chatfield, the long labor of single authors is being supplanted by collaboration. The writer's garret has been supplanted by the more sociable writer's room familiar from TV shows like *30 Rock,* not to mention the creative writing workshop (though the fields of Iowa may, ironically, be where the myth of the author as solitary genius makes its very last stand).

It is increasingly fashionable to say that even those of us who are not primarily collaborators—the writers of poems, stories, novels, essays—do not work alone. David Shields's manifesto *Reality Hunger* is a compilation of quotes that makes the implicit argument that to remain relevant, writers must seize the means of appropriation and bring larger and less digested chunks of "reality" into their work, shunning the tired artifices of fiction, whose reality effects are all worn out. Shields lists an interesting constellation of artworks that suggests the porous boundaries of the new genre or anti-genre that he sees forming (the term he seems happiest with is the "lyric essay" associated with John D'Agata, whose statements are cited liberally throughout Shields' book):

> Jeff Crouse's plug-in *Delete City.* The quasi-home movie *Open Water. Borat: Cultural Learnings of America for Make Benefit Glorious Nation of Kazakhstan.* Joe Frank's radio show *In the Dark.* The depilation scene in *The 40-Year-Old Virgin.* Lynn Shelton's unscripted film *Humpday* ("All the writing takes place in the editing room").... *Curb Your Enthusiasm,* which—characteristic of this genre, this ungenre, this antigenre—relies on viewer awareness of the creator's self-consciousness, wobbly manipulation of the gap between person and persona.

You get the idea: these are fundamentally fictions that trespass on the real, that rely for their aesthetic effect on the viewer's awareness of the manipulation of actual events. Of course you've noticed that all of Shields' examples thus far come from pop culture and visual media. He's on shakier ground when he finally gets around to discussing the literary equivalent of this sort of reality-performance:

> The appeal of Billy Collins is that compared with the frequently hieroglyphic obscurantism of his colleagues, his poems sound like they were tossed off in a couple of hours while he drank scotch and listened to jazz late at night (they weren't; this is an illusion). *A Heartbreaking Work of Staggering Genius* was full of the same self-conscious apparatus that had bored everyone silly until it got tethered to what felt like someone's "real life" (even if the author constantly reminded us how fictionalized that life was). At once desperate for authenticity and in love with artifice, I know all the moments are "moments": staged and theatrical, shaped and thematized. I find I can listen to talk radio in a way that I can't abide the network news—the sound of human voices waking before they drown.

Billy Collins? Really? Is he the best example available of a poet who satisfies the new craving for "reality"? It seems to me a very long distance between Collins' easy-listening poetic and the highfalutin' Eliotic allusion with which Shields ends this passage. But Collins is one of the few genuinely popular poets out there, and Shields' manifesto craves and ratifies, more than reality, what is popular. (He could easily have swapped titles with Steven Johnson, whose book is called *Everything Bad Is Good For You*.) The Billy Collins persona is that of a sensitive, semi-educated Joe Sixpack; there's just enough erudition and self-consciousness in there to flatter the intelligence of his NPR-listening readers, while at the same time the slapdash, self-satisfied quality that makes me wince is a pleasing mark of the poet's just-folks "authenticity." Shields' attack on fiction (notice the snide implicit assault on the postmodern "self-conscious apparatus" of writing that is *un*tethered to "real life") can sound uncomfortably close to an assault on imagination itself.

Yet the man is on to something. What he calls "reality," to take a cue from Wallace Stevens, is really just another level of imagination, except that what's crucial to this antigenre is its arousal of and dependence on the *reader*'s imaginary participation in the work. It's a kind of bait-and-switch: the overt, self-conscious presence of the *meta* in these works creates the illusion of something incontrovertible and real that the meta qualities of the work floats intangibly above, as metaphysics presumes physics. These texts and entertainments undo, to a greater or lesser degree, the suture between authenticity and artifice and invite their audiences to fill the gap, to take pleasure in a sort of sublime. I say "sublime" because the reality effect Shields is after depends on the indeterminacy of the suture: pure documentary with its adherence to verifiable fact is incapable of arousing this emotion, which as Kant tells us depends on the defeat of the understanding and what he calls "vibration": "a rapidly alternating repulsion and attraction produced by one and the same object." We feel reality's presence in the work, but that presence is unquantifiable (if quantified and found wanting the resulting disappointment is titanic; cf. James Frey, who comes up for frequent discussion later in Shields' book).

There is a connection to be drawn between the devolution of literature as we once understood it, a semi-autonomous realm of authors whose ownership of their work was sufficient guarantee of its authenticity (and look how much aura yet clings to authorial names like Joyce, Woolf, Faulkner, and Beckett), and the rise of the paraliterary antigenre that Shields celebrates. Though his celebration strikes many readers as a capitulation, we must take seriously the nexus that Shields' book unfolds between the transformation of literature on the genre level and the transformation of the field of the literary as such into one more facet of an increasingly level media landscape in which the lines between producer and consumer become ever more blurry. The question for writers now, it seems, is whether to join Shields at the barricades of the lyric essay and memoir; to fight a residual action, harkening back to the heroic artifice of authenticity that bears the name of modernism; to write genre fiction (more popular than ever); or to surf the wave, captured by no single authorial identity, finding opportunity in crisis without yielding too quickly to cynicism, curmudgeonliness, or the reality bandwagon.

My intuition suggests, however, whatever paths open or close to individual writers in the next twenty years, that *collaboration*—in myriad forms—is here to stay, and will be at the center of art's vitality going forward. For artists themselves now assume the role of the "pieces of reality" that compose what continues to be the most compelling and versatile legacy of the twentieth century: the assemblage, the collage.

The future, like the past, belongs to poets who *perform* the self, who manifest their corporeality, shame, and will-to-power on the page. The poets Arielle Greenberg and Lara Glenum have named this practice, or an aspect of it, "the Gurlesque"; its most ambitious practitioners walk the line between poetry and theater, as in the work of Trisha Low or Cecilia Corrigan. Male poets too play with and riff on their poetic selves, theatricalizing their own gawky vulnerability, sometimes through displays of virtuosity (I think of the ghazals of Anthony Madrid) but more often through an appealingly inclusive shagginess (Dana Ward's *The Crisis of Infinite Worlds* strikes me as exemplary). Perhaps most urgent and new-seeming in this register is the work of black poets such as Tyhembia Jess, whose *Olio* is an astonishingly theatrical and carnivalesque presentation of American history through the re-presentation of the work of African American musicians in the years between Reconstruction and World War I.

Even on the page these poets asks us put aside the page and close our eyes. To bring us into the presence of the oracular, the medium, the stance of he who testifies to something beyond. A stance that's never merely ironic, for the poet's own body is at stake.

The public has always responded to the writer's personality, or the performance of that personality, and writers have always done a striptease with how much or how little of the "authentic" self and its experience can be located in a given work. The Romantics, broadly speaking (Goethe-Wordsworth-Byron through Dickinson-Whitman) can be defined at least epiphenomenally by the performance of persona, though the grandiosity of the High Romantics is nearly impossible to imitate without irony. It may be the work of Low Romantics like John Clare, combining precision of observation with a performance of abjection and self-consciousness that gets linked, appositively, to the objects of that perception, that may offer a way forward now:

> I am: yet what I am none cares or knows,
> My friends forsake me like a memory lost;
> I am the self-consumer of my woes,
> They rise and vanish in oblivious host,
> Like shades in love and death's oblivion lost;
> And yet I am! and live with shadows tost
>
> Into the nothingness of scorn and noise,
> Into the living sea of waking dreams,
> Where there is neither sense of life nor joys,
> But the vast shipwreck of my life's esteems;
> And e'en the dearest—that I loved the best—
> Are strange—nay, rather stranger than the rest.

Poets are no longer famous, yet they go on performing their personalities, just like the just-like-us "stars" of reality television. Some of them still lay claim to craft, subject matter, something to say, like the contestants on *Top Chef* or *Project Runway*. The purer breeds, coming and going interchangeably on shows like *The Bachelor*, stand as naked as Clare, "the peasant poet" taken up to his detriment as fashionable by the literary culture of his time, into "the nothingness of scorn and noise, / Into the living sea of waking dreams" to delight and scandalize. Poets like poems are disposable (but recyclable) commodities. Poems interrupt the prose of life (as the formatting of poems in *The New Yorker* has always taught us), indistinguishable from cartoons or advertisements.

Really the only difference between poetry and reality television is that reality television is *popular*. As David Shields or one of his citations puts it:

Warhol's Marilyn Monroe silk screens and his *Double Elvis* work as metaphors because their images are so common in the culture that they can be used as shorthand, as other generations would have used, say, the sea. Marilyn and Elvis are just as much a part of the natural world as the ocean and a Greek god are.

But the gods have not returned, and neither has "nature." Celebrities no longer have the iconicity they once had, any more than poets do. (High Romanticism = the Hollywood studio system. Low Romanticism = YouTube.) As Warhol predicted, everyone is equally (un)famous, equally (un)worthy of performance and attention. Romantics of all stripes mine our nostalgia for a glamor, heroism, gods, nature that the individual, even a famous individual, never can possess. (I wish I was Cary Grant, said Cary Grant.) As Schiller says, the *sentimentalisch* poet always defines himself by self-conscious difference from the naive poet. It doesn't matter whether or not naive poets actually existed. We have had to invent them, as we have invented media to which we deform and conform our lives. Because mimesis, like the sublime and beautiful, is not a quality of objects or artworks. It is a faculty of the self.

When I say "collaborators" I mean the decentering (as opposed to the death) of authorship, the defederalization of the author. But I am also thinking of the *épuration légale* of French women having their heads shaved in 1944, marching in ignominy to social death past jeering crowds, bearers of the shame of collaborating with power, sleeping with the enemy, doing what it took to survive.

> I long for scenes where man has never trod;
> A place where woman never smil'd or wept;
> There to abide with my creator, God,
> And sleep as I in childhood sweetly slept:
> Untroubling and untroubled where I lie;
> The grass below—above the vaulted sky.

The Tripod:
Three Modes for Twenty-First-Century American Poetry

Too much of the discourse around American poetry is hampered by its own Americanness, the most pernicious form of provincialism in that it doesn't know that it's provincial. I've devoted far too much energy to trying to classify various tendencies—flarf versus conceptualism, mainstream verse versus the post-avant—and the results have always generated more heat than light. If I feel myself lured, once again, into the fatality of a Cartesian grid of the social forms of poetry, at least let me be guided this time by the work of Adam Zagajewski, a Polish poet whose 2004 essay collection *A Defense of Ardor* offers a rousing defense of a strain in poetry that is too often silent or obscure on the American scene.

In the title essay, Zagajewski refers to his "four periscopes": eyes on differing strains or lineages that guide him as a poet. "One, the main one, is turned toward my native tradition [of Polish literature]. The other opens out onto German literature, its poetry, its (bygone) yearning for eternity. The third reveals the landscape of French culture, with its penetrating intelligence and Jansenist moralism. The fourth is aimed at Shakespeare, Keats, and Robert Lowell, the literature of specifics, passion, and conversation." The particular contents (or, I suppose, seas) surveyed by these "periscopes" matters less, I think, than their multiplicity: Zagajewski implicitly contains multitudes that comprise not just grammars but literatures and histories that capture an enormous swath of his European heritage.

From this generous humanism Zagajewski goes on to adopt two signature characters as stand-ins for powerful opposed tendencies in Western thought: Lodovico Settembrini and Leo Naphta, the angel and the devil on the shoulder of Hans Castorp, the protagonist of Thomas Mann's *The Magic Mountain*. These two characters illustrate the modern schism in "the poetry of the cosmos" via "Naphta's demonic whisper and the humanitarian discourse of Settembrini." Zagajewski summarizes one of the major arguments from the philosopher Charles Taylor's book *Sources of the Self* to illustrate the schism: "in our age, Enlightenment values triumphed in public institutions, at least in the West, whereas in our private lives we abandon ourselves to Romantic insatiability. We go along with rationalism whenever public, social issues are at stake, but at home, in private, we search ceaselessly for the absolute and aren't content with the decisions we accept in the public sphere." Since Zagajewski wrote these words, we've witnessed a troubling reversal of these positions: the refusal to accept limitation, the "Romantic insatiability," has been adopted by the political right in direct proportion to its disdain for Enlightenment values. Facts and reason are now at best quasi-public, a web of affiliations referred to quaintly by a George W. Bush administration official as "the reality-based community"; the passionate intensity of the political worst sidelines rationalism and pursues absolute goals without regard to the values and hesitancies of the rest of us. Yet there remains an important kernel of truth in Zagajewski's claim, that too often poetry, as the sphere in which expression at its most private intersects with the public, has lacked "Ardor, metaphysical seriousness, the risky voicing of strong opinions." He puts his finger on a dissatisfaction I've come to feel with American poetry as I found it in the early twenty-first century, a dissatisfaction which has only grown.

Zagajewski's essay helps me track a number of trends as well as my own dissatisfactions. It seems to me that the aesthetic Left—most especially Language and post-Language writing—with its affinities for European literary theory, Marxism, and intellectualism generally, represents a surge of public-Enlightenment values into the private-Romantic sphere reserved for poetry, an incursion which causes continual outrage on the private-Romantic side that manifests alternately as pooh-poohing, anti-intellectualism, sphincter-tightening, and genuine worry that the private sphere defined by the Romantic poem (often but not necessarily connected at least unconsciously with the values of private property) might vanish or stand revealed as the fragmented nexus of consumerist desires. Poetry, in short, that is explicitly concerned with the social, and which either in itself or in its mode of production represents a challenge to the model of poetry as either a private and ephemeral pleasure or, more seriously, as a genuine, arduous, and singular path toward vision and transcendence. I yearn for some kind of combination of the two modes, as presented half-cynically by the full title of Bruce Andrews's book *I Don't Have Any Paper So Shut Up (Or, Social Romanticism)* or more ardently and openly by the likes of Adrienne Rich. I hazard the following triangle as a step beyond the usual easy dualism of us versus them, innovative versus mainstream, et al, ad nauseam:

A. *Social formalism*, which tends to be critical, antimetaphysical, constructivist, and politically engaged (both in terms of content and in terms of the scene of production). It can dry, abstruse, conceptual with a deliberately dissociated or repellent surface; it can also often be very funny. Flarf and other forms of the anti-poem serve largely to illuminate the social field of poetry as such, but at their furthest aperture they drench all manner of meaning-making machinery from the puerile to the perverse in pitiless light. Logopoetic practically by definition; friendly to melopoeia, which it finds generative; takes a hostile or ironic stance toward phanopoeia and indeed all forms of representation that reproduce the world it would like to tear down. Negative capability is a prerequisite for further construction. Language poetry was the most dynamic manifestation of this mode, and has been carried forward into the twenty-first century by conceptual poetry and not infrequently by prose.

B. *The private-romantic*: the poem as guarantee of some minimal subjectivity (legroom in coach) through a stage-managed epiphany that claims to stand free of the social largely by virtue of its ragged right margin or a louche earnestness. Its authority, such as it is, derives from some institutional structure whose hegemony it serves to conceal: this is the sort of thing favored by young fogeys like Adam Kirsch and David Yezzi, a stance toward poetry that starts from the question, What to make of a diminished thing? Its practitioners tend to make a fetish of accessibility and tastefulness, though there is also a subgroup—one might call it B posing as A, and its embodiment is Frederick Seidel—which flaunts its tastelessness as doggerel, a kind of nihilistic shrug in the face of social forces that it outlines without opposing. Phanopoetic image-making is its stock in trade; its melopoeia is facile where it isn't rigid; its logopoeia generally restricts itself to allusions and heavy-handed allegory. Its negative capability derives principally from exhaustion, from indifference, or else it doesn't exist at all and yields happily to dogma. Anti-modernist or symptomatically postmodernist.

C. The *metaphysical-romantic*. These are the rare poems that dream big, whose private clearing begets a cosmology, whose withdrawal from the social is truly generative of vision, and return to the social, as it were, *armed*, like the speaker of Blake's "Jersualem." It enacts what Zagajewski, drawing from Plato, calls "*metaxu*, being 'in between,' in between our earth, our (so we suppose) comprehensible, concrete, material surroundings, and transcendence, mystery." It's difficult to privilege any one aspect of the three major dimensions of poetry for this mode, but I would say it goes primarily by ear, with logopoeia serving to generate an intellectual context (something like a "poetry of ideas") and phanopoeia generally providing relief, a touching place on the earth. Its negative capability most resembles Keats': a mode of attentive listening. In the twentieth century it's best represented by the strain of modernism emerging from Rilke, Yeats, H.D., and Stevens.

Whereas the trouble with Poetry B is, for me, self-evident, the trouble with A is that it tends to deny C or else attacks it as bourgeois and complacent about social conditions (including of course the social conditions of poetry). Poetry C can be mistaken for its unambitious cousin B, for the compositional space of such poems is generally conceived of as private; at the same time, though, that space is metaphysical and ex-centric, not a stake plunged into the hard turf of tradition but a launching pad. It brings the highest ambitions for poetry as public voicing within the private-spiritual sphere to which poetry has traditionally been allocated—whereas Poetry A seeks to explode or implode the private as a mere symptom of the private property it would also like to destroy. To imagine a blending of A and C is to flirt with theology, or at least the religious: it supposes that poetry could serve to organize a *polis* aspiring toward a particular transcendent fact, neither entirely private nor public—a congregation, a "visionary company."

As always there's the interesting question of audience: I think most people, when they *need* a poem, need something like Poetry C. Sometimes they find it, sometimes they settle for B. The average literate person is simply not aware that social formalism exists, and when they stumble across it they are usually repelled by its rebarbative and conceptual surface. This in no way invalidates A: it stands far more strongly for some kind of alternative to life as sheer exchange value than B does, though such is B's pose; the difference may boil down to the underexamined faith in individualism that a B poet assumes, a kind of Emersonianism *manqué*. The risk of C is quietism: it can stand at too great a distance from the social in its pursuit of its orphic goals, getting high on its own supply of transcendental vision. At its worst it can mirror the cliché: "spiritual but not religious." At its best I still think it has vital work to do, and may even be the "soul" of poetry as such. Or is A closer to that soul, if the soul of poetry is Talmudically to contest its own boundaries?.

What I have inelegantly labeled "metaphysical romanticism" does not lend itself very well to talk of schools and filiations, though the "New Gnostics" grouped around the journal *Talisman* comes close. It can fall into anti-intellectualism almost as easily as B can. But it cannot and should not become the sole property of the Right. I think there must be a place for metaphysics in poetry, even provisional metaphysics: a poetry that proposes meaning, and language as ground for meaningfulness. It may take the revival of a missing term to link the realms of the social and the metaphysical, the civic and the orphic:

what poets used to call Nature. But if Nature has disappeared, as many seem to believe that it has, on what ground can the social and the individual be reconciled? Not a metaphysical politics—that way lies Fascism, a road the West seems to be once again hurtling down. But not, for this poet, a pure politics either, as badly as we need a renewal of the spirit of Enlightenment. Not Nature, maybe, but the common, the ground for speech and shared existence, for humans and nonhumans alike. An intuition to pursue.

Richard Hugo's Constructivist Moment

Down where the ladders start—that's where you'll find the workshop of Richard Hugo's much-beloved book on writing, *The Triggering Town*. More nakedly than any American poet I know, Hugo writes about the task and function of poetry from a position of sheer abjection. "The self as given is inadequate and will not do"—that statement stands at the core of his disarmingly ad hoc poetics, outlined in chapters with titles like "Assumptions," "Nuts and Bolts," and "Statements of Faith." At first and probably even second glance he looks like an advocate of confession and the unified lyric "I"—not least because he himself is a compulsive confessor. We learn about his traumatic experiences as a World War II bombardier; we overhear English Department infighting and gossip; and between the lines we discover Hugo as a painfully shy, immature, sexually inhibited, passive-aggressive alcoholic. And if this weren't embarrassing enough, Hugo also implicates the reader in his vision of the poet as awkward failure.

Borrowing his terms from Hemingway and Faulkner, Hugo characterizes all poets as being either "Krebs" or "Snopes": "In Hemingway's story, the protagonist, Krebs, by birth and circumstance is an insider. As a result of his experiences in a war and his own sensitivity, he feels alienated and outside. In Faulkner's story, the protagonist, Snopes, a little boy, by birth and circumstance is an outsider who wants desperately to be in." These are not appetizing choices, but they suggest a number of appalling truths. One is the usually unspoken question of class in American poetry that separates poets into self-deprecating MFA insiders and resentful nonacademic outsiders. Another is the fact that any poet, even the most successful, is likely to feel herself an outsider in a culture where most literate people are cheerfully oblivious to poetry—they literally don't know what they're missing.

Hugo's book is for those who know or suspect that they need poetry, who are—why not admit it?—nearly always poets themselves. That need, that state of abjection, is Hugo's given, and if you take it as your own, he can teach you how to write a poetry that transcends your inadequate self. Again and again Hugo warns poets against defended writing—against "writing what you know." The central metaphor of "the triggering town" is the jumping-off point, the subject—for Hugo, always a town that has seen better days, "the town [that] will have become your hometown." A piece of the world, something glimpsed from a car window or from inside a bar, is the start of every poem for Hugo.

But the world inevitably sends you to language—to *your* language: "you are after those words you can own and ways of putting them in phrases and lines that are yours by right of obsessive musical deed.... Your words used your way will generate your meanings. Your obsessions lead you to your vocabulary. Your way of writing locates, even creates, your inner life. The relation of you to your language gains power. The relation of you to the triggering subject weakens." In spite of the relentless repetition of "you" and "your" in this passage, note that it's the relation of "you to your language" that gains power and not the "you." The implication is that "you" will only discover yourself beyond your givens: "give up what you think you have to say, and you'll find something better." The "something better" is the poem, but it's also perhaps a version of the self beyond what you *think* of yourself and what others think of you. The outsider, Krebs or Snopes, can disappear into the poem if the poet can just "get off the subject, I mean the triggering subject." The self as given is the triggering town: the point of departure. The destination is in the poem.

In spite of his instinctive aesthetic conservatism, Hugo's insistence on going beyond the self can serve as an imperative for poets to go beyond the mere ratification of subjectivity in their poetry. This stance has the latent pathos—and latent Modernism—of T.S Eliot's much-quoted prescription against personality in "Tradition and the Individual Talent," including its often omitted follow-up sentence: "But, of course, only those who have personality and emotions know what it means to want to escape from these things." Of course this does not mean that Hugo himself did not believe in an authentic "inner self" ("Quest for self is fundamental to poetry," he writes), only that he was persuaded that we cannot access it directly—that experience must lead to language before language can be an experience.

"A good teacher can save a young poet years by simply telling him things he need not waste his time on, like trying to will originality or trying to share an experience in language or trying to remain true to the facts." Like the small towns that have seen better days, for Hugo a given poet's will, experience, and knowledge of "the facts" are just materials, triggers, with no intrinsic value in the world of the poem. This radical democracy of the given can look like cynicism, just as Hugo's humility can look like a cunning pose. Actually, it's a profound faith in the imagination as an intrinsically redemptive force. "It is impossible to write meaningless sequences.... In the world of imagination, all things belong. If you take that on faith, you may be foolish, but foolish like a trout."

The last chapter of *The Triggering Town* is titled, "How Poets Make a Living" and it takes the form of a story Hugo heard while he was working at Boeing—the only story from his working life Hugo ever put directly into a poem. It was about a homeless man—"the Admiral"—and his wife who were squatters on company land, who were eventually evicted and driven in a truck full of trash ("old pieces of dirty rags, hunks of wood, maybe even stones, anything that might show a hostile world that he was not destitute") to the Monroe Valley, where they were eventually abandoned by the side of the road. It becomes clear by chapter's end that Hugo identifies with the Admiral—his defiance, his incoherent letters to the management of Boeing, his desperate attempt to make a semblance of life from garbage. There's a sentimentality here that's easy to turn away from, but there's truth, too, about the poet's human condition and what we must all be prepared to give up—to be good poets, yes, but also simply to be good.

Read at the right angle, *The Triggering Town* can help bridge the gap that now yawns so wide between a poetry of subjectivity and a poetry that foregrounds the operations of language, that seeks to demonstrate the fragile constructedness of our selves and the world. For Hugo, doing one necessarily leads to the other. "All truth must conform to music" is Hugo's constructivist gamble, and if that attitude is right, he still has a job to do.

Return to *Howl*

Reading Ginsberg again. I don't even *like* the Beats, I keep telling myself. I'm not an angst-ridden teenager any more. I'm old enough to see through their genius for self-promotion, the easy recuperation by the culture of their attack on the forces of patriarchy, conformity, and capitalism. (Spontaneous Bop Capitalism, we ought to call it.) Kerouac wore khakis, Burroughs was a lowlife, Ginsberg wrote three or four indelible poems and was otherwise a bearded self-referential embarrassment. What keeps me coming back?

For all their shaggy ecastic optimism, Ginsberg's poems are saturated with what he as an American Jew of extraordinary sensitivity could understand of the Shoah. Allen Grossman puts it this way:

> The characteristic literary posture of the postwar poet in America is that of the survivor—a man who is not quite certain that he is not in fact dead.... 'Since so many like me died, and since my survival is an unaccountable accident, how can I be certain that I did not myself die and that America is not in fact Hell, as indeed all of the social critics say it is?' Ginsberg's poetry is the poetry of *a terminal cultural situation.* It is a Jewish poetry because the Jew is a symbolic representative of man overthrown by history.

"Ginsberg's chief artistic contribution in *Kaddish,*" Grossman writes, "is a virtually psychotic candor that affects the mind less like poetry than like some real experience that is so terrible that it cannot be understood. In America, which did not experience the Second World War on its own soil, the Jew indeed may be the proper interpreter of horror." "Virtually": what we have here are paired and opposed virtualities: the virtuality of "the bitter logic of the poetic principle" (poetry's effacement or erasure of the actual in its pursuit of representation) versus "virtually psychotic candor," a break not with representation but with reality itself. *Kaddish,* in other words, may come as close as any poet who was not himself a survivor can to presenting the Shoah's horror as a lapse in his mother's own acute consciousness, something which can otherwise only be given in the testimony of survivors, the scream unbarred by the Adornian dictum "To write poetry after Auschwitz is barbaric."

It's personal. When I posted a photo of Ginsberg recently on Facebook, someone commented that it looked a lot like a younger version of myself. And while I don't have the genes to become bald or grow a beard, that simple fact—that when I was a young poet I could find so easily an image for myself reflected in the world—still means something.

Just look at the guy. You can see the charisma, but in spite of the black and white and the cigarette or roach he's smoking, there's nothing *cool* about those glasses, the intensity of the gaze, the shockingly sensuous mouth. If Ginsberg embarrasses he embarrasses by his warmth and vulnerability and nervous joy in living. His words and image made it possible for my younger self to imagine that my inability to be cool, to live indifferent and defended, might not mean my automatic and inevitable destruction.

Or rather, that it might be possible to live with the knowledge of destruction. For Ginsberg is one of the most-death haunted poets I know. It's all over *Howl* and it's the reason for being of *Kaddish*, an unbearably personal poem, not least for me because my own mother, although far from mad, exhibited qualities of depression and narcissism that marked me for life, and then of course she died young, as it happens less than a mile from the "The mental hospital—state Greystone," one of the several grim palaces in which Naomi Ginsberg was treated, generally unsuccessfully, for her mental illness. (It's also where Woody Guthrie spent his last years losing the battle with Huntington's; Bob Dylan visited him there before the singer died.)

When Ginsberg addresses Carl Solomon in *Howl,* when he says, "I'm with you in Rockland," he's really talking to his mother. She is the muse he cannot deny, who terrifies and threatens him, the possessor, in Allen Grossman's formulation, of "an insane idealism of which her son is heir," and for whom he musters a truly astonishing compassion. In one of the most uncanny passages of *Kaddish* he embraces, almost literally, the stench of mortality and sadness that has come to surround her flesh, as it surrounds all flesh, though we pretend not to smell it:

> One time I thought she was trying to make me come lay her—flirting to herself at sink—lay back on huge bed that filled most of the room, dress up round her hips, big slash of hair, scars of operations, pancreas, belly wounds, abortions, appendix, stitching of incisions pulling down in the fat like hideous thick zippers—ragged long lips between her legs—What, even, smell of asshole? I was cold—later revolted a little, not much—seemed perhaps a good idea to try—know the Monster of the Beginning Womb—Perhaps—that way. Would she care? She needs a lover.
>
> Yisborach, v'yistabach, v'yispoar, v'yisroman, v'yisnaseh, v'yishador, v'yishalleh, v'yishallol, sh'meh d'kudsho, b'rich hu.

Birthdeath, "the Monster of the Beginning Womb," revolted only "a little, not much," followed by the Hebrew that only comparatively late in life am I beginning to get a feel for, if not comprehension of: *Blessed and praised, glorified and exalted, extolled and honored, adored and lauded be the name of the Holy One, blessed be He.* Something I say, or ought to say, every December 21, on the anniversary of my own mother's death.

As with Ginsberg, my mother represents a portal to the incomprehensible cruelty of the past. In Naomi's case, she is haunted, sometimes comically, by the specter of Adolf Hitler—"she saw his mustache in the sink." Mom was a Holocaust survivor, born in Budapest in 1942, hidden with her grandparents in the ghetto while her own parents, my grandparents, Ernest and Eva Montag, were sent to Auschwitz-Birkenau. Miraculously, both survived, and returned to Hungary to collect their little girl, waiting together a few years in the British DP camp in Bergen Belsen before emigrating to this country. Mom grew up in the long shadow of her parents' trauma, surrounded by other Hungarian Jews, in darkest Queens.

In the summer of '65, not long before my mother met my father in New York City, restless traveler Ginsberg managed to get himself kicked out of two socialist countries in succession (Cuba and Czechoslovakia). He described these events in a long and entertaining letter to Nicanor Parra, a letter in which he also describes, in an unsettlingly brief and casual way, a visit he paid to Auschwitz: "Then a week in Krakow which hath a beauteous cathedral with giant polychrome altarpiece by medieval woodcarver genius Wit Stoltz, and car ride to Auschwitz with some boy scout leaders who were trying to pick up schoolboys hanging around the barbed wire gazing at tourists." This borders on bad taste: is the perpetually horny Ginsberg unable to notice anything at the camp other than the vaguely predatory behavior of the "boy scout leaders" with whom he is inexplicably traveling? And who the hell was Wit Stoltz? Google turns up only Ginsberg's letters and, if you don't use quotation marks, footage of Eric Stoltz as Marty McFly in unused footage from *Back to the Future*. (Further research reveals the artist's actual name to have been Veit Stoss; his altarpiece is a mad Gothic tower of carved wooden figures in relief, an overwhelming Molochian mass. I stand there in the chilly cathedral taking it in, listening for the echoes. A few candles in gray light. Humped, homogenous Poland swirling blondly past on the streets of Krakow.)

Sixty years after *Howl* and fifty-six years after *Kaddish* and fifty years after Ginsberg made nothing, at least nothing obvious, of standing on the ashen ground of Auschwitz, and eighteen years after Ginsberg's death in New York, I paid my own first and so far only visit to the museum at Auschwitz-Birkenau. There is a snack bar in the center of the parking lot and postcards on sale in the gift shop; the ironies are too large and too obvious to be ironies. Young Israelis wrapped in blue and white flags pose for photos on the train tracks on which my grandparents arrived in the camp to be processed, both strong and healthy enough to survive the initial *Selektion*. The foundations of barracks stretch across the bald Polish plain. The ruins of crematoria, picturesque as any other ruin. What shocks me, though it shouldn't, is the proximity of the camp to the town. The camp *is* a town. It is the precise inversion of the Aryan utopia the Nazis tried to create: a Berlin, a Vienna, a Paris without Jews. Hell is empty. The devils are still here.

Implicitly, maybe explicitly, Grossman criticizes Ginsberg and other American poets for reducing the disasters of the twentieth century to the *personal*. But from what other ground does a fundamentally lyric poetry (and I believe that Ginsberg *is* a lyric poet, in spite of the length of his most famous poems) have to work? Put another way, I feel myself as a poet forever trying to reconstitute the conditions that ground my imagination and its powers, however limited. Perversely, I feel called beyond the bounds of what poetry can say to capture this groundless ground, having written one novel that tries the mental life of my mother as survivor, while in another, hybrid text I retell the story of the infamous love affair between Martin Heidegger and Hannah Arendt as a kind of ground zero moment of the twentieth century's failed project to think the political alongside the sublime of techno-capitalism. Ginsberg is not, apparently, present in these projects. And yet for me there's never any getting away from him; poetically speaking he's my gay grandfather, *mon hypocrite semblable*, whose drolly encompassing prosody seems to promise, as Grossman suggests, not a description of experience but experience itself. A kind of wit matched with the darkest recesses of experience, intended not to aggrandize the self but which makes the lyric I into the imperiled traveler (a drunken boat) we all are.

Standing on that bare ground, in Poland, my head bathed by the smokeless air, I encounter neither Allen nor my grandparents nor the angel of history but sheer contingency, fragility, the monster of beginning, incomprehensible ground of all poems that find their way from fate.

Baroque Nation

Poetry is nation-building by other means, a shadow government that arises wherever a people is denied access to its own institutions, cut off from its own powers, its very language de-authorized. Yeats and his compatriots in Ireland before (and perhaps even more crucially, after) independence; Akhmatova in the Soviet Union quietly defying Stalin; the vast and complex tradition of poetry and anti-poetry in Latin America that has led to the murder and disappearance of poets who dared to represent the people against the power of the state. In this country poetry on the page hasn't often played this role, but rap and spoken word has. Chuck D once called rap "CNN for black people" and an album like Kendrick Lamar's *To Pimp a Butterfly* lives up to that painful and necessary poetic charge. Consider the cover, on which one of the most marginal and vulnerable groups in America—young black men—have taken over the White House lawn in joyous carnival, brandishing fistfuls of Franklins while a John Roberts-type lies KO'ed in the foreground with X's over his eyes. It is the unconscious made visible of the White House of Barack Obama, the President so cool that he needed an "anger translator," who has since been replaced by the sort of walking white man's id that utterly denies the humanity here on display. The unbearable whiteness of the White House, on display in this image, has only grown more unbearable, and more inescapable, since the election of Donald Trump.

 The album itself is angrily, emphatically, gloriously baroque: excessive, combinatory, enfolding layer upon layer of black musical history in every groove, talking back to it, culminating in a quasi-imaginary interview between Lamar and his hero Tupac. Never not political, it nevertheless meets the Yeatsian standard for poetry: "We make out of the quarrel with others, rhetoric, but of the quarrel with ourselves, poetry." Lamar's album has hit me hard, as few albums do, because of that dialogic, self-confronting quality that I associate with the strongest lyric poetry, going back at least as far as the English Metaphysicals—that is to say, poets of the Baroque period as it expressed itself in England: Herbert, Marvell, Donne. It rewards re-listening. I'm listening to it right now.

The Baroque is in the air. Originally a product of the Counter-Reformation, it stands for an art that exceeds all boundaries, so as to subvert the very ideology that sponsors it, which that art was created to legitimate. *To Pimp a Butterfly* is a dialectical attack on the conditions that made the album necessary; the racism it roots out goes too deep not to uproot the subject position of its speaker. The gold chains that he can now afford to wear are still chains, and the violence of the speaker's language is directed toward an ambiguous "you" in these lines from "The Blacker the Berry":

> I'm the biggest hypocrite of 2015
> Once I finish this, witnesses will convey just what I mean
> Been feeling this way since I was 16, came to my senses
> You never liked us anyway, fuck your friendship, I meant it
> I'm African-American, I'm African
> I'm black as the moon, heritage of a small village
> Pardon my residence
> Came from the bottom of mankind
> My hair is nappy, my dick is big, my nose is round and wide
> You hate me don't you?
> You hate my people, your plan is to terminate my culture
> You're fuckin' evil I want you to recognize that I'm a proud
>   monkey
> You vandalize my perception but can't take style from me
> And this is more than confession
> I mean I might press the button just so you know my discretion
> I'm guardin' my feelings, I know that you feel it
> You sabotage my community, makin' a killin'
> You made me a killer, emancipation of a real nigga

Look at that album cover again: a "riot" or should I say a *mattering* of black male bodies (#BlackLivesMatter) almost obscuring the symbol of legitimate democratic government, a symbol (and a government) that was badly undermined by the relentlessly racialized opposition to its lawfully elected occupant, Barack Obama—an opposition that has continued, like a virus seeking a new host, into the Trump Administraiton. It's a dialectical image, representing the greatest fears of white supremacists but also calling into question the adequacy of our existing institutions when confronted with the structural violence and rapacity of our society. Can poetry—written poetry, poetry on the page—ever top this? Should it even try?

In 2014 Stephen Burt wrote a review-essay in *Boston Review* called "Nearly Baroque," criticized at the time for its provincial American focus and for his vaguely Protestant emphasis on the values of rigor, restraint, and tastefulness. Burt has a knack, or maybe just a predilection, for grouping poets under labels intended to get around or under the armed camps of post-Language poetry and mainstream lyric; way back in 1998 his article on the so-called "elliptical poets" became a calling card for poets who had adopted some of the techniques of language poetry without sacrificing the positionality of the lyric "I." On its face, the "nearly baroque" is even more wishy-washy; nevertheless, I embrace the re-emergence of the baroque as a critical category, celebrated by Burt for its performative "femme" qualities of ornament and artifice. Some of the poets he mentions, including Geoffrey Nutter and Robyn Schiff, are among the most purely talented poets working today. However, it's the closing paragraph of his piece that re-connects the aesthetic excess of nearly baroque poetry with its political potential:

> I have been trying to recommend these poets: I admire them very much. Yet I have also been laying out, almost despite myself, a way to read them skeptically, as symptoms of a literary culture that has lasted too long, stayed too late. *Engagé* readers might say that the nearly Baroque celebrates, and invites us to critique, a kind of last-gasp, absurdist humanism. We value what has no immediate use in order to avoid becoming machine parts, or illustrations for radical arguments, or pawns for something larger, whether it is existing institutions or a notional revolution. And we must keep moving, keep making discoveries, as the scenes and lines and similes of the nearly Baroque poem keep moving, because if we stop we will

see how bad—how intellectually untenable, how selfish, or how pointless—our position really is. The same suspicious readers might say that these nearly Baroque poems bring to the surface questions about all elite or non-commercial or extravagant art: Is it a waste? What does it waste? Can it ever get away from the violence required, if not to produce it, then to produce the society—yours and mine—prepared to enjoy it? The rococo is the art of an ancien régime: it may be that the nearly Baroque poetry of our own day calls our regime ancien as well. It does not pretend to predict what could replace it.

Burt's argument for—and here, against—the "nearly Baroque" or "almost rococo" hinges on a conception of this elaborate and ornamental poetry as a conquest of the useless that paradoxically evades poetry's uselessness, or any notions of the useful, so we won't discover "how bad ... our position really is." I'm not sure that's an adequate description of either Schiff's or Nutter's poetry: Schiff is not only formally inventive but concerned with the deep histories of objects in an at-least Benjaminian way, while the elegiac qualities of "Purple Martin," the Nutter poem that Burt quotes, are to my ear sharply and self-accusingly ironic, smartly engaged with the two-edged sword of phenomenological precision and fascist obfuscation that is the poetic legacy of Heideggerian philosophy.

But this may matter less than Burt's incisive question about "the violence required, if not to produce [this poetry], then to produce the society—yours and mine—prepared to enjoy it?" There is, first of all, a kind of violence done in postmodern Baroque poetry (I prefer this term, as hackneyed as it is, to Burt's overcute coinages "nearly Baroque" or "Baroque Baroque"), directed at the anti-eloquent plain speaking English that dogs and cats can read that in its hegemony over our culture wipes out nuance, difference, and the sites in which either historical memory or the genuinely new are most likely to emerge. That violence can be directed inside the poem, at the lyric self itself, as in the work of Finnish poet Tyttie Heikkeinen that Burt discusses in another 2014 review-essay, "Poems About Poems," or in the work of poets associated with the Gurlesque—the violent femmes of the postmodern Baroque. It might also be a prophylactic violence, the both-ways violence Burt describes in his discussion of Daniel Borzutzky's *The Book of Interfering Bodies*. More disturbing is the implication that our enjoyment of the postmodern Baroque is an enjoyment of the very structural violence that this poetry seeks to take refuge from. The unappetizing alternatives appear to be a Baroque that renders violence spectacular and consumable (Caravaggio-style) or a Baroque conditioned by the violence it conceals and evades.

Burt soberly remarks that "We may want poetry to do what it cannot do, to perform a magic in which we no longer believe or a political efficacy that no longer makes sense," before going on to remark that in Borztusky's poems, "we are brought up short and discover that poetry is the despised Other of more consequential textual forms such as the PowerPoint slideshow." More *consequential*, not more *legitimate*—PowerPoint is the language of power (I am reminded of articles in the *New York Times* a few years back about how the limitations of PowerPoint as a medium may have led to some of the costlier decisions made by the American military—I imagine each and every proposed drone strike is PowerPointed, so as to pre-empt every consideration of what might otherwise escape such euphemisms as "civilian casualties"). It seems to me that culture is not, in the end, separable from its legitimation function—for how else except through culture do we come to recognize or critique our own values?—and the crisis is indeed centered on the assumption that our institutions can somehow run on autopilot, no matter how obstructed (on the legislative level), or detached from everyday life, or structured by repression. How can we "reform" the police when their actions merely express the consequences of the white majority's refusal to recognize the humanity of dark-skinned people? The current President is embarked on a profoundly (un?) American experiment premised in the delegitimization of all institutions that do not center in his own person or that are not primarily characterized—as is the military, as are the police—by the violence of the state. Skeptical as he was of Borzutzky's work, Burt has come to reluctant acceptance of its importance under the new regime, writing in his 2016 essay, "Reading Yeats in the Age of Trump" that "Daniel Borzutzky, with his new National Book Award, looks better, and more frightening, than before."

Burt worries that his love of the baroque and rococo may have been pre-empted by "the wrong kind of rococo" of President Trump: "not delicate craftsmanship as a blow to misogyny, but the gilding of every conceivable surface, the flaunting of a wealth he has used to hurt others, as a boastful public spectacle. Trump represents the end of liberalism, the end of self-restraint and public kindness delivered through flawed, long-lived institutions, at least on a national scale." But has the baroque ever been about liberalism, especially if we understand liberalism now to be precisely a kind of technocratic institutionalism unsupported by ideology?

In its excesses the postmodern Baroque has the capacity to theatricalize poetry's abjection, to make manifest the violence of ideological flows, or the even more violent vacuum that goes by the name of the democratic "norms" that Trump has travestied, but which for poets like Kendrick Lamar were always already obviously hollow. The Baroque can help us to recognize our abjection as citizens subject to dictatorship, a fragility mutually recognizable (though not of course evenly) between white people and black people, gays and straights, migrants and natives. Call it the unsettlement of the Baroque. It can also, in spite of everything, make a place for beauty—not a resigned, detached, or decadent beauty but a complex, self-questioning beauty that emerges from conflict and is never a refuge from it. The Baroque is the other of power, but never of politics, because politics happens when people organize—on any level, including the level of language—and find means of directing that organization against the hollowness of power. If revealing the nakedness of the emperor does not, in this historical moment, diminish one whit the emperor's control of the war machine—and that is a terrifying and deeply uncomfortable truth—it is nevertheless necessary to the imagination of alternatives. Including, most simply and radically, the imagination of alternative relations to our own selves, as more complex, more thoughtful, more diverse, more perverse, more impoverished, and more capable of forging connections than we might otherwise ever have realized.

A much-bandied quote of the moment is Martin Luther King Jr.'s "A riot is the language of the unheard." We condemn riots for their violence, especially their violence to property, and yet a riot—or an uprising—has the potential, the barest potential to be *heard* (as opposed to processed as spectacle, which is what the mainstream networks have been busily doing, putting the riot's historical rootedness on mute). And that capacity to be heard is rooted in excess, in moments of beauty as in the image above, as well as in the more distasteful and horrifying moments that are inseparable from the beauty. The postmodern Baroque, in poetry and out of it, has the capacity for making these connections legible, recalling us, just possibly, to the poem's lost power of the legitimation of personal and political desire. *When shit hit the fan, is you still a fan?* asks Kendrick Lamar. It's the question of this new Baroque nation.

The Transcendental Circuit

Plato saw poets as intrinsically corrosive of the values of his ideal state; they are dangerous to the republic because the poet "awakens and nourishes and strengthens the feelings and impairs the reason." The poets exaggerate and lie; they imitate virtuous action without real knowledge of virtue; they excite ignoble passions and are indifferent to the guidance of the law; they are "the eulogists of tyranny." In this dire political moment that description should give us fresh pause; it seems to describe not a poet in the usual sense of the word but the means by which a person sufficiently lawless and sufficiently intuitive might achieve enormous power. I am talking, of course, about Donald J. Trump and his peculiar way with words. In a speech a few weeks before the 2016 election, the tech billionaire and Trump supporter Peter Thiel—a man who used his enormous wealth to sue the news outlet Gawker out of business—summed up Trump's rhetorical appeal in a few now notorious sentences:

> I think one thing that should be distinguished here is that the media is always taking Trump literally. It never takes him seriously, but it always takes him literally.... I think a lot of voters who vote for Trump take Trump seriously but not literally, so when they hear things like the Muslim comment or the wall comment, their question is not, "Are you going to build a wall like the Great Wall of China?" or, you know, "How exactly are you going to enforce these tests?" What they hear is we're going to have a saner, more sensible immigration policy.[1]

What does it mean to take Trump's language, or anyone's language, "seriously but not literally"? Is there not a dark echo here of Shelley, of unacknowledged legislation hiding in plain sight? Is there not a kind of perverse poetry to be ascribed to the rhetoric of a man who continually invites his listeners to insert their own darkest fears into

---

1   https://www.theguardian.com/technology/2016/oct/31/peter-thiel-defends-donald-trump-muslim-ban-mexico-wall

the sinister repetition of bland statements like "There's something going on"?

American society, if not the whole of the West, has reached a tipping point, marked by the fecklessness and moral bankruptcy of our elites and the mounting rage and despair of masses of people who have been led to blame people of color, Muslims, immigrants, refugees, and women for the very real decline in their social and economic prospects brought about by the inexorable logic of global capitalism. In the run-up to this election we saw how the best not only lacked all conviction, but lost themselves in the echo chamber of social media, which turned out to be a driver of the legacy media's narrative that Trump could not possibly win rather than any sort of reality check. Meanwhile the worst have brought their passionate intensity to the cause of a man who campaigned against language itself, in a kind of grim parody of old deconstructionist arguments about the endlessness of the signifying chain: "There's no such thing, unfortunately, anymore of facts." When it comes to Trump and his language, and its appeal to millions of white voters who feel themselves to be disenfranchised, and who are coming to an appalling new consciousness of themselves as white, we cannot really be concerned with a *defense* of poetry. We are looking at something much more like an *attack*.

Does the hatred of poetry translate, all too easily, into the poetry of hatred?

I.

"Poetry," Ben Lerner writes near the beginning of his very brief, much-discussed new book, "arises from the desire to get beyond the finite and the historical—the human world of violence and difference—and to reach the transcendent or divine." We are already in difficulties, for before we can encounter the core of Lerner's argument—basically, that the unheard melodies of *poetry* are inevitably sweeter than the heard melodies of any actual *poems*—we must contend with this surprisingly narrow claim that a desire to transcend is central to the poetic impulse. To define poetry as "the desire to get beyond the finite and the historical" restricts poetry, if not actual poems, to the category of the anti-civil or the orphic, heedless of the long history of Horatian and other discursive poetries concerned with the deeds of men. More problematically, it seems to leave out the kind of political or civic poem that inscribes historically excluded and oppressed persons into the language—we might call this the poetic task of creating a usable linguistic personhood for those at the margins of society. Lerner's attempt to recover this dimension of poetry later in his argument, with a discussion of Claudia Rankine's *Citizen*, centers on that book's un- or anti-poetic qualities: citing the book's conjuring of "the experience of depersonalization—numbness, desensitization, media saturation," Lerner remarks, "What I encounter in Rankine is the felt unavailability of traditional lyric categories; the instruction to read her writing as poetry—and especially as lyric poetry—catalyzes an experience of their loss, like a sensation in a phantom limb." The suppression of the speaker's lyric presence—the feeling, sensitivity, and contemplative solitude associated with the Wordsworthian lyric self—enables a troubled and troubling transcendence of the speaker's historical particulars. In his discussion of one of the many scenes of racial micoaggression documented by *Citizen*, Lerner focuses on her substitution of the second person for the first person, which performs in effect a reverse transcendence on the (white, male) reader: "My privilege excludes me—that is, protects me—from the 'you' in a way that focuses my attention on the much graver (and mundane) exclusion of a person of color from the 'you' that the scene recounts." The "American lyric" of the book's subtitle operates as a zone of indeterminacy, a pathos triangulated on its (black, female) author's distance from the status of being a fully "American" citizen but also her inability—maybe anyone's inability—to occupy the curious position suggested by "lyric citizen." This extrapolation is a contradiction in terms that mirrors the historical contradiction of "Black American citizen" explored and exploded by the book. The question for Lerner, and for us, is whether the contradiction suggested by "lyric citizen" is historically contingent or something closer to an ontological fact, a fatal flaw inside poetry itself.

Joshua Corey

Lerner's argument centers on the practice of poetry as a *via negativa* aimed not at God but at Marianne Moore's "place for the genuine," a kind of transcendental location canceled or obstructed by actual poems. Only through suppressing the specifically lyric qualities of actual poems can the phantom limb of poetry make its throb be felt, a throb that we recognize as the pathos of limitation. I am reminded here of something William Empson says in *Some Versions of Pastoral* regarding what he identifies as the deeper truth beneath the otherwise "bourgeois ideology" of Thomas Gray's "Elegy in a Country Churchyard": "it is only in degree that any improvement of society could prevent wastage of human powers; the waste even in a fortunate life, the isolation even of a life rich in intimacy, cannot but be felt deeply, and is the central feeling of tragedy" (5). Gray's poem naturalizes the "mute, inglorious Milton[s]" of its titular churchyard; "Full many a flower is born to blush unseen / And waste its sweetness on the desert air." But the "you" of Rankine's *Citizen* was not "born" to be either unseen ("I didn't see you" is a recurring phrase in the book) or else to be seen as some kind of inhuman, monstrous or animalistic threat (detailed most memorably for this reader in Rankine's meditations on the racism directed at tennis star Serena Williams). The dialectic of black invisibility and hypervisibility is historically contingent, that might and must be otherwise, and Rankine's widely acclaimed *Citizen: An American Lyric* is a blow struck on behalf of that "otherwise."

Poetry's marginality, and its ability to capitalize on its minimal means—all you need to write a poem is a pencil and a scrap of paper, all you need to publish or perform it is a social media account or a YouTube video—seems intrinsic to its peculiar political power of voicing the otherwise. Transcendence is still important to this kind of poetry, but it is a specific transcendence of particular historical conditions that would otherwise bar utterance. Transcendence, in other words, is not a destination for such poetry but a *route* that returns the poet to the historical world, gifted by the powers of language with a face or name.[2] This Adamic capacity of poetry to name is a political capacity, as demonstrated by this poem by Danez Smith:

---

2 I am thinking here of George Oppen's poem by that title: "There is a force

The Transcendental Circuit

ALTERNATE NAMES FOR BLACK BOYS

1. smoke above the burning bush
2. archnemesis of summer night
3. first son of soil
4. coal awaiting spark & wind
5. guilty until proven dead
6. oil heavy starlight
7. monster until proven ghost
8. gone
9. phoenix who forgets to un-ash
10. going, going, gone
11. gods of shovels & black veils
12. what once passed for kindling
13. fireworks at dawn
14. brilliant, shadow hued coral
15. (I thought to leave this blank
    but who am I to name us nothing?)
16. prayer who learned to bite & sprint
17. a mother's joy & clutched breath[3]

Smith's poem resonates because it anticipates and speaks for the political moment for which Ferguson, Missouri is the metonym—in spite of the fact that the poem first appeared in the March 2014 issue of *Poetry*, five months before Michael Brown was murdered by the Ferguson police officer Darren Wilson. (Consider this a politically charged variation on the Eliotic "ideal order" of "existing monuments ... modified by the introduction of the new [the really new] work of art among them.") The poem's power derives from the absence gestured at by the "alternate names" it offers, none of which, of course, are actually names but represent the displacements of personhood and

---

of clarity, it is / Of what is not autonomous in us, / We suffer a certain fear." Oppen's version of "Objectivist" poetry comes very close, tonally, to the anti-lyrical depersonalization that Lerner identifies in Rankine: "All this is reportage." "Route," from *Collected Poems* (New Directions, 1975).

3 https://www.poetryfoundation.org/poetrymagazine/poems/detail/56843

citizenship suffered by "black boys" in American society. Personhood, agency, a seat at the civic table—these things are as out of reach as the names that the poem metonymically evokes without providing. The ache of this is made felt, in part, by the lyric beauty of some of the lines and images, warped with the weft of the unbeautiful: "monster until proven ghost" is the most succinct possible summary of the dialectic of (in)visibility that Rankine requires an entire book to unfold.

What Lerner, adapting a phrase from Allen Grossman, calls "the bitter logic of the poetic principle" is not a merely structural bitterness but a historical one. This is something that Lerner sometimes seems to forget; though his book can be read as a trot or distillation of Grossman's complex and rebarbative prose, when Lerner intones that "the poet is a tragic figure" the phrase lacks the specific gravity of Grossman's texts. Consider, for example, what Grossman has to say about Allen Ginsberg and the relation of Ginsberg's poetry to his Jewishness. "The Jew," writes Grossman, "like the Irishman, presents himself as a type of the sufferer in history; "the Jew is a symbolic representative of man overthrown by history." On the other hand, "For Ginsberg the poetic identity must supersede the ethnic identity if the poet is to survive." Grossman here seems to confirm the idea implicit in Lerner's statement, that the poetic reaches down to some fundamental ground—or up to some transcendental height—beyond historical, ethnic, identitarian particulars. Insofar as I am fallen into any historical identity, I can identify with the symbol of "the Jew." And yet Jews can only be the bearer of this alleged symbolic capacity because of the actual secular history of their oppression and diaspora, and because of their theological and linguistic response to that history; as Grossman puts it in another essay, "the Jew's place is the word," Torah, a word that "strictly speaking, is One (holy, sacred, *kadosh*), and is unlike all other words in that it does not signify by difference but rather serves the Master who *is* difference—which is to say, existence itself." Or as every teacher of creative writing knows: the royal road to the universal is difference. We can only take root in humanity by way of identity, which is always political and specific. Any "transcendence" of identity by poetic means can only be accomplished by a paradoxical form of sublation, preserving and remembering that identity in a different form.

"Poetry," Grossman writes in the preface to *The Sighted Singer*, "is a principle of power invoked by all of us against our vanishing." That sounds like a universalizing gesture, one Lerner seems to follow when he claims that "we are all poets simply by virtue of being human.... Since language is the stuff of the social and poetry the expression in language of our irreducible individuality, our personhood is tied up with our poethood." Lerner writes that "the falling away from poetry [is] a falling away from the pure potentiality of being human into the vicissitudes of being an actual person in a concrete historical situation." No wonder Lerner repeats with Marianne Moore that "I, too, dislike it." What is the value of a writing that can only succeed by its failure to present "pure potentiality"?

One answer might be in how poetry's potential powers—another name for the virtual—metonymically resemble the virtuality of personhood itself. Lerner's argument somewhat clumsily encapsulates what Rankine puts much more clearly in *Citizen* as the distinction between "historical self" and "self-self":

> A friend argues that Americans battle between the "historical self" and the "self self." By this she means you mostly interact as friends with mutual interest and, for the most part, compatible personalities; however, sometimes your historical selves, her white self and your black self, or your white self and her black self, arrive with the full force of your American positioning. Then you are standing face-to-face in seconds that wipe the affable smiles right from your mouths. What did you say? Instantaneously your attachment seems fragile, tenuous, subject to any transgression of your historical self. And though your joined personal histories are supposed to save you from misunderstandings, they usually cause you to understand all too well what is meant.

What did you say? A momentary slip of the tongue, a slip of the mask, yields up the gap between the transcendental "self self" and the immanent "historical self," as Rankine and her friend are forced to confront language's painful power to simultaneously address and erase. As Rankine puts it elsewhere in *Citizen*, paraphrasing Judith Butler, "Our very being exposes us to the address of another, she answers. We suffer from the condition of being addressable. Our emotional openness, she adds, is carried by our addressability. Language navigates this." Needless to say, there is a mirroring pain evoked here, the pain of exclusion from an address: the appeal of Trump and his epigones to "real Americans" with the nostalgic fantasy that they will "make America great again" excises and excludes Americans of color, gay Americans, immigrants, and everyone else who understands that the phantasmic America of the past Trump's language hints at is an America without them. And I might include in that list of the excluded the educated, and within that group—the excluded of the excluded—intellectuals; and beyond even them, excluded to the third power, poets, and their (phantasmal?) readers.

II.

Politicians are expected to campaign in poetry and to govern in prose. In the case of Trump I am expecting a catastrophic attempt to govern in the apocalyptic reality-show poetry of his campaign; the man seems incapable of "prose" if we define that word by its connotations of seriousness, sobriety, and the management of day-to-day affairs. As W.H. Auden warned us in his essay "The Poet and the City," "All poets adore explosions, thunderstorms, tornadoes, conflagrations, ruins, scenes of spectacular carnage. The poetic imagination is not at all a desirable quality in a statesman." Auden's essay anticipates a number of Lerner's concerns; Lerner even echoes the scene in which Auden confesses his embarrassment at admitting he's a poet to "a stranger in the train" when he writes of the "awkward and even tense exchange between a poet and non-poet—they often happen on an airplane or in a doctor's office or in some other contemporary no-place." Auden centers the problem on the lack of social position for a writer-qua-writer: "the so-called fine arts have lost the social utility they once had"; not only that, but "in a society governed by the values appropriate to Labor ... the gratuitous is no longer regarded—most earlier cultures thought differently—as sacred." His solution therefore to the problem of the stranger on a train who asks him what he does, "satisfactory because it withers curiosity, is to say *Medieval Historian.*" This is amusing and telling; though Auden's own imagination was industrial rather than pre-Raphaelite, the Middle Ages persist in our fragmented historical memory as our most consistent image of a society organized on the principle of the sacred—a principle we now relegate, with increasing uneasiness, to the category of culture.

Lerner too is embarrassed by poetry's lack of social utility; "If my seatmate in a holding pattern over Denver calls on me to sing, demands a poem from me that will unite coach and first class in one community, I can't do i.t" But the "contempt" that poetry evokes from this straw-man "seatmate" is strongest in Lerner himself, an internalization of the much larger problem of the sheer power of anti-intellectualism in American life. Much of Lerner's essay bears the marks of this internalized contempt, expressed wryly or anxiously by turns: "Anybody who reads (or reads the *SparkNotes* for) *The Republic* is imbued with the sense that poetry is a burning social question." The parenthetical deprecation speaks volumes: the "hatred of poetry" alleged by Lerner's title is a parochial manifestation of the hatred of education itself—a phenomenon acutely expressed by Trump's most ardent supporters, whose votes were in part an expression of hatred for the academics and other educated elites that have ignored or condescended to them for so long. No poet or troubadour spoke for or to this group (the best Trump could do was Ted Nugent, while Beyoncé, Jay-Z, and Bruce Springsteen all sang for Hillary Clinton); given both the president-elect's documented contempt for literacy and the politically liberal leanings of most American poets, it seems unlikely that his inauguration will be graced by a poem, and the contents of such a poem are in any case unimaginable unless parodic.

In any case, as I have been hinting, Trump's rhetoric seems to be poetry enough for his supporters, in large part because it is a virulent address to the grievances of a politically potent minority which as of this writing controls the levers of power in all three branches of the federal government and the overwhelming majority of the states. It is a poetry of coach versus first-class; never mind that it leaves behind vast numbers of Americans who are disadvantaged historically, economically, and socially. What it names it excludes. Consider for example one of the most notorious pieces of Trump's rhetorical poetry, taken from his announcement of his presidential bid in Trump Tower on June 16, 2015:

> When Mexico sends its people, they're not sending their best. They're not sending you. They're not sending you. They're sending people that have lots of problems, and they're bringing those problems with us. They're bringing drugs. They're bringing crime. They're rapists. And some, I assume, are good people.

The mobility of the *they* in this passage is typical of Trumpian poetics: it starts out as a referent to Mexico itself, suggesting without being definitive that Mexican immigration is a policy of the Mexican government. The *they* mutates in the fourth sentence: in the first clause it's still referring to Mexico but in the second clause it seems to refer to the migrants themselves, and this shift is accompanied by a strange deformation of the preposition in that clause: "*with* us" instead of "*to* us." It's tempting to dismiss this as the kind of prepositional mutation all too typical in undergraduate papers, or else to say that Trump misspoke. But I read this *with us* as a kind of echo or semantic rhyme of "You're either with us or against us"—an echo of the exclusionary rhetoric associated with the last Republican president, George W. Bush. The *with* also suggests the insidiousness of Mexican immigration: the "they" is trying to get *with* us, to sexually invade the pure (white) body politic of the "you" and the "us" repeated in this passage of Trump's speech. This sexual interpretation is made explicit by the penultimate sentence, "They're rapists," a gasp-inducing line that the speaker then pseudo-apologizes for by ending the passage with the phrase "good people." But this move is not enough to restore the humanity of Mexican immigrants because the sentence, like all the other sentences in this excerpt, is not addressed to them. It is addressed to a you and us that implicitly includes the "best" and excludes the *they*.

The natural objection is that Trump is not a poet, nor do his deliberately vague and repetitive speeches count as poems. But let me write out the passage again, using the pauses in Trump's delivery as indicative of line breaks:

> When Mexico sends its people,
> they're not sending their best.
> They're not sending you.
> They're not sending you.
> They're sending people
> that have lots of problems.
> And they're bringing those problems
> with us.
> They're bringing drugs,
> they're bringing crime.
> They're rapists. And some
> I assume are good people.

Written out in this form—and verse, it should be noted, has a natural advantage over prose in its ability to replicate speech on the page—we notice the contesting end words: *people* (three times), *best, you* (twice), *problems* (twice), *us, drugs, crime,* and *some*. As I hear Trump's delivery, *rapists* comes in the center of the penultimate line before a caesura, and the *some* is enjambed to emphasize the exception Trump is making. But the *people* at the end echoes the *people* at the beginning—the dehumanized *people* of an *its* who are not *best*. The poem uses repetition effectively—notice the five uses of variations on *send* and *sending,* which is then echoed by the three uses of *bringing,* effectively and frighteningly closing the distance between the pure *you* and the impure *them*. There's even some subtle alliterative play at the end: the *p* and *s* of *rapists* are echoed and redistributed in the words that are supposed to take back some of its venom: "And some / I a*s*sume are good *p*eo*p*le." It's the poetry of demagoguery, the demagoguery of poetry. And it works. It has "social utility," though that utility in this case is the utility of a dagger aimed at the heart of the ethnically inclusive social contract that many of us thought to be the promise of America.

Poetry, as Yeats reminds us, makes nothing happen; it is a *way* of happening; it is a mouth that can both speak (and thus acknowledge) and needs nourishment (and be itself acknowledged). The mouth of Trump is a bottomless pit into which his listeners pour themselves; they feel themselves to be unified in his other-excluding song. They transcend, for the moment, the sense of alienation that they attribute—with some justice—to the indifference and contempt of educated elites. But a transcendence that does not return to real historical conditions, that is not itself changed by those conditions, is either a white supremacist fantasy—transcendence as erasure and restoration—or straight-up nihilism.

So I return to the notion of poetry as transcendental route, or river, that returns us to the world as it is, with a view of how it might be otherwise.

III.

We can thank Ben Lerner and his essay for fostering conversation about the role of poetry today, even as we might deplore the shallowness of his argument or the provincial narrowness of his references (there are few or no references to poets who do not write in English, for example). For a book that covers some of the same territory but in more intricate, certainly more loving detail there is Reginald Gibbons's *How Poems Think,* the title of which suggests a task for poetry undreamt of in Lerner's philosophy. Lerner, after all, is primarily concerned with how poems make us *feel,* and takes as a given that what we are most likely to feel in the face of actual poems is fear or resentment, while reserving a muzzy sort of reverence for the *idea* of poetry. Gibbons, on the other hand, is concerned with how poetry might shape ideas, or rather how its pec uliar forms of play with language constitute realms of ideation distinct from the capabilities of prose. The tones of the two books could also not be more different. Lerner's essay has an aw-shucks tone recognizably akin to the first-person narrators of his two novels, *Leaving the Atocha Station* and *10:04,* both of which center on their protagonists' painful skepticism about their, or anyone's, ability to have "a profound experience of art" (*Atocha 8*); he seems embarrassed not only by poetry but by intellectuality itself; it is a book written from a defensive crouch. Gibbons, however, opens his book with a moving autobiographical excursus about his experiences as a student of poetry at Stanford in the 1960s, in which he is not afraid to portray himself as a young man in pursuit of his soul, in reaction to and in tune with his times. The suggestion, always, is that we might judge the present on the basis of examples offered by the past, and rarely or never the reverse.

The central drama of Gibbons' book is articulated in the character of his mentor Donald Davie, the English critic and poet whom Gibbons presents as sharply as the hero of a novel. Gibbons quotes Davie commenting tellingly on his own work: "It is true that I am not a poet by nature, only by inclination; for my mind moves most easily and happily among abstractions, it relates ideas far more readily than it relates experiences. I have little appetite, only profound admiration, for sensuous fullness and immediacy; I have not the poet's need of concreteness." This passage is a key to Gibbons' book, which in essence divides poems into two kinds: the poetry of "sensuous fullness and immediacy," the poetry of named persons, things, and places, which he holds to be central to the tradition of poetry in English; and another poetry that Gibbons terms "the apophatic," which works to evoke the non-physical and non-present; even, indeed, the non-thought, or rather the thought that can not be paraphrased or imagined by non-poetic means. Much of Gibbons' book pursues the apophatic in poetries other than the English; French poetry, Spanish poetry, Greek poetry, and above all Russian poetry offer alternatives to what Gibbons calls the "cataphatic" or the poetry of naming and showing. "We can see the implications for poetry," Gibbons writes, "in the contrast between an active, Adamic, cataphatic artistic impulse to evoke the visible world by naming it and a meditative, apophatic artistic impulse to evoke the invisible, the elusive, the absent, the not quite conceivable, the unnameable."

The active and the meditative; we can begin to pin down here some of the stakes for poetry in these terms, evocative of the *vita activa* and *vita contemplativa* that return us to the question of poetry's social utility. But let us return for the moment to Donald Davie and the last paragraph of the passage from which Gibbons quotes:

> For a true poem can be written by a mind not naturally poetic—though by the inhuman labor of thwarting at every point the natural grain and bent. This working against the grain does not damage the mind, nor is it foolish; on the contrary, only by doing this does each true poem as it is written become an authentic widening of experience—a truth won from life against all odds, because a truth in and about a mode of experience to which the mind is normally closed.

"There is a larger grain than the poet's own," Gibbons comments, "and that is the language the poet speaks." Davie's predicament—almost his tragedy—is not that he is not a natural poet but that he is, or so Gibbons seems to suggest, a naturally *apophatic* poet writing in English, a *cataphatic* language. Davies denigrates certain poems he has written as "not truly poems, simply because the thought in them could have been expressed—at whatever cost in terseness and point—in a non-poetic way." A poet like Keats yearns, as he wrote in one of his famous letters, for "a life of sensation rather than of thoughts"; that yearning is a mark of his sense of distance from the sensuous world, and Keats's poetry is thus the heroic record of his astonishingly successful struggle to close that distance. Davie by contrast has "little appetite" for the sensuous; he is instead committed to writing a "true poem ... an authentic widening of experience" by means of specifically poetic means of *thought*.

Such are the means of thought that Gibbons seeks to explore in his delightfully wayward book, in which Donald Davie represents one lodestar and the other, somewhat surprisingly, is the French feminist theorist Hélène Cixous, whose emphasis on Joycean linguistic play goes against the grain of French poetry as surely as Davie's intellectualism goes against the grain of English. But Gibbons is not particularly interested in being evenhanded; his experience as a translator, most particularly of Russian poetry, has left him more interested in the poetics of apophasis and the intangible, which seems to come close to the Grossman-Lerner concept of poetic virtuality, but without the bitterness. Perhaps neither Grossman nor Lerner have looked far enough outside the cage of English to recognize the possibility of an actual poem that can do the work of a more generalized "poetry" in creating a space for "pure potentiality." Yet Gibbons is also interested in what he calls "the necessary and productive self-alienation of the poet" who must use "his or her little canon as a self-chosen challenge rather than as a source of approval." He or she "must work in words so closely, and with such openness to language, that only by coming to see the words on the page, and to hear them in the ear, as belonging as much to themselves and to the language as to the poet who composes them, can the poet discover *how* to think *with* them and *through* them, beyond the artistic limits of the ingrained individual habits of language and poet thinking, and beyond the limits imposed by the poet's self-positioning within culture" (9, emphasis in original). The poet, in other words, can choose neither the "self self" nor the "historical self" to write from; there is a third position that we might call the linguistic self, or the point of view of the poem itself. It is the position, Gibbons argues, that makes possible the transcendent route of the poem, making it a kind of circuit that connects all three selves, and the intimate, historical, and linguistic communities that encompass them.

Nowhere are the stakes for this made clearer than in a section in the book's second chapter where Gibbons discusses "the relevance and value of self-alienation" in the work of three very different writers, Frederick Douglass, Emily Dickinson, and William Carlos Williams, all of whom, Gibbons persuasively claims, were alienated from the very communities to and for which they most wished to speak: Douglass because the vast majority of black slaves were illiterate; Dickinson because her "poetic innovation and mastery" were beyond both her Amherst intimates and the supposedly more sophisticated literary community of Boston; Williams because of the gap in "functional and cultural" literacy between himself as physician and the immigrant families "about whom he sometimes wrote with intense acknowledgment of their fullness as human beings." These writers do not abandon their audiences so much as address a point of alienation and otherness that a part of themselves also occupies. "Rimbaud's formulation of poetic liberation, *je est un autre*," Gibbons writes, "might be not only a given or sought-for psychological state—as we all take it to be—but also a social effect of the very act of writing." The hatred of poetry—more commonly phrased as the question of poetry's *inaccessibility*—may be intrinsic to the need for transcendence, not for transcendence's sake but for the sake of a kind of thought for an alienated community that includes oneself.

I lack the space to summarize the richness of Gibbons' succeeding chapters, except to say that they wind an idiosyncratic course, evaluating the capability of various poetic techniques and constraints to act as modes "of producing discovery, improvisation, liberation, ideas, and otherwise unattainable articulation." Rhyme is one of these techniques, or it can be; Gibbons distinguishes between merely "ornamental" rhyme and rhyme as a goad for cognition: "The sound leads the thinking." Other chapters explore in detail the "apophatic poetics" of the unnameable, which English in its "word-thinginess" can have difficulty in accessing (though Gibbons rightly names Dickinson as one of the greatest poets of apophasis). Other chapters of the book preoccupy themselves with demonstrating the persistence of poetic *technē* in the most ancient Greek and Latin poems, rooting that persistence in the essential orality of the poem, its origins as ritual and song. Another chapter, "Simultaneities," speaks to the poem's ability to move along various lines of thought and temporality simultaneously through repetition, etymological play, allusion, and visual as well as aural rhymes. Throughout the book he quotes from a generous range of poets: in a single paragraph on intensified sound patterns he cites Wallace Stevens, Robert Hayden, Lorine Niedecker, Bruce Weigl, Nathaniel Mackey, Ellen Bryant Voigt, Natasha Trethewey, and Alexander Pope. There is an appealing catholicism, in the old sense of the word, to Gibbons' generous tastes in poetry; I would not necessarily have expected him to have much interest in the work of a poet like Robert Duncan, but he gives over three pages to quote "At the Loom—*Passages 2*" in full, the better to demonstrate its "thematic and sensuous" weaving of "sounds, rhythms, word-forms, structures of language, and threads of thought and story in language" with "the sensuous 'imagery' of sight, sound, touch and taste."

Lerner speaks much less than Gibbons to particular *techniques* of poetry; he is mostly concerned with partial or deformed encounters with poems, as though *all* poems were apophatic demonstrations of something they are not and could never be. To quote Lerner quoting the narrator of his own *Leaving the Atocha Station,* "I tended to find lines of poetry beautiful only when I encountered them quoted in prose, in the essays my professors had assigned in college, where the line breaks were replaced with slashes, so that what was communicated was less a particular poem than the echo of poetic possibility." Though he does provide nominal close readings of poems by three poets—the notoriously talentless 19th-century Scots poet William Topaz McGonagall, John Keats, and Emily Dickinson—he collapses the considerable distance between them by arguing that they all, in different ways, "make a place for the genuine by providing a negative image of the ideal Poem we cannot write in time." The limitation of Lerner's thought may center on that word *image*: though he dutifully remarks on the prosody of Dickinson's "I dwell in Possibility," he seems deaf to the actual music of poems, focused as he is on what he calls, quoting the critic Michael Clune, the "images of virtual music" in a poet like Keats. Lerner scorns the claims of critics who argue that "the music of [Keats's] lines induces a trance"; "I've never seen any critic in a trancelike state," he quips. My trouble with this rather arch, self-defended stance is that by discarding the sweetness of "Heard melodies" in favor of "those unheard," Lerner discards not profundity but experience itself. And as Gibbons takes pains to show, it is the experience of reading actual poems—not gauzy appeals to the "pure potentiality" of poetry—that makes possible the circuit from self to alienation and back to enlarged possibilities of thought and sympathy. This may or may not be a "profound" experience but it is certainly an *experience,* of and by language unfolding in time and not in an image.

Gibbons' work as a translator of Russian poetry, often in collaboration with the Russian poet Ilya Kutik, leads him to assert that "Russian makes it possible for poetry to think a meaning that includes, rather than chooses between, opposites, and also to apprehend a verbal negative space (analogous somehow to such space in sculpture) that is created by paradox, absence, negatives, and invisible qualities and entities rather than visible ones." Implicit here is that not only the Russian language but Russian poetic culture is friendlier to the alienation-in-language central to the poetic route than the Anglo-American culture taken for granted by Lerner. And yet the English title of the contemporary Russian poet Kirill Medvedev's collection of poems, essays, and "actions," *It's No Good* (originally published in English by Ugly Duckling Presse in 2012; a second edition came out in 2016), suggests something of the same unhappy alienation from his own medium that worries Lerner; in the case of Medvedev it is the closed horizon of Putinism that seems to foreclose the revolutionary and elegiac potentialities of great predecessors like Pasternak, Manstelshtam, Brodsky, and Akhmathova, with her singular promise of her poet's ability to record and remember the atrocities of Stalinism. The expression of Medvedev's alienation has come in his disavowal, circa 2003, of anything resembling a "literary career," as well as refusing the copyright to his own work: he is still writing and performing poems of an appealing casual shagginess, often centering on his own sense of disorientation and unease in a society where the suture between poetry and politics is continually coming undone. At the same time, I read Medvedev's writing as more of a rebuke to Lerner's stance than in harmony with it, as when he attacks "critics":

> who write
> that what's lacking in my poems
> according to them
> is some kind of depth of experience

> jesus christ
> depth of experience
> (I think that wanting depth of experience from a poem
> means not having any inkling of your own worth)
> …
> I think
> that my poems are some kind of test;
> a trial
> for perfection or rather at est
> to determine the capacity for perfection
> to determine
> THE CAPACITY
> to see and accept yourself
> as you are;
> miserable, ugly, worthless,
> vain, selfish,
> head hanging low in a vast space
> over some sparkling stinking abyss
> (I think that for somebody hanging over a stinking abyss—
> and the majority of people are—
> "deep thoughts" are
> beside the point)

And with that stinking abyss I must circle back, at the close of this essay, to the poetry of hatred—to the tweets and effusions and neo-fascist ejaculations of our President, Donald J. Trump. The anxiety after "profundity," like the anxiety over "deep thoughts," may be beside the point when we consider the sheer dangerousness of poetic language *as image*—detached, that is, from the poetic techniques that perform the necessary circuit of transcendence and return I have tried to describe in this essay. What is Donald Trump's America—the one he's going to make great again—but a radically and violently simplified virtual image of the America his language carves out of a texture infinitely more complex and contradictory than he or his supporters seem to find bearable? If "the United States themselves are essentially the greatest poem," as Whitman said, it is that poem—America as multi-ethnic, polyglot, diverse in thought and expression—that is essentially most hated. The "poetry" that Lerner seeks to catch like the wind in his rhetorical net is a phantom that I fear he fails to sufficiently separate from the "Make America Great Again" white supremacist transcendence that is an end in itself for Trump, and for all the critics, well-meaning or not, who call for a magical restoration of the transcendental and universal in poetry, the kind supposedly accomplished by Robert Lowell or Robert Frost or some other equally acceptable flinty or neurotic white male New Englander.

In an article that he composed a week before the election, in expectation of a Hilary Clinton win, the political commentator Matthew Yglesias wrote, "The cliché is that you campaign in poetry—and Clinton is, frankly, a lousy poet." Clinton, Yglesias goes on to say, is a master of the prose of governance—but before you can govern, "you really do need to win the election first." That takes a poetry that goes beyond the "micro-targeting" of various political constituencies; it does require something like Lerner's deprecated poem "that will unite coach and first class in one community." "I suspect that," Yglesias writes, "somewhat paradoxically, continuing to put forth candidates of color may be crucial to speaking more compellingly to white voters since they can speak credibly about a cross-racial politics without sounding like they are trying to sideline nonwhite people's concerns."

The route of a genuinely inclusive politics, and an inclusive poetics, passes through a circuit for which transcendence can never be the goal, only a means. And it may well be that any poetry or politics worthy of the label "progressive" will best succeed at this moment if it is put forth by "candidates of color." White men—like Lerner and Gibbons and myself—who wish to write against a Trumpian poetry of hatred will have to renounce any hatred of poetry that centers on discomfort at the poet's ambiguous status. It is not the white male poet's burden to elevate or be elevated by "the song of the infinite" only to be "compromised by the finitude of its terms." That leaves such a writer prey to the kind of *ressentiment* that helped to elevate

Trump to his present appalling perch. Let us instead look to poems that think, through and into the otherness of otherness, as Rankine and Medvedev do by their very different means, and as Gibbons does with his thoughtful, quirky survey of the past two thousand years of poetic *technē* in a universe unbounded by English.

IV
Reginald Shepherd: A Dialogue

Reginald Shepherd: A Dialogue

Blogging brought me many gifts over the years: interested readers, the occasional invitation to publish an essay or poem, and always, the scary but exhilarating prospect that comes from thinking on a tightrope. One of the most meaningful gifts I received was friendship with a poet I never met, the late Reginald Shepherd. Starting in 2003 with an e-mail that he sent to me in response to something I had posted on my blog, and later via posts on his own blog, we engaged in a challenging and remarkable conversation about the stakes for poetry as we saw them. I had read some of Reginald's work before he reached out to me and had been impressed by the rigors of its prosody, which he deployed in an almost classical, fiercely Apollonian project of self-fashioning that turned a gay Black kid from the Bronx into a figure formidable for the sharpness and grace of his intelligence. Without detracting one iota from his seriousness—he was, in every sense of the words, a serious character—I thought that he practiced a kind of dandyism of the intellect that was as dialectical and unnervingly pointed as Oscar Wilde's. He showed love, I think, through argument; we hadn't written back and forth for very long before I began to appreciate that his sallies were charged with a kind of wry affection and respect. (I appreciate this even more now than I did at the time, wincing as I sometimes do at the more naive and jejune dimensions of my correspondence.) We engaged each other on and off for five years, by blog and by e-mail, until just before his unexpected and heartbreaking death on September 10, 2008 at the age of 45—a year younger than I am now. But I will always think of him as a kind of elder brother whose moral and aesthetic gravitas and dry sense of humor have served for me and, I know, many others, as a kind of beacon—an example of what it means to live in, with, and for poetry.

Reginald's first e-mail arrived out of the blue in March, when my blog was only a couple of months old, and I was engaged in what in hindsight seem rather petty discussions of what Ron Silliman used to call the "School of Quietude"—the aesthetically conservative "mainstream" poetry published by the larger university presses and a few New York houses that seemed to those of us with commitments to more innovative aesthetics to bestride the American poetry scene like some sort of tinpot colossus. Like I said, petty. Reginald, who married a deep love of the Anglo-American poetic tradition with a warrior's spirit, took exception to the claims I seemed to be making, and here's what his first e-mail to me said about that:

> I am writing because I was quite disturbed by some comments you made regarding the relationship of poetry and politics in your recent entries. I have already written the substance of these comments to a friend who pointed out the comments, so I thought that I might as well share my thoughts with the comments' author.
>
> Your assertion that a conservative poetics leads to a conservative politics shows a simplistic view of the relationship of literature and politics (I had thought that deconstructing such one-to-one correspondences, art as mirror of the world, was one of the tasks of the avant-garde—certainly the Modernists were hard at work at it) and furthermore ignores the history of Anglo-American modernism. The Anglo-American moderns are notable for their conservative and even reactionary social-political stands: Yeats's contempt for democracy and the mob, Eliot's Anglo-Catholic monarchism and anti-Semitism), Pound's fascism (including massive doses of anti-Semitism). Gertrude Stein's hatred of FDR, socialism, or any egalitarian political programs. There are certainly exceptions, William Carlos Williams most prominent among them (with Stevens occupying a kind of middle ground but still, with regard to the Italian invasion of Ethiopia, being in his words on the side of the coons and the snakes versus the Dagoes). It's interesting, because aside from the Italian Futurists, Celine, and some but not all of the German Expressionists, most continental European modernists were socio-political leftists (though often of a rather amorphous variety), which got them in trouble with Herr Hitler and, earlier, with a Russian Revolution which after some hesitation decided that it liked its art safe, accessible, and obedient to orders social, cultural, *and* aesthetic.

In academia today, pseudo-political talk too often substitutes for talk about poetry (and literature in general)—and it's certainly easier than actually reading and thinking about poems. And of course political talk about culture ('cultural activism') is *much* easier than political action, which might require *doing* something in the real and messy world. Though I am no admirer of his poetry (quite the opposite), I actually thought that it was rather brave of Billy Collins to come out publicly against mauling Iraq, given his government sinecure. Since Congress is busily renaming French fries (which are actually Belgian) "freedom fries" and "French toast" "freedom toast," along with enacting various economic measures against France (how dare they have an opinion of their own!), they will no doubt soon get around to abolishing the post of poet laureate as punishment for Mr. Collins' impertinence. Or perhaps, though, they'll just strip him of his laurel crown, like Vanessa Williams deposed as Miss America and sent off in disgrace, though not nearly so attractive....

My point is that such simple and simplistic correspondences between art and society do not exist and never have. It is odd that an aesthetic-intellectual tendency which insists so on poetry as an autonomous language practice also so often insists on a view of literature as nothing more than an ideological epiphenomenon of society (which, as Marx reminds us and too many *soi-disant* leftists forget, is *not* a seamless totality, but riven, rifted, and conflicted). Adorno, for one thing, presents a much more nuanced view of the complex and shall we say over-determined nature of the relation between these two entities. Even Althusser's tautologically totalizing system allows for the semi-autonomy of art.

I responded:

First of all, I'm not sure I ever conflated conservative poetics with conservative politics in the way that you say. I'm fully prepared to concede that there are poetically conservative poets with impeccable left-wing credentials, who have found the language and the tradition more or less as given adequate to their purposes, and of course the Modernists you mention were no democrats (more on this below). There is of course no one-to-one correspondence between one's aesthetics and one's politics. But I do recognize a continuum between the big-P Political language that is being utterly debased for quasi-fascist purposes ("regime change," "shock and awe," "possible war") and the small-p political or cultural language that may be coming from the East Wing of the same White House ("there's nothing political about American literature") or from the desk of a self-appointed cultural commissar like Joseph Parisi who "sees just about everything" at his $100-million magazine. I think a poet who approaches language with a remaking rigor, with a desire to either show how dirty it's become (what I've elsewhere called "re-representation") or else to break through its clotted surface to express what's been covered over, is better equipped poetically, and *perhaps* politically, to produce a text adequate to the crisis. I'm glad you mention Marilyn Hacker, whose work I respect a great deal: I'm not sure I would call her poetically conservative because I feel her formalism (aside from having a great ear behind it) has that breaking and resetting rigor that I demand from a poem right now. I am passionately interested in formalism, which is why I once wrote sonnets like "Kimono"; it's just that I became interested in different sources and traditions of formalism (from Baudelaire's prose poem to Pound's poem including history to Olson's projective verse to Language poetry) than those espoused by the New Formalists.

Your point about the generally fascist tendencies of many of the high Modernists is well taken, but relies perhaps on an overly symptomatic reading of their work. As I initiate myself into Modernism studies, I am continually struck by the connections to be made between the poetry and prose of Stein, Eliot, Lawrence, et al, and the thought of Martin Heidegger, both early and late. The late Heidegger's arguments for aesthetic autonomy, for the world-founding powers of art, resonate with the early Heidegger's insistence on achieving authenticity in one's life through one's Being-towards-death, which is supposed to perform the work of "clearing" that makes it possible for Dasein to shape its individual destiny—a destiny that is most vivid outside of the socio-phenomenological boundaries that form the ordinary distracted person's world. A large part of the Modernist project seems implicated here, and the dissertation I'm working toward formulating will probably be devoted in part to showing how Heideggerian the poetics of the Modernists is. Of course, invoking Heidegger exposes and makes more plain their fascist tendencies, and I do not want to shy from this. Fascism has left an ineradicable stain upon the Modernist project, but I want to argue that there are strains of repressed resistance in Heidegger that manifest similarly in the poets. Just as Levinas' ethics of the face is impossible without working in, through, and against Heidegger's thought, the poetically and politically radical work of the Objectivists, the Black Mountain poets, and of course the Langpos is inconceivable without the high Modernists. Whatever the political sentiments of Eliot, Pound, and Stein (sentiments that I would concede are not extrinsic from their work), they have opened an aesthetic realm in which the poetical and the political can make contact and influence each other in new ways. Stein may have rejected the New Deal, but her work clears a space for a powerful feminist and lesbian poetry far more radical than anything Roosevelt dreamed of. Pound was a fascist and an anti-Semite but his work makes Charles Olson's rediscovery of lost American histories in his poetry possible. Eliot's politics were stultifyingly conservative and his loathing of the sexual body almost comical, but *The Waste Land* is probably the first and best model in English of a poem that deconstructs different socio-political registers through an almost Benjaminian dialectical pastiche.

The poetics/politics or aesthetics/ethics nexus has been troubling my sleep for years, now. The dissertation is one place where I'm hoping to work out some kind of strategy for dealing with the divide, and the blog has become another.

Reginald's response was an education, one I probably should have paid more attention to; in particular, I think he could helped me achieve much greater clarity with regard to my feelings about Heidegger a whole lot sooner than I did:

> You have misinterpreted my point about the Anglo-American Modernists, with whom I have lived in a happy agon for quite a long time; my position regarding the relationship of their too-frequently very dubious politics (the conservatism of which often involved a recoil from the unfamiliar and the Other seen as threat to the integrity of the beleaguered self) to the interrogations and explorations of their poetry (which occurred and for readers still occurs in exactly that land of unlikeness) is exactly the opposite of that which you seem to impute to me. I also wish to make it clear that I don't consider conservative or even reactionary positions as equivalent to 'fascism,' a term that is thrown around all too casually as an all-purpose political pejorative. Conservatism, at least in Europe, is often antithetical to fascism, which is after all a phenomenon of modern mass society, exactly the thing that someone like Yeats despised. I call Pound a Fascist because he proclaimed himself one, and did the work for Rome Radio to prove it. I don't think that precise thinking can occur without precise speaking and writing.
>
> Allow me to clarify. I disagree vociferously with those—unfortunately a dominant party in the current academy—who dismiss the work because of the personal or political failings of its author, or at best read the work as a symptom of the author's opinions, feelings, or social position: in fact, regarding literature itself as a social symptom. (As Eliot wrote, poetry is not the expression of personality and emotions but the escape from these things—with the understanding that only having these things, occupying and being occupied by a subject position, could impel one to wish to get out of or out from under them). I would argue strenuously (and in several published essays have done so) against those who read Eliot's poems, say, as symptoms of his politics (or his misogyny or repressed homophobia or what-have-you), or what could be called (borrowing from Dali) the paranoiac-schizophrenic collage method of *The Cantos* (in which each element automatically calls to mind

an association that the poem, whatever the fragmentation of its surface, insists is intrinsic and intrinsically meaningful) to Pound's clear personal need to control everyone and everything around him, which is obviously one source of his attraction to Fascism and its specious claims to order and make meaningful every aspect of life. On the contrary, I consider those aspects of these writers to be the most mundane and _uninteresting_ things about them (as I responded when one of my Cornell students asked whether Yeats was a misogynist, "Yes, and that's the least interesting thing about him").

The Anglo-American modernist cohort was not and is not distinguished from the mass of people of their time or, sadly enough, of ours by their socially normative racism, homophobia (sometimes internalized, and with the conflicted exceptions of figures like HD and Hart Crane), sexism, classism, elitism (which I mean in the social and political sense rather than in the too-loosely tossed around high cultural or artistic sense, in which latter sense, 'cultural elitism,' I, as a gay black man who grew up in Bronx housing projects and was to a large extent rescued by Eliot, just don't believe—whatever the frequent and specious assertions to the contrary, poems don't oppress people, though social, political, and economic systems, including other people wielding and/or being the instruments of power, certainly do) (at the risk of being hyper-parenthetical, in this regard I quite object to pseudo-political pejoratives like 'cultural commissar,' as Mr. Parisi has no state-sanctioned or otherwise power to censor or silence, simply because he chooses only to publish certain kinds of work, work in which you might not be interested, in his journal—that is, actually, a part of rather than antithetical to freedom of expression). It's that their work, while rising out of their subject positions as socially situated individuals, also rises above those limitations (while still of course bearing their scars—Adorno calls style in art one of the scars of history), reflecting them in negation. As Adorno says (and I find Adorno a much more salutary thinker on art in itself and on art's relationship to society than Heidegger, who is too often deliberately mystifying and obfuscatory about frequently banal notions of authenticity and truth, his articulations of which I do often find disturbingly conservative in their social implications), art takes the alienation on which capitalist social relations are based and sublates it, in the Hegelian sense, into the objectification on which aesthetic relations are based—with regard to lyric poetry, it alienates language from its alienation in everyday use, negating exactly that debased use of language (with the emphasis on use, and thus on mis-use) that we both, I believe, despise and fear in its power over our daily lives and the lives of millions of other people who are not lied to on a minute-to-minute basis but cut off from the means of apprehending and articulating their own experience in any terms but those shoved down their throats and ears. Certainly some poets (hello, Billy Collins, and goodbye too) and other 'cultural producers' (a telling term) also participate in that process of debasing language and thus occluding the world and our experience of it, however honorable their political intentions (I would grant no honor to Mr. Collins' poetic intentions).

For William Carlos Williams, poetry was a mode of attention—anything could become not only the subject of a poem but a poem in itself (a note pinned to the icebox, for example) if the proper attention were paid to it, and this is a model of living in the world and actually seeing it (the life springing up along the muddy borders of the road to the contagious hospital that is death), that realm of things existing not as the objects of what Horkheimer and Adorno call instrumental reason and Lyotard calls performativity which Kant calls the kingdom of ends, freedom itself. Whatever Eliot may have "thought" (and his best poems, at least, exhibit a mind too find to be violated by ideas, as he wrote of Henry James, in the sense that they enact the process of feeling/thinking rather than laying out the conclusions to which one comes after one has discarded that process—this latter state of certainty afflicts the Four Quartets, much to their detriment), his poems enact that same exploratory openness to an experience of word and world. Having recently taught "Prufrock," "Preludes," "Rhapsody on a

Windy Night," and *The Waste Land*, I was struck by the way in which the last section of *The Waste Land*, What the Thunder Said, in contrast to those other poems which are willing to enact their multiple dilemmas—social, historical, psychological (and, yes, spiritual), economic, sexual, aesthetic—without claiming to be able to resolve them, pulls back from the presentation and exploration of situation into the attempt, however tentative or tenuous, to claim possession of A Solution, which turns out to be "Find God": a real let down from the rest of the poem's willingness to explore rather than merely answer questions. As Yeats said, poetry is what we make out of what we *don't* know. But again, as I tell my students all the time, we only care about any of these author's personal or social opinions (including Eliot's Christianity—even if one were a believer, Christian, Buddhist, or Hindu, to name the three possibilities the end of *The Waste Land* offers, one wouldn't need to read Eliot's poetry for the sake of faith) because we care about their poems.

It's exactly art's semi-autonomy that allows it to both posit a realm beyond the imperatives of capitalism in particular and social/political/economic power in general and to acknowledge and even insist on that realm's impossibility or at least its present inaccessibility—when it doesn't acknowledge this, when what Adorno calls art's promise of happiness claims that it can be fulfilled in the world as it is, it's not art but mere escapism, a lie that tells a lie rather than a lie that tells the truth. Speaking of Barnes and Noble, to which I myself much prefer Borders, and speaking also of the odd and unexpected circumstances in which one can find a glimpse of truth (and only, as in Frost's poem, a glimpse, and momentary—for once, then, something), last week a banner in the music section of Pensacola's local branch displayed a remarkably and apparently utterly accidentally Adornian quote from someone of whom I've never so much as heard, one Edward H. Howe: "When people hear good music, it makes them homesick for something they never had, and never will have." I would say that thing is freedom, where people and things exist for their own sakes and not for the sake of profit or power or some other end extrinsic to the actual existence of the entities of the world.

So on the issue of the Modernists and their heritage, I believe that we are in agreement. I was simply questioning the implied equation I read in your web log between aesthetic tendency and political tendency.

I was already interested in Adorno, but it was probably Reginald's intervention that led me to take him as seriously as I eventually did—and, as he suggested I ought, as a necessary counterweight to Heidegger. I wrote back:

> It does in fact look like we are in fundamental agreement about the importance of the Modernists and the "happy agon" (a happy phrase) many contemporary poets have with them. I was interested and moved by your statement that you felt yourself to be "rescued" by Eliot—he and Stevens were the two poets who had the most impact on me when I was a teenager and it's a tribute to poetry as an art form that they can and do stimulate and provoke "a gay black man who grew up in Bronx housing projects" as much as they did this straight white Jewish boy from an affluent Jersey suburb.
>
> I've been planning to read Adorno's *Aesthetic Theory* for some time, and your e-mails only make my encounter with his thought seem that much more urgent. I'm familiar with Adorno—I've slogged my way through *Negative Dialectics* and *Minima Moralia* is one of my favorite books of philosophy—but it's becoming clear to me that his contribution to aesthetic theory will be crucial for my understanding of the topic. One reason Heidegger has appealed to me, for all his wilfull obscurantism and Nazi utterances, is that his notion of art is one that builds something (*bilds* something?) in the world, something that newly arranges human relations both to other humans and to the self, as well as to that vexed and nearly forgotten thing called Nature (this is what he calls somewhat ponderously the "fourfold" of man, the gods, the sky, and the earth).

Adorno's essential negativity frustrates me, even as his "corrosive postmodern no" provides a devastating and necessary critique of the administered world (something nearly equivalent to Heidegger's "world-picture" or technological "enframing"—he has a lot more in common with Adorno than the latter would like to admit). So I haven't given up on the notion of art's at least having an influence on the actual world (as much, surely, as the actual world has upon it), on its ability to press back on "reality" with all the considerable force of the Stevensian "imagination," and on its role as a vehicle for imagining other possibilities, even if a genuine utopia must always be no place. This is why pastoral interests me and will probably become the organizing trope for my dissertation. I believe that Modernist poetry contains the seeds of both a negative pastoral and an erotic pastoral. "The Waste Land" might be a negative pastoral, in that it suggests an unrecoverable but much-longed-for whole through its mosaic of fragments—a mosaic which as you point out is falsely resolved in the poem's final section. This kind of pastoral is death-haunted, constructing a Being-towards-death for the speaker who arrives at his authenticity at the cost of a sociality which always contains an erotic dimension ("Prufrock" is another good example of this). Erotic pastoral is the strain in Modernism that celebrates rather than recoils at the tropes of the Heideggerian inauthentic (idle chatter, curiosity, ambiguity), that finds new worlds in which the possibility of a heroically "inauthentic" sociality become possible. Stein and Woolf's opening of a field for women, the domestic sphere, and a specifically feminine/lesbian eroticism is a good example of this kind of pastoral. Perhaps the most paradigmatic Modernist for what I'm talking about would be D.H Lawrence: [in *Women in Love*] Birkin's weird conception of marriage as two stars locked in orbit around each other yet somehow "unaffected" by each other is a tortured attempt at a compromise between a valorization of the authentic self being-towards-his-death and a valorization of being-with-others, of erotic and ethical engagement with them. Negative pastoral rejects the inauthentic, which means it rejects all possible political spheres except perhaps for a single collective blut-und-boden; erotic pastoral does engender an ethics but it puts an emphasis on privacy that can make the political seem irrelevant. Williams might offer a useful alternative: his Arcady is Paterson, N.J., and grounding erotic pastoral in a particular place with a particular history might open up non-authoritarian political possibilities. I'm still working these ideas out, obviously, and I expect they will change considerably, perhaps beyond recognition, as I continue to research pastoral, aesthetics, Modernism, and Modernism's Romantic/Victorian precursors.

Later that month, another exchange. Reginald:

I recently read Myung Mi Kim's *Commons,* which is an interesting book, rather severe and fractured (though rather conventionally syntactical for the most part) but with a strong lyrical strain running through it. I must say, though, that I'm beginning to think that fracture is too easy and even evasive, that rather than just cutting things up or claiming that they just *are* cut up (a simplistic view of art as a reflection of the world which is shared by many *soi-disant* avant garde writers, at least in America: didn't Picasso say that art is called art because it is not life?), it's much more difficult and interesting to put things together despite or in the face of fragmentation, not to create false whole or a false confidence in wholes, but to see and show that things *are* related, how random and chaotic their surfaces and appearances may be. That randomness is an ideological illusion, and this response is as much the Marx in me as the John Crowe Ransom. Totalities may be (always are) contradictory, but they are totalities, and we live in, among, and with them. Part of the work of thought, and the work of poetry, is to trace out their lineaments-for me, poetry, language, and thought (to obliquely refer to your beloved Heidegger) are about relating things, about making the connections among disparate things often seen as disconnected or even opposed or contradictory, because contradiction is a relation too, as is opposition.

Sometimes I tire of experimentation for its own sake—it comes to seem like a form of keeping up with fashion, never wear the same outfit twice, make sure you're wearing next season's clothes. Those trendy outfits also bear a strong resemblance to the clothes they wore in the teens and twenties, which people too often forget. So many of the 'experiments' in which our avant-garde engage were performed by Eliot, Pound, et alia, long before any of us was born. There's nothing wrong with using techniques that have already been developed (the English language is one of those techniques, after all), but there's something rather unseemly about claiming that you came up with them yesterday. The avant-garde frequently forgets that Pound's injunction to "Make it new" contains two parts—they concentrate so much on trying to be new (which ends up as a cult of novelty that mirrors the planned obsolescence of the consumer culture it claims to critique, a consumer culture my main criticism of which is that it isn't in fact available to all) that they neglect the necessity to make something, that newness is not a value in itself (no human being is 'new,' though each is unique) but a means to the rejuvenation of aesthetic experience (and thus, analogously at least, of our experience of and in the world).

I wrote back:

I envy, or think I envy, your attitude—I won't call it detachment—toward this dismal war. It seems like a healthy peasant's attitude, the attitude of someone who keeps doggedly plowing their field while the latest warlord, as in his father's father's time, conducts the latest bloody and meaningless war in which the peasant is too wise to let himself be conscripted. Of course wisdom in itself is no defense, and there is a narrow but deep generational gap here. I inherited my parents' (really my mother's) skepticism about government more or less uncritically: Reagan was obviously and manifestly evil in her world and so in mine, which is why it puzzles me to this day to see how venerated he's become. I was a toddler when my parents watched Vietnam and Watergate on TV: my cynicism about that era is a hand-me down from their old satirical albums and Doonesbury comic books. The horror of the present is fresh and I feel implicated when I wake up to the news, and when I see a flag, and when I pay my taxes. The situation does make me feel more acutely every day the insufficiency of any poetic response and the lack of any significant ethical privilege that could possibly be accorded toward avant garde forms. What an aesthete, what a formalist I am! Perhaps I simply find most conventional poetry boring because it's not formally interesting, and not because it reifies a dead, scabby language. Not that much experimental poetry isn't boring too: disjunction for disjunction's sake, as you point out. So I'm trying to get closer to your headspace: in Tom Waits' words, to get behind the mule and plow. Even though my blogging has slowed to a crawl I am at least writing poems, which perhaps share the same miniscule yet crucial value of any protest: a sign of life, a glimmer of the unadministered world.

… Your message has me thinking about the question of experimentation for experimentation's sake, and about the word "experimental" and how it's being loosely applied as a genre classification. I wonder if it would help if there were openly acknowledged genres of poetry—if there were signposts to direct the general reader. Would this be a meaningless exercise in subdivision that would only further insure that different camps can remain in happy ignorance of each other, or would it stimulate poets to try and work in genres whose existence they hadn't quite intuited before? We already have the strange division "Poetry" and "Popular Poetry" at Barnes & Noble: the latter's where you'll find books by Mattie Stepanek and Kahlil Gibran and the like, whereas the former somehow manages to encompass everything from Angelou to Zukofsky.

Perhaps we could avoid invidious subdivisions of "experimental" poetry and "formalism" by taking over the categories of genre fiction. What would "crime" poetry look like? "Thriller" poetry? "Romance"? "Fantasy"?

At any rate, while I appreciate your suspicion of the very real tendency some poets have to fetishize the new, and their tendency to forget the "it" in Pound's formula, I myself will not utter a discouraging word about formal experimentation. New forms are constantly being discovered, and 20th-century techniques like disjunction and the new sentence are already transforming themselves beyond prescription and mannerism and into the tradition: one more tool in the tool-box next to alliteration and enjambment. Perhaps the question is not where to draw the boundaries but rather how to teach young poets the uses of boundaries. How do you instill students with a desire for formal rigor—how do you get them to discover their own limitations so that they might eventually transgress them? This is not an idle question: I'll be teaching creative writing this fall for the first time in years and I want to empower and challenge my students in equal measure. I'm not going to pretend to be unbiased, but how can I create an atmosphere that encourages a student who does the kind of writing I find boring to at least articulate his or her assumptions and expectations? Is it enough to demand a statement of poetics from them after showing a few examples? This is a wandering paragraph, but you can see why I'd move from the general question of experimentation to the question of teaching. I feel reasonably well-equipped as far as my own creative explorations go, but what are the best and most useful tools I can give to students? What's a creative writing classroom for, anyhow?

The conversation lapsed after this into something a bit more personal, stored on an e-mail account to which I, alas, no longer seem to have access. The Internet giveth, and the Internet taketh away.

*

In the spring of 2005, while Reginald was in the throes of editing the first of the two anthologies he would edit, *The Iowa Anthology of New American Poets,* we had another series of exchanges on the question of "teams" in American poetry that I republish here as we sent them:

To: Joshua Corey
From: Reginald Shepherd

Joshua Corey

Date: 4/26/05

Dear Joshua,

This is just a brief note to let you know that you should be receiving your contributor's copies of *Bayou* very soon. I think that it's a very interesting assortment of rather diverse writers; I hope that you'll be pleased to be among them. I also wanted to send you an essay on which I've been working—it's a longer, more polemical version of the introduction to *The Iowa Anthology of New American Poetries*.

I am more and more disturbed by the reflexive dichotomizing among avant-gardeners (a great phrase) between avant-garde work (too often and easily equated with real poetry) and *soi-disant* "School of Quietude" poetry (i.e., everyone and anyone who's not in my club and doesn't wear my uniform), and not only because it seems that by definition (I'm published by a "mainstream" press) I would be SoQ. So often it seems that work is not judged on its own merits (and that the possibility that different kinds of poetry might be doing different and equally worthwhile kinds of things is not even considered), but pre-judged and preemptively dismissed or lauded in terms of the author's institutional affiliations. Ron Silliman is the most egregious practitioner of this kind of smug, self-satisfied dismissal and praise, which is a shame because he's not an unintelligent man, just a highly and willfully blinkered one. Given the avant-garde's supposed commitment to exploration and the acknowledgment of the unknown, such prejudgments are particularly glaring. (And yes, I do realize that a degree of prejudgment is an unavoidable and necessary part of mental functioning as such.) After all, when Prufrock says that he has known them all already, known them all, it's a lament, not a boast.

You at least grapple with the problem as a problem, though I think that you also are too willing to accept such categories as "School of Quietude" (a phrase that frankly I've come to despise) and to dismiss work accordingly (I'm not sure how Ron Silliman's poems are going to more effectively save or even change the world than Marilyn Hacker's, and frankly I find most of her work more compelling as poetry than his, though many of his essays are very interesting), and also too willing to praise work based on its author's intentions and affiliations rather than the work itself. I frequently see little difference between work labeled "avant-garde" and work labeled "mainstream"—too often it's all in who one's friends are.

What gets lost in all this territorialization (and didn't Deleuze & Guattari teach us that was bad bad bad?) is *poetry*, and more specifically, actual *poems*. You definitely care about (and even enjoy, something else that gets neglected, perhaps because it seems unsophisticated) poetry, and not just poetry, but real poems as experiences and aesthetic artifacts. I don't get the feeling that many people do, though. Does Ron Silliman? I don't see how one can when one has always already read any poem (or rather, any poet—the poems themselves tend to disappear) one comes across, which it seems that he has.

>   Take care.
>   peace and poetry,
>   Reginald

*

>   To: Reginald Shepherd
>   From: Joshua Corey
>   Date: 4/27/05

Dear Reginald,

Thanks for your e-mail and essay; I haven't had a chance to read it yet, but your reservations about the SoQ designation and clubbishness and pleasure have already stirred me to some thought, reflected indirectly in my latest blog post (last night's). I am always searching for a flexible yet strong critical instrument to separate wheat from chaff; at the same time I am convinced that disinterested aesthetic evaluation is neither possible nor desirable. Questions of affiliation and publication history—what Tim Yu calls "the context of production"—are always going to be part of the mix, though not, I hope, overdetermining ones. I myself am perhaps a little hard to track when it comes to evaluating my context: both my books are on small presses, but they're also both contest winners, with the judge of one being a former poet laureate and the judge of the other being one of the best known experimental poets in Canada. Plus my ambitions for a larger audience mean that I am going to seek more established presses for at least some of the books to come: I'd like to publish *Severance Songs,* for example, with a good university press or even—why not?—a big publisher like Knopf. I may yet write other things more suited to a small press; I think the new book, *Fourier Series,* is perfectly suited to the micropress that's publishing it. Anyway, I think about this stuff, as I'm sure you do too, because it's impossible to appreciate the gem without being affected by the medium in which it has been set.

All best,
Josh

*

To: Joshua Corey
From: Reginald Shepherd
Date: 4/27/05

Dear Joshua,

I did indeed read your web log of last night, which I found quite interesting and thought-provoking. We are clearly diametrically (though cordially) opposed in our views on the question of text and context. All artworks have contexts, but we only care about the context of a work because we care about the work, or at least that's as it should be—I am old-fashioned enough to believe that all response should start with and return to the text. If one is interested in the context for its own sake, then one is interested in biography or history or sociology or economics, et cetera, but not in literature. All of these interests are completely legitimate, as long as one is clear about what one's interest is. (And of course all of these things relate to literature in various overdetermined ways—but they do not define it as such, and literature's being in relation to these forces and structures doesn't distinguish it from, well, everything else in our society or any society which has ever had such a category of discourse as 'literature.') I recently read a very interesting and somewhat polemical book on Postmodernism by Christopher Butler (part of Oxford University Press's" A Very Short Introduction" series) in which he discusses the problem of artworks whose entire meaning (or, in some case, even their existence as artworks) depends upon their accompanying critical apparatus. As Susan Stewart points out (I quote this in the essay I sent you), "art practice that proceeds under the shadow of theory is doomed to be mere allegory [or illustration]; and ... theories of art bound to particular historical practices are doomed to [be] apologetics."

As for the "mode of production" of poetry, the analogy simply doesn't hold, and it trivializes real economics and real politics while aggrandizing poetry writing as some sort of political act (why not aggrandize it as an aesthetic act?). To talk about the mode of production in relation to poetry is pseudo-economics, pseudo-politics, and pseudo-Marxism. Poetry is not an economic good. In this regard, its use in intellectual discourse resembles the bandying about of the term 'cultural capital,' a glaringly imaginary—dare I write 'ideological'?—construction, except that at least in the case of poetry one can point to actually existing poems. In economic terms, poetry has no exchange value and no use value, nor is surplus value extracted from labor in the pursuit of profit in the writing of poetry. Indeed, Marx discusses the artist as an example of unalienated labor, and Adorno points out that art sublates social alienation into artistic objectification. And in more general social terms, art and high culture in general have never had the kind of legitimating functions in America, which has been proudly philistine and anti-intellectual from its colonial inception, that they've had in much of Europe. I sometimes feel that people forget in their wholesale importation of European theory that America is in fact not Europe, for better and for worse.

If one is interested in politics, one should engage in politics (as I know that you have to a certain extent), not the metaphorical (at best) or compensatory (at worst) 'politics' of 'cultural activism'—posing at politics, as social commentator Adolph Reed so trenchantly calls it. There is such a thing as politics, and it is distinct from art, whatever their interconnections. Actually engaging in political, social, or economic action is much harder than sitting around talking about containment and subversion.

I think that we're in agreement that poetry's greatest gift is its uselessness, its refusal to bow before the demands of utility and profit. Poetry is an example of all that's in excess of necessity, of all that escapes social and political definition and domination. Poetry defies what Adorno called instrumental reason and what Lyotard calls performativity: the demand that everything do something, that everything be "good for" something. It's an end in itself, rather than a means to an end, and in that way it's a model of the ideal life and the ideal world, in which things exist for their own sake and not for the sake of anything else. Kant called freedom the kingdom of ends, and that's what I think poetry presents the possibility or at least the image of: freedom, which is always an asymptote, an unattainable aspiration toward which we're still obligated to strive.

What poetry *does* is add to the world, presenting us with an image of a world (the poem) in which each element exists both for its own sake and as part of a larger gestalt in which each part contributes to the whole and the whole enriches every part. But this is a creative and not merely a critical task: it's too often forgotten that Adorno's relentless negativity, his refusal of things as they are, was in the service of a great hope, the possibility, however often deferred, of a just society, a world to which one could freely assent.

These days many people have transferred their hopes for social, political, and economic change into the cultural realm, out of despair and out of (frankly) laziness and unwillingness to do the hard, dirty work that's involved in trying to change the material world in which we live. It's a lot easier to critique art for being a bourgeois mystification or ideological occlusion than to fight for fair labor laws or clean water or civil liberties. I also think that kind of transference is a mistake: it places inappropriate demands on art (culture isn't the source of oppression in the world, no matter how many "cultural activists" claim that it is) and it deprives art of what it can truly give us, of what it truly can do for us. As Gary Indiana wrote, as democracy seeps out of our social and political lives, it invades our cultural lives, where it doesn't belong.

Since I seem to be on a rant, I might also mention that I've grown weary of experimentation for its own sake—it comes to seem like a form of keeping up with fashion, never wear the same outfit twice, make sure you're wearing next season's clothes. Those trendy outfits also bear a strong resemblance to the clothes they wore in the teens and twenties, which people too often forget. So many of the 'experiments' in which our avant-garde engage were performed by Eliot, Pound, et alia, long before any of us was born. There's nothing wrong with using techniques that have already been developed (the English language is one of those techniques, after all), but there's something rather unseemly about claiming that you came up with them yesterday. The avant-garde frequently forgets that Pound's injunction to "Make it new" contains two parts—they concentrate so much on trying to be new (which ends up as a cult of novelty that mirrors the planned obsolescence of the consumer culture it claims to critique, a consumer culture my main criticism of which is that it isn't in fact available to all—if this were truly a society of over-abundance, I wouldn't have much of a problem with it) that they neglect the necessity to make something, that newness is not

Joshua Corey

a value in itself (no human being is 'new,' though each is unique) but a means to the rejuvenation of aesthetic experience (and thus, analogously at least, of our experience of and in the world).

I do wonder, with regard to judging work by its author's institutional/social affiliations versus judging work as a text (as a, dare I write the New Critical words, autotelic artifact), what is the difference between Jane Miller and Michael Palmer (or, from his more recent work that I've seen, between Michael Palmer and Charles Simic?). Inquiring mind wants to know.

Take care, and know that though we disagree quite profoundly on many questions I appreciate the serious thought that you put into them (it's quite rare), and your obvious love of poetry and poems, which is not so widely shared among those who call themselves poets (and I include poets on either side of whatever fence you care to build).

>   peace out and about,
>   Reginald

Haunted by Reginald's claim that "many people have transferred their hopes for social, political, and economic change into the cultural realm" (a claim that seems as or more resonant in the age of Trump as it did in during the reign of Bush II), I mused on my blog:

> The man has a point: no amount of cultural activity, however well-meaning or "radical," can have an immediate, direct impact on our increasingly shitty world. You can try to detour around this question; for example, many people who take a populist apporach to poetry and its promotion believe that if poetry were somehow removed from the embrace of a decayed "high" culture it would have a more immediate appeal—that it could have the same impact on our political scene as, say, a Bob Dylan song in the 60s. The problems with this idea are obvious: for one, whether or not you're willing to stand up for high culture, to strip poetry of

a large dimension of its possibilities (for engagement with literary tradition, for requiring concentration and negative capability from its reader) is to neuter it. For another, can we really give Bob Dylan or any other "protest singer" (Dylan is actually far too ambiguous an example—how about Buffalo Springfield?) credit for bringing about, say, the end of the Vietnam War? Or can we only credit them for the morality of their response to that war? Still, though I readily concede that poetic activity is no substitute for political activity, I'm troubled by Reginald's separation of the two spheres, which strikes me as a version of Plato's banishment. That is, since poets create alluring representations that may distract citizens (especially young citizens) from the real work of polis-building— even fool them into thinking that art-making and polis-building are the same—they must be kicked out of the Republic into a hazy zone of autonomy. The benefit of this is that poetry then becomes what Reginald so beautifully quotes Kant as calling the kingdom of ends. But doesn't this vision, especially if it becomes the active locus of intense imaginative activity, have *some* impact on the polis it lurks below and above? If you believe that poetry, being physical, alters however slightly the physical body of the one who reads it by rewiring neural pathways, then our own bodies become the bridge between polis and poetics. It's my belief that poetry with a social orientation of whatever description, especially poetry that tarries with the negative, will tend not to anesthetize its readers/writers but aestheticize them: activate more nerves, help them experience that the bounds of their own body extend into the larger world, renewing their resolve to care for it more actively. That's why I object to middlebrow poetry that circulates exhausted pieties, covers up uncomfortable truths, and encourages passive resignation. I have a more ambivalent relation to what we might call poetry of praise, the poetry of the beautiful—my dissertation is one attempt to discover if beauty can be in some way progressive— if Keats' equation of truth and beauty is somehow correct. So I will continue to read my contemporaries with antennae tuned to this overall project—while trying to remain open to the likelihood that I won't always recognize it when I see it.

Cultural politics, it turned out, was to draw far more energy from me and from many other poets in those years. The other Silliman-fostered term being thrown about in those days—the "us" that was positioned in opposition to the School of Quietude's "them"—was "post-avant," an absurd term; I much prefer the term that Reginald references above, which he took from another Ron, Ron Slate: "avant-gardener." The question of the avant-garde, and its viability as a concept for the twenty-first century, nagged at us both. Reginald returned to this theme and to the invidious team-building exercises to which it led in an e-mail a few days later:

Reading some of the responses to my comments and others on your web log reminds me that I really should use the internet only for email and buying things. The misreading of my comments is impressive and depressing. But then, in general it seems difficult these days to make a nuanced argument—people see things only in black and white, and insist on reducing one's arguments to simplistic parody. Tim Yu seems particularly determined to willfully distort everything I wrote, as evidenced by his cheap attempt to smear me with the Billy Collins brush, a strategy to make everyone who might disagree with him equally dismissible.

Simeon DeDeo thinks that I am a categorizer like Ron Silliman when I have been quite vociferously arguing against such fence builders as Silliman. As Tim Yu seems to have completely missed, my point in comparing Marilyn Hacker and Ron Silliman's poetry was that neither is going to change the world politically or socio-economically, but that Hacker's work provides a more satisfying poetic, aesthetic experience than does Silliman's—and that is, after all, what poems are supposed to do, isn't it? The scare quotes around "mainstream" were precisely and obviously to indicate that it is others, again like Tim Yu, who would so characterize and dismiss me, not that I so characterize myself or my work. I might also add that the word "mainstream" referred to my publisher.

Since I began reading poetry in the 1970s, I have always been opposed to what I saw as contemporary mainstream American poetry, because it was boring and because in its neglect of poetry's verbal resources it was out of the mainstream of English language poetry from the Elizabethans through the Metaphysicals to Keats and the Modernists. These are the writers who made me want to read and to write poetry in the first place, whose work is still the standard by which I measure my own work and that of others. But historical memory is also something that tends to fall by the wayside.

Also contra Tim Yu, I have indeed read Ron Silliman's blog and his readings of various poets and poems, but have usually found them unconvincing. Silliman has a lot of smart and interesting things to say, but his readings tend to be motivated more by his agenda than by a close attention to the text. I am sometimes hard pressed to tell the difference between the poems that he praises and those that he dismisses, except, again, on the basis of their context and the poets' affiliations. And his tendency to give a special pass to poets from approved ethnic minorities (like Tsering Wangmo Dhompa, whose poetry I rather like but don't find to be particularly "avant-garde") is just patronizing and condescending.

Such misreadings as I have responded to above are examples and results of exactly the kind of relentless, dismissive dichotomizing and categorizing that I've been arguing against. I think of Prufrock's complaint about "The eyes that fix you in a formulated phrase." As Prufrock plaintively asks, "when I am formulated, sprawling on a pin..../Then how should I begin...?" But even though I would much rather that your various web friends read my poetry than my comments on your web log or even my published essays, I do want to clarify a couple of things before I withdraw from the fray. So please feel free to copy this letter onto your web log.

First, when I wrote of the misplacement of politics onto poetry, I wasn't intending to privilege politics—if anything, the opposite. Though I keep myself more informed than I would like to be, I tend to avoid political involvement, mostly because I see the world and this country in particular as more and more utterly and irredeemably hopeless. My main goal is to survive as long as possible. Poetry can and should, of course, engage politics as it can and should engage any of the material of this world, but poetry's function is, as I've tried to make clear, is not to be either a branch of or a substitute for politics. Picasso said that art is called art because it is not life, and I don't see why politics can't be politics and poetry be poetry—two distinct names for two distinct things. Poetry and politics are related, yes, but no more so (actually, less so, in material terms) than refrigerators and politics. Why can't poetry be allowed to be and do what it is and does? The demand that poetry be something else seems to me a symptom of the pervasive and long-standing denigration and devaluation of art in this country, so that even those who defend art feel that they have to do so in terms of something else more obviously important.

Second, I do understand that objectivity isn't possible, and that defining oneself against things that one isn't (or perceives or conceives of oneself as not being) is an important way in which identity is produced both as a person and as an artist. I certainly did a lot of it when deciding I wanted to be a poet in the late Seventies, aligning myself with Modernism as against the then-utterly-inescapable aesthetic of transparency, what Charles Altieri calls the scenic mode. But I also think, in literature as in life, that it's important to at least make the attempt to be objective, because even if it's not achievable it can be approached in a meaningful way (as you can probably tell, I'm also not a relativist), and again, literature, and art in general, to me is about expanding the realms of the possible, not shutting them down, and I've often been surprised by what I've found in a piece of literature about which I'd had preconceived notions. And even though texts can't escape their contexts, they can transcend them (in the Hegelian sense of sublation); if they can't, I honestly don't see what the point of art is at all, or how it could communicate anything to anyone. I don't remember the exact phrasing, but Allen Tate wrote once of literature as a realm in which two contradictory things can both be true at the same time.

Third, when Tim Yu says, and you concur, that we are all post-avant-garde, what he means is that we are all post Modernist, in the strict chronological sense: we are all in the wake of the Modernists, of Modernism, especially when seen as an international phenomenon. All the poetic avant-gardening in the past thirty years or longer has basically been a process of people rediscovering the Moderns, turning over the soil, if you will, and rediscovering things that had been buried or at least lost sight of. (I include in that process re-seeing a figure hiding in plain sight like Eliot, who in his poetry and in much of his critical prose is far from the conservative curmudgeon he's made out to be or that he later made himself out to be.) I don't see anything—and I do mean anything—in so-called avant-garde work that wasn't done by the Modernists: collage, montage, pastiche, quotation, parody, juxtaposition ironic and non-ironic, fracture and fragmentation, ungrammaticalities and syntactic deformation, decentered subjectivity, non-referentiality (whatever that can mean as applied to language, which only exists as such as the nexus of concept, sound, and physical mark), critical or celebratory incorporation of popular culture, critique of mass society and capitalism, critique of art as a social institution, etc. There is nothing in the so-called avant-garde, from the New Americans to the Language poets to whatever the contemporary crew wants to call themselves besides "too good for everyone else," that wasn't done by the Modernists. There's nothing wrong with this per se (as someone said once, there is nothing new under the sun)—after all, none of us invented the English language either, or the Roman alphabet, which doesn't mean that we don't have the right to use them or the potential to do interesting things with them. But as I said in one of my previous emails, there is a lot wrong with pretending that one came up with these techniques and approaches oneself, especially when one then goes on to congratulate oneself for one's daring and perspicacity.

Joshua Corey

If one is in the "avant-garde," then one is part of the leading formation of some army or another. Besides questioning at the teleological nature of such a conception (toward what goal is one moving? what exactly is the goal of poetry in this progressivist conception? I feel a grand narrative coming on), I also wonder just what one imagines oneself to be in the vanguard of? Why, to mention two of my favorite poets, is the work of Jorie Graham, whose work at its best is as complex and challenging as anyone's, not "avant-garde," while the work of Ann Lauterbach is? (Or is Lauterbach not because she is published by Penguin?) I am asking about the work, not the people (though at this point Lauterbach is only barely less established than fellow MacArthur Award winner Graham). And why, for that matter must interesting, challenging, difficult poetry be labeled or accountable as "avant-garde" in order really to be taken seriously? You've acknowledged the danger that the term "avant-garde" turn into a synonym for "what I like" or even just "good poetry," but too often that's exactly how it's used. Perhaps you're right that it's time to retire the term.

And now I think that I will turn my energies to more fruitful endeavors, like reading some actual poems. The Canadian poet Tim Lilburn is quite amazing, if you've not encountered his work—I highly recommend *Kill-site* and *To the River*. I've been a bit disappointed in Christopher Dewdney's *The Natural History*, which I bought on the basis of your praise on your web log. It has many lush and lovely passages, but: besides being a bit repetitive and having a few too many big empty words like "mysterious," "profound," "vast," "unearthly," "eternal," and "infinite" (all this from one section of "The Cenozoic Asylum"), it plays a bit too fast and loose with natural fact for my taste. I'm a stickler for accuracy.

peace and poetry,
Reginald

I found myself responding to the stickler in a somewhat muddied fashion; in hindsight, I see myself struggling against my own Romanticism, to which I have since more or less happily surrendered:

> You are of course correct that few of the poets I've favored with critical attention are avant-garde in the strict sense defined by Bürger. However, I've come to believe that avant-gardening is a continuum: pure avant-gardeners are rare because few of us have the courage or cojones or insanity to erase every barrier between art and life. But I do think there are a number of strategies—repurposed Modernisms, if you will—by which artists selectively attack that barrier and put it into question. For example Rankine's naive stance, which rankles you as false, strikes me as an attempt to portray how vulnerable we really are to mass media and the extremely limited and limiting categories it offers us for subjectivity, especially collective subjectivity. Instead of a poem which either ignores mass media entirely (as most middlebrow poetry does) or asserts a self strong enough to surf its waves without damage (Frank O'Hara and his postmodern epigones), Rankine gives us a poem in which the speaker takes on the challenge of being affected, shaped, and then goes on to try and reshape her damaged self with only the language of her sympathetic imagination. In other words, her poetry stages a vulnerability to "life" (modern mediated life) and is willing to at least partially compromise its autonomy to do so; this strikes me as legitimately avant-garde, maybe a 6 on a 1 to 10 scale with 1 being utterly conventional, 9 being Duchamp's *Fountain* when it still had power to shock, and 10 being something probably never yet achieved—maybe the Situationists came closest.

At this point I'm becoming interested in another dimension of the question which I suspect leads to a lot of misunderstanding between people: the poetry of transcendence vs. the poetry of immanence. (I know, another bloody dichotomy: well, I'm assuming that like all dyads, this one too can be dialecticized.) I saw a blog post recently by a writer calling himself Sisyphus Walking, claiming that what we really have in these discussions is "poetry of the religious mind" and "poetry of the irreligious mind." The first, which the writer clearly favors, seeks after some kind of positive meaning, which he or she seems to conceive as existing in some "out there" and we just have to go find it. The second is purely negative: "Because these minds find meaninglessness in the world, their poetry's attitude (and likely their own) exhibits disdain for the human population at large. It is a poetics not for the many. Examples would be any Post-Structuralist poetry, most commonly Language poetry." I think this is hogwash but it might be rephrased more usefully as a post-Romantic vision of poetry as religion by other means versus a post-Modernist poetry that is concerned with this-worldliness and sees all meaning as a human construct (which is by no means equivalent to "finding meaninglessness"). Neither type of poetry has an exclusive claim on political virtue or aesthetic quality, but the post-Romantic sort is less likely to feel that formal breakage and re-making is necessary to its project; instead it seeks some sort of continuity with a tradition that is nonetheless inadequate as is. I don't know whether I for one have an "irreligious mind"; I still like what Fanny Howe has said about how atheists take God more seriously than those who insist on personalizing him. But I do tend to agree with Vico (who said that we ought to be able to understand our world since we are the ones who made it) and Marx (who said that changing the world, not understanding it, is the point). I think we are just beginning to catch up with the implications of the Modernist project, which recognized the fungibility of the world and reflected that in its artistic techniques. So I continue to favor an experimental, innovative, post-Modern poetry with avant-garde tendencies as having the best chance of being the axe to break up the frozen sea (of reification, of mediated life) within us and between us. Which is not to say that I'm completely unmoved by the post-Romantic poetry of quest and redemption that a few poets still have the heroism to practice (Jorie Graham is one). And I'm interested in the blurry line between them, as suggested by the career of someone like John Ashbery, celebrated by Harold Bloom and post-avants alike.

Reginald:

With regard to my comment that Tim Yu's assertion that "We are all post-avant" would be more accurately phrased as "We are all post-Modern," I don't think that he is referring to the historical avant-garde at all; his horizon seems much narrower than that. It seems quite clear that what he means by saying that we are all' "post-avant" is that we are all post-Language poetry, and it was that context to which I was referring when I said that his statement would be more accurately reformulated as we are all post-Modernist (as in, in the wake of). There's a quote from Robert Archambeau in the Samizdat review of *The Mechanics of the Mirage* that sums it up very well: "all poetry being written in America now could usefully be discussed under rubrics that attach one prefix or another to the term 'modernist': anti-modernist, late-modernist, post-modernist, neo-modernist, maybe even pop-modernist."

With regard to Peter Bürger's conceptualization of the avant-garde, I don't think that any of the writers you've discussed admiringly, however interesting some of their work is (I don't share your high opinion of Claudia Rankine, for example, whose work I find banal and often sentimental; the faux-naivety of *Don't Let Me Be Lonely,* as if the narrator had just turned on her television and found out that the world isn't a happy place, actually offended me), is engaged in the project of breaking down the barriers between the institution of art and the praxis of life that Burger attributes to the historical avant-garde. In that sense they are all modernist or 'experimental' writers, not avant-garde writers. I'd be hard-pressed to think of anyone writing in America today, whether I think their work is successful or not, who is participating in such a project. As a matter of fact, it's hard to imagine just how any purely literary endeavor would even go about trying to do such a thing—Dada and Surrealism were, after all, not primarily literary movements.

In fact, it's clear that whatever avant-garde has been around since World War II at the latest, excepting as you say the Situationists and some of the "critical art" of the 1970s and 1980s (and perhaps Warhol, though Duchamp had already erased the material difference between the art object and the mundane object long before Warhol's Brillo boxes, which were after all not even *real* Brillo boxes, unlike at least Duchamp's first urinal), has *not* been engaged in the project of destroying the boundaries between the institution of art and the praxis of life Burger attributes to the historical avant-garde, nor has it particularly been trying to do so. It's not so much a failure as a difference in aims altogether. I frankly don't think that this is such a bad thing. I like art, and I wouldn't want to see it disappear. I think that the world is a more interesting place for containing a variety of phenomena, and I wouldn't want to level out that variety (though I would certainly like to pick and choose—there are many phenomena I would happily see disappear). And as Burger points out, so long as the praxis of life remains that of capitalist instrumentality, to subsume art into the praxis of life would be a defeat, not a victory—that's exactly what capitalism is already doing: "the culture industry has brought about the false elimination of the distance between art and life, and this also allows one to recognize the contradictoriness of the avant-gardiste undertaking." It's a double-edged sword that turns on its wielder.

I think that the dichotomy you set up (yet another one, as you acknowledge) between a this-worldly and an other-worldly would be usefully formulated in terms of what Charles Altieri has called the distinction between an immanentist and a transcendentalist aesthetic with of course the understanding that most writers would fall somewhere in between—it's a continuum or spectrum, not a binary. But to the more I think about what you wrote, the more muddled and confusing it becomes. I end up not being sure what exactly the distinction you're drawing is, or what the relationship between your premises and your conclusions is. I don't know what you mean when you say that the Modernists recognized the fungibility of the world, since fungible means interchangeable, and is usually used to refer to commodities (as my Merriam-Webster Dictionary uses as an example, "oil, wheat, and lumber are fungible commodities"). I would think the opposite, that the modernists were interested in pointing out the uniqueness of the world, its irreducibility to categories and definitions, let alone to tokens of exchange. Nor do I see why "formal breakage and re-making" are antithetical to "some sort of continuity with a tradition that is nonetheless inadequate as is". That was exactly the Modernist relationship to tradition, and indeed the relationship of any strong poetry to tradition: if the tradition were complete and utterly adequate in itself, there'd be no need to write anymore. And if one tried to have no relation to the tradition (an impossibility), there'd be nothing to break or remake. There's no poetry of any interest whatsoever that either slavishly repeats the tradition or attempts to ignore it. The poets whom you champion (I won't call them "the avant-garde") simply have a different version of the tradition than that of "the Poets Whom You Don't Like"—what Harold Rosenberg calls the tradition of the new.

I'm also not clear why Jorie Graham is not *both* post-Romantic and post-Modern in your terms. She has certainly engaged, on several occasions, in what Helen Vendler calls "the breaking of style," and *Swarm,* for example (her worst book, in my opinion), is rife with fracture and fragmentation, un-making and un-doing. I think that *The End of Beauty* is one of the best books of poetry of the past twenty-five years, and it is all about unraveling given narratives and undoing social, historical, and epistemological certainties. Graham is also interested in what might replace those inherited and imposed certainties, if that's what you mean by "[seeking] after some positive meaning." But it's obviously impossible to live without some sense of positive meaning, and you clearly have much of your own— it's the basis of your critique of what I shall just call "the Poetry That You Don't Like," and of the social world you see that poetry as standing in for. Contingent, ironized, or otherwise, you believe that the things you think are true, as does everyone. You are more open than most to the possibility that they are not, but that still presumes such a thing as truth, as positive meaning. Again, human life would be impossible without such, from my belief that when I put my foot down while walking the ground will be there to meet it to my belief that murder is wrong. As for the notion that truth is a human construct (which is somewhat obvious—as Wittgenstein wrote, the world is composed of propositions about the world; that is, we see the world through our ideas about the world), as John McGowan puts it in *Postmodernism and Its Critics,* "We moderns spin our truths out of our own bowels (to paraphrase Yeats), and the conviction that this is so engages modernity in its endless polemic against truth claims that deny their human origin; but this polemic has no force if the fundamental insistence that humans make rather than find truth is not accepted as an unalterable truth."

And if you're talking about quest and redemption, what is what you call the attempt "to break up the frozen sea (of reification, of mediated life) within us and between us" but a redemptive quest of the highest order? When Marx writes that the point is not to understand the world but to change it, clearly this change is a version of redemption. (After all, presumably he doesn't want to make the world worse, which would also be a version of change.) There is a wholly non-pejorative way in which Marxism can be accurately described as millenarian—that's a huge part of its point and its appeal. Certainly all the critical efforts of Language poetry have that behind them, as does Adorno's relentless negativity (a point I've made before). Otherwise they're just pointless caviling.

*

The last exchanges I wish to reprint here were more indirect, based upon comments we made on our own blogs about something the other had said on his. This kind of extended conversation presents, I believe, the brief age of blogging at its very best: a series of overlapping conversations and meditations that were digressive in nature, and thus more creative than argumentative. These begin with a post I wrote on the political stance of a poet with whom I am sometimes confused, if only because of the similarity of our names, back in November 2006:

Joshua Clover laments the foolishness and ideological blindness of other poets (and, as his second post makes clear, this poet in particular) who ran out to vote for, as he puts it, "candidates more conservative than the Republicans they found beyond revulsion twenty years ago" and who now dance pathetically in the end zone celebrating a Democratic Congress. Apparently I didn't express nearly enough skepticism to satisfy him: indeed, his tone makes me think he lives in a world comprised of a virtuous Berkeley-Marxist-anarchist minority who are all "in the know," and who behold the majority of marks and suckers with mixed pity and contempt. There's hardly any distinction to be made between liberal marks and conservative suckers in the bargain, since both by voting at all vote to perpetuate the system. Those of us who, in spite of our misgivings about a badly damaged political system, joined the less-than-half of the eligible population who voted (does that mean in fact that 60 percent of the electorate are Marxists and anarchists rather than apathetic? Would that it were so!), discover that we did not in fact vote for change, for some kind of brake on an incoherent, compulsively violent, and reckless administration, but for more of the same. The "personnel," as Joshua would have it, are all empty signifiers, so that by his own lights he can plausibly plug in "Condoleeza Rice" for my "Nancy Pelosi." It's a gross misinterpretation: I am not celebrating the rise of any old woman to the post of Speaker of the House, but the rise of a specific woman who is probably more sympathetic to Berkeley-style politics than anyone in the new Congress (with the notable and welcome exception of Bernie Sanders, I-VT). Joshua takes such a long view of our admittedly disastrous era that individuals and institutions scarcely matter: we are all fiddling while Rome burns and it signifies little who takes the part of lead violin.

Perhaps he is right. And I have nothing to say to anyone who is actually pursuing an alternative politics: who doesn't just stand aloof with jaundiced eye but actually works for radical change. I don't see myself as someone who does this, at least not yet: I am at best a sympathetic fellow traveler, reading Rexroth and Bookchin, trying to formulate an adequate response to the crises of the world I find myself in, while at the same time unwilling to make the complete separation from the mainstream—the world where most of my friends and family and ordinary people live—that the radical position seems to demand. I criticize myself constantly for not being more active, more courageous, more clear-sighted. But when I look at the world I find more questions than answers. I am not satisfied by any single political program that I've ever become aware of. And I persist in seeing difference where Joshua sees identity: Democrats, even conservative Democrats, are *not* Republicans, for the simple reason that they've been out of power for the past six years and have had no significant influence on the ghastly policies of Bush-Cheney. I want opposition to those troglodytes on almost any terms, because I think they are way, way beyond the ordinary ghastliness of neo-liberalism: they are fanatics personally responsible for the loss of more than half-a-million Iraqi lives. And maybe I really have been suckered—"please don't throw me in that briar patch!"—maybe the neo-liberal machine will simply function more smoothly and destructively now that we have divided government. But maybe not. I'm taking a chance on "maybe."

We Americans do need to imagine something new, we do need to take on responsibility appropriate to our power to affect the world. But right now I want to slow down the pace of destruction: when the big crisis comes, the Depression-equivalent that I'm expecting sometime in the next decade or so, I don't want the damage to our environment to be utterly beyond repair. I don't have the answers, or a fully consistent political philosophy. But given the simple choice between casting a vote that *might* do something to impede the flow of greed and and arrogance and fanaticism, and not voting—irrespective of what other activities or criticism I might be able to muster—I chose to vote. And I am provisionally pleased with the results.

Reginald's own post, from January 6, 2007, was titled "Salon des

Psuedo-Refuseniks," and rather concurred with and amplified my feelings:

> In a post from his November web log, Joshua Corey, who is both a very talented poet and an insightful and committed thinker about poetry, refers to two posts on Joshua Clover's web log attacking the foolishness and blindness of those who are naïve or ideologically deluded enough to vote. Corey has a very smart and eloquent response, but I wanted to add my own.
>
> I am sick to death of these more-correct-than-thou types who claim to hold themselves utterly aloof from a world they see themselves as completely above, particularly those who assert that voting doesn't matter because all candidates and all parties are the same, or even that voting is a manifestation of false consciousness because it constitutes buying into the system. How anyone can believe that after over six years of George W and his accomplices despoiling pretty much the entire world is beyond me, except that their smugness and self-righteousness makes it impossible or unnecessary to actually see the world, since they always already know all about it anyway, unlike us poor benighted souls who are, as Joshua Corey so aptly points out, both to be pitied and to be held in contempt. It's interesting how much such types despise the very people for whose liberation they claim to hope, though apparently not to work.
>
> I certainly don't know what these people, so many of whom seem to spend most of their time casting a jaundiced and superior eye down on the rest of us, are doing to bring the *soi-disant* revolution any closer. Perhaps they believe that salvation is not by works but by faith alone. The intellectual and political Puritanism, and self-righteousness, of pseudo-purist leftists does bear striking resemblances to Calvinism at its ugliest.
>
> On the question of what is to be done, and of what is being done, one major problem with the Manichean ultra-leftist worldview (besides its all too common hypocrisy) is that if there is on the one

hand only total purity and on the other hand only total corruption, then nothing can be done, because any action will inevitably sully the purity of the intention. Between the intention and the act falls the shadow, as T.S. Eliot wrote some time ago. Thus the quietism and passivity of such types, who sit back and criticize others' actions (for what action is perfect?) while doing nothing themselves. Clean hands are idle hands. They are also never as clean as their bearers think they are.

So many Americans who consider themselves leftists or progressives would prefer nothing to something if the something isn't utopia. Or, like the several varieties of worsists, they would actually *like* to see disaster befall our society, or they think that they would, no matter how many people suffer, because that would trigger the revolution. Such types like to consider themselves totally outside of that which they claim to critique. Perhaps this is why is never occurs to them that they too will suffer in their implicitly-hoped-for worst case scenarios. But not voting is still participating in the system. By not voting, you are simply giving more weight to the votes of those who do bother to vote, however deluded or brainwashed they may be. In practical terms, you are voting for whoever happens to win.

Those who question or even deny the value of voting tend to be from those groups, social, economic, and racial, that have been able to take voting for granted. But people died so that I could have the right and the opportunity to vote. I don't intend to throw that opportunity away.

From politics we moved on to the perennial question of creative writing as an academic discipline and what its purpose might be. The poet G.C. Waldrep, with whom I would later collaborate on *The Arcadia Project,* wrote me a long e-mail in March 2007 that I posted on my blog, but which boiled down to what he had taken from his experience teaching creative writing to undergraduate students: their "desire for 'authenticity.'" I will reprint here one of G.C.'s most important paragraphs, which makes a convincing link between that fundamental desire and the craft of poetry:

> What I have tried to get across to my students, increasingly, is that if authenticity of (a) self can be achieved in language, then craft matters. The host culture has sufficiently colonized our brains with language—we are awash in media—that the seemingly simple act of stripping away cliché from one's writing can take years of self-conscious, often discouraging effort. That through solving problems of craft a writer is not distracting him- or herself from that authenticity, but rather finding ways to deepen that authenticity: of voice, of form, and yes, in the end, of self. I'm one of those characters who doesn't know what he means until he sees what he says, so for me the idea of a self coming into being even as the words unspool is a potent one, at least in theory.

Reginald followed up on G.C.'s remarks with "What Is Creative Writing For?":

> Some of the discussion in Joshua Corey's recent posts of creative writing's function as an affirmation of the self, and particularly his quote from a long and eloquent email message from the fine poet G.C. Waldrep, author of *Goldbeater's Skin*, regarding creative writing pedagogy, has prompted me to post this excerpt from a longer piece I have written on the teaching of creative writing. I hope that it will prove illuminating or at least interesting.
>
> Many students attend college for no reason other than having been told that is what they should do after high school, and perhaps with the hope that they will make more money if they have a college degree. They tend to feel simultaneously resentful ("Here I am stuck in this stupid class") and entitled ("I'm not in high school anymore, now I'm an adult"). Students often see creative writing classes as the antithesis to their other classes, in which they are forced to absorb and regurgitate all kinds of information in which they have no personal interest or investment. In a creative writing

class, they can be themselves, because anything goes in a poem. (The idea that they might not yet have "selves" to "be" does not occur to them, nor does the idea that selfhood might be a process of becoming, not a fixed state of being.) Concomitantly, they also believe that poetry is too subjective to judge, because it's all opinion and personal preference.

To acknowledge that personal preference and opinion are always factors while still maintaining that specificity, particularity of image and language, precision, concision, and avoidance of cliché are aspects of all good poetry (as sometimes needs to be pointed out, vagueness is not a style) sometimes seems beyond them, especially since they are convinced and have often been taught that if they think something then it must be true. (One great problem in American education isn't what students don't know, but what they know that isn't true.) My partner has a bumper sticker on his office door that reads "Don't believe everything you think." It's a caution that many might profitably take to heart.

We live in a culture which robs people of social, political, and economic agency, making them feel as if their experience counts for nothing, while simultaneously insisting that everyone's every passing notion and experience is of supreme importance because it happened to *them*. These two aspects are concomitant with one another, the second offering an imaginary (that is, an ideological) compensation for the first. Much of the boom both in creative writing programs and in slam poetry, performance poetry, stand-up poetry, and the like, has more to do with a cult of the public performance of personality (à la Oprah Winfrey and Jerry Springer), on the one hand, and with the scarcity of outlets for genuine feeling and expression in our society and an ever-increasing sense of the impotence and insignificance of the individual, on the other hand, than with an interest in poetry as an art form.

The turn to creative writing, and to versions of poetry in particular, is a way of saying "I matter" in a wholly ritualized and conventionalized format, and is wholly understandable (if somewhat misdirected) as such. But again, this has to do not with an interest in the art of poetry, but rather with a sense that poetry is a mode of personal expression unsullied by commerce or social constraints. (And of course poems are shorter and thus apparently easier to write than novels or even short stories, another aspect of their appeal in a society that seeks quick results but shuns effort.) So the recent rise in the popularity of poetry doesn't contradict poetry's marginality in our culture any more than does the use of the word "poetry" as an all-purpose honorific: Michael Jordan, as they say, was poetry in motion on the basketball court. I prefer to think that poetry is poetry and basketball is basketball. Indeed, it is one of the functions of art to help us see things as and for themselves.

Canonical poetry, or literary poetry, or Modernist poetry, or post-Modernist poetry, or any poetry grounded in a practice of language and of writing as such, rather than one of personal expressivity and/or identity confirmation, still isn't much read. Rather, it is disdained as one or another variety of stiff academicism, insular, "elitist" and oppressive, as opposed to the authentic expression of slam poetry or some similar construction. In this model, "creativity" is just another commodity which anyone can procure, on credit if necessary.

Another poet-blogger with whom we used to have commerce, K. Silem Mohammad, intervened at this point in the conversation with a post that is no longer extant. Reginald responded with "More on Creative Writing Pedagogy":

> "Breaking the Self-Affirmation Barrier," a recent very articulate and thought-provoking post on K. Silem Mohammad's blog, at least partially a response to my recent post "What Is Creative Writing for?" on creative writing pedagogy, has in turn prompted me to post another part of my essay on the teaching of creative writing, one that addresses some of the issues he so saliently brings up, though from a different angle of vision.

Due to the heavily policed institutional borders between creative writing and criticism or literature, the interrelationship of the two is often obscured. Creative writers, seeing themselves as the keepers of the sacred flame of literature, engage in frequent polemics against the invariably destructive encroachments of theory on creativity, while theorists largely ignore or at best disdain the unselfconscious effusions of authors who refuse to accept the news of their death. This state of affairs has always troubled me, for I have never felt the chasm between my writing and my critical intellect (or that between my emotions and my thoughts on which it is based) that so many seem not only to take for granted but determined to enforce on others. Other literary works, both those with which I have felt affinities and those toward which I've felt great antipathy, have always been both inspirations for and challenges to my own work and the work I aspired to do. Indeed, I never would have considered writing poetry without the impetus of reading deeply in it, wanting to comprehend, apprehend, and wield the power I found in it. Complementarily, criticism and what is sweepingly and too vaguely called "theory" have been crucial in thinking through and thinking anew my writing. Such critical thinking has been central to my development as a writer, and has helped me work through many an impasse in my work.

Most literary academics have no idea how to read a poem, having imbibed the conviction that close reading or textual explication is reactionary or simply passé without ever having informed themselves just what such reading might entail. While poetry writing programs have burgeoned, poetry has fallen by the wayside as an object of literary study in favor of the examination of novels as social documents.

Many literary scholars and theorists believe that writing cannot or should not be taught, that talent is some immeasurable intangible. Such academics share many students' sense that there is nothing to teach or be taught in a creative writing class, that writing literature, unlike, presumably, analyzing or theorizing it, requires no knowledge or training. Reified notions of innate genius which have been thoroughly deconstructed with regard to the literatures of the past are still too often unselfconsciously applied by writers and by critics to dismiss the possibility of training the writers of future literatures. Some people have a greater aptitude than others for musical composition or performance, for dance, for science or mathematics, yet no one asserts on that basis that these practices cannot be taught. Nor would many argue against the assertion that both those with more of an inclination and those with less of an inclination toward such pursuits can benefit from such education and training. But among both writers and critics, canards like "Keats never took a writing workshop" are freely tossed about, although the most cursory scan of literary history shows that developing writers and artists have always engaged in formal and informal processes of apprenticeship and training, of learning from and being guided by more experienced artists and writers. Perhaps it is the wider availability these days of such apprenticeships to *hoi polloi* to which critics of creative writing programs object. Historically, Keats is one of the few poets born in the working classes to have been able to take advantage of such apprenticeship and patronage.

The idea that writing cannot be taught is a more sophisticated version of the emptied-out pseudo-romanticism pervasive in our society: the assumption that everything one needs is inside one, that thought is the enemy of creativity and of feeling in general, that self-awareness is antithetical to art. As Ann Lauterbach has put it, "There's a familiar split in the notion of what a creative act is. That split, in our culture, involves an idea of creativity as being natural and expressive: a poet has no need to have thought about anything in order to make a poem; the enemy is the analytical. This is a long-standing divisive space, certainly within the academy but also in the culture at large." But self-awareness, the capacity to step back and analyze not just the world but oneself, is what defines us as human, and art is the material embodiment of that self-awareness, of the capacity to separate oneself from one's immediate existence and see it as if from the outside. In that regard, art and science, often conceived of as opposites, have a great deal in common: both are about not taking for granted things as they appear, neither the world nor oneself, about investigating and exploring the universe rather than simply existing in it, about delving through the surfaces of things to understand their true workings. Things are not always what or how they seem, and we are among those things.

In English departments there is little or no attention paid to contemporary literature, except for that literature which can be scrutinized (as distinct from being actually read) as a social symptom, minority and women's literature for the most part. (I must add, though, that as a black gay man who has taught at three different universities and been a student at several more, I have never encountered the caricatured straw institution so prevalent in right-wing anti-academic screeds where minorities are pandered to and Hopi chants are taught instead of Shakespeare.) In most creative writing programs, only contemporary literature is read, and there is a pervasive neglect of the literature of the past (especially of anything written before the twentieth century) among both students and faculty, who tend to consider it irrelevant or even (if they are a bit more intellectually hip) oppressive. This is not to say that individual students may not make efforts to educate themselves, but they are rarely given any context or structure in which to do so, or any incentive for their efforts.

In creative writing courses and programs, student writing is too often expected to emerge from the vacuum of inspiration (a vacuum too easily filled with prepackaged formulations and received ideas, from popular music, television, and movies, among other sources). The intention of the writer is conflated with the intention of the poem, because no other context is provided or produced for the work: thus the role of the creative writing teacher is simply to facilitate the student in finding and perhaps refining his or her own voice. This voice, like the self it stands in and expresses, is assumed to be pre-existent, needing at most to be shaped and developed. (This is a recent and socially constructed notion of selfhood and subjectivity, one that would have been alien, for example, to Shakespeare.) Each student brings an idiosyncratic and haphazard canon and set of assumptions to the class, basing his or her ideas of poetry on what he or she happens to have read or to have heard on the radio (for many students, popular music lyrics are their main model of poetry). Rarely have they read enough to have made informed choices among the possibilities of writing practice or to have questioned choices made solely on the basis of "what I like." I have heard creative writing instructors say that they specifically exclude outside reading from their classes in order to focus on student work, as if that work came forth with no connection to anything else that had ever been written.

The unacknowledged assumptions underpinning both student reading and student writing (the reification of taste, the valorization of sincerity, the enshrinement of self-expression) block the development of each individual's writing, leaving students in cul-de-sacs inescapable precisely because they are invisible. Even students engaged in experimental modes tend not to have read anything outside those modes, any of the work that led up to or even negatively instigated that work. Moreover, they are frequently unwilling or unable to recognize what is still radical (in both senses of the word) or experimental about writers like Sir Thomas Wyatt or Christopher Marlowe, should they take the occasion to read them. Many young writers' conception of "the experimental" seems a concoction of received ideas about "language" poetry (as if other kinds of poetry were made of something other than language) and an attenuated romantic notion of idiosyncratic individualism. Thus such writers are often also ignorant of and uninterested in the historical and intellectual underpinnings of those modes, seeing them only as matters of style. Anti-intellectualism and an indifference to literary history are rife among both mainstream and avant-garde writers.

I tried to synthesize my own ideas in response to Reginald and

Joshua Corey

Kasey with a March 21, 2007, post titled "The Rigor of Poetry and the Pleasures of Theory." I see now that I was then, as I perhaps still am now, primarily concerned with bringing together two powerful tendencies in my own personality that were often seen by myself and others as somehow opposed: the intellectual and the poet.

There's been a lot of discussion recently of creative writing pedagogy, an extension of sorts of the conversation I began on the two cultures of AWP. I think it's worth recapitulating here the four "minimal requisites" that Kasey proposed for a creative writing program that would not "perpetuate the whole predatory pedagogical system":

1. Some degree of grounding in various historical and intellectual contexts for the production and reception of poetry.

2. Some degree of immersion in contemporary poetic theory, as well as relevant political and philosophical studies.

3. Some degree of engagement with the social and communal aspects of the poetic life, especially insofar as this involves stepping out of the institutional framework and looking critically at what it means to be within it in the first place, and what it means for other writers to be outside it.

4. Some degree of consideration of what lies beyond "craft" as defined above: under what conditions might vagueness be considered a "style" worth taking seriously? when do the protocols of "precision, concision, and avoidance of cliché" fall short, and what might be the value of deliberate unwieldiness, ugliness, or banality in certain contexts? and what else is out there?

Kasey's ginger touch with the word "craft" (note the scare quotes) points to the history of that word's being used as an ideological bludgeon, and I think his stipulations in general reframe the conflict that Reginald's first post puts in professional terms (scholar-academics vs. poet-academics) as "craft" vs. "theory." It ought to be obvious what a false distinction this is, and yet the two words are routinely used to represent opposed positions that grind exceeding small back and forth, giving and losing meager amounts of ground, flung like mortar shells into the trenches and foxholes of English departments all over this land. The participants in this battle get the mud of pettiness and spleen all over themselves and their positions, though very occasionally it is transported to a more elevated plane: I'm thinking here of the famous confrontation between Robert Duncan (here standing for "craft" in its most occult aspects) and Barrett Watten (ditto for "theory") at a memorial for Louis Zukofsky at the San Francisco Art Institute in 1978. Duncan, aggrieved enough to respond aggressively to Watten's aggressively cerebral approach to Zukofsky, is supposed to have said at one point, "Can't we just have fun?" To which Watten replied, "But Robert, this is how some of us get our fun." At which point the debate collapses into *de gustibus non disputandum*—and yet I am amazed how often those who turn "craft" into an ideological position attack scholars and theoretically minded writers for being puritan killjoys blind, deaf, and dumb to the pleasures of the text. The possibility of taking intense pleasure in reflective and critical activity doesn't seem to occur to them—more pernicious still is the belief that taking pleasure in critical thought somehow dulls one's senses to the kinetic and lingual pleasures of poetry.

There's no craft, or any practice of any art, without theory: the only question is whether or not one is conscious of the theory of poetry that you've adopted, or that's adopted you. Reginald's second post is an account of the difficulties of getting beginning writing students to accept even the most basic theory of creative writing: namely, that one has an audience in mind. The students come to a creative writing class with a romantic theory of spontaneous self-expression that must be gruelingly unlearned for them to get at the next level of sophistication, the theory of craft. The strength and weakness of this theory lies in its vagueness: the impoverished critical vocabulary of the "earned" ending, the image that "works," etc., can force the more persistent and inspired student into inventing his or her own critical idiom. At best, it steers the student clear of overdetermining vocabularies; at worst it itself overdetermines a complacent response to aesthetic givens. The theory of craft can be reified into an ideology with a Procrustean tendency to fit poems into whatever categories are most fashionable in a given academic community; without active and adventurous questioning on the part of the instructor or students, poems end up being measured against an imaginary normative given, and get either stretched or chopped so they fit.

A theory of craft is essential to any poet: it's the cognitive leap from a belief in one's own natural expertise to a respect for language as a material that offers up considerable resistance to expression. The next step—and this I think is what Kasey's program tries to address, since even most graduate programs don't address this level of thinking—is the crafting of theory, the cultivation of the skills necessary to articulate one's own poetics and place them in some kind of active relation with the numerous other poetics that are out there. Among other things this requires a sense of history, which means doing a lot more reading and a lot more work. It requires, above all, an instructor who is thinking and working on this level—but there are still many creative writing teachers out there, some of them in prestigious programs, who reject the very idea of theory, and instead instill a more-or-less rigid ideology of craft in their students. Of course the smartest or most stubborn students will react appropriately to this dogmatism, but if one of the goals of creative writing instruction is the promotion of critical and imaginative skills—if we believe that the study of creative writing should be an asset to the majority of students who will not go on to become professional writers—then we have to work to promote this more critical-theoretical model of pedagogy, and fight against the laziness and anti-intellectualism that characterizes so much of our culture, inside the academy and out.

It seems to me that the best teachers (and students) approach craft seriously and simultaneously with questions that belong properly to the realm of theory: what are different sorts of poems for, what effects are possible, what histories of poetic discourse are we bearing in mind, how can language be made responsive to identity and vice-versa. At the same time, I think the ideal poet's education would include megadoses of the canon (or canons—I certainly wish my own education had required me to study the poetry of another language, for example), the study and practice of traditional-closed and experimental-open prosodies, study of the history and practice of poetic distribution (small presses, little magazines), and the encouragement to follow an ultimately self-directed path through the contemporary scene. This poet's education can and does work in harmony with what I'd term an intellectual's education, defining as "intellectual" the preoccupation with analysis of the given (in literature, in politics, etc.). Although potentially synergistic, they are two very different practices: as practitioners of poiesis—as *makers*—poets challenge the given with very different tools than intellectuals. They stand somehow between the philosopher who seeks to understand the world and the activist who seeks to change it.

It is not truly necessary for a poet to be an intellectual, but I have a strong inclination toward those who embrace the "and" of my title, though they might emphasize one more than the other at times. The antagonism between the two falls away, I think, if one embraces the real rigor of poetry and turns away from the thoughtless model that equates poetry with pleasurable spontaneity and intellectualism with puritan drudgery. Which is not to say the conflict can be totally wished away, especially when it's internal. As someone who participates in any number of awkward hyphenates (MFA-PhD, poet-scholar, writer-critic) I sometimes myself am caught up in the trap of participating in a restricted economy in which the resources allocated to one dimension of work are stolen from the other. For most of my experience, though, they've actually enlarged each other. When I was at the University of Montana some of my fellow students in the MFA program bemoaned its rather minimal academic requirements: "I just want time to write!" they said. Meanwhile, I was finding that the literature seminars to be as stimulating as the workshops, sometimes more so. There was a real synergy between the two kinds of thinking, the two strategies of knowing: making and analysis, craft and theory. It's still true for me now, though the intellectual labor of a PhD program demands considerably more of my energy and time, and I do find myself wishing for pure "time to write."

Well, I see I've lapsed into personal anecdote and I don't expect such to be especially persuasive to anyone not similarly inclined. But I do believe in the rigor of poetry and the dignity and pleasure to be taken in intellectual work, and I think they ought to be put in productive relationships with each other. I believe in a limitless general economy of thought, and I would like to share that sense of abundance and possibility with my students, however I can.

I fear this is an at-best-fragmentary, where it is not redundant, reconstruction of the conversation that my brief contact with Reginald sparked. And yet I see my own intellectual history, and the work that the essays in this book try to do, everywhere in our exchanges. I simply wouldn't be the poet and thinker about poetry that I am today if it hadn't been for his provocative, lively, and ethically unerring voice. Peace and poetry, Reginald. You are much missed.

V
THE POET'S NOVEL

My Poet's Novel

Now, Ariel, rescue me from police and all that kind of thing.
—Wallace Stevens

What *is* the poet's novel? Is it something distinct, a genre in its own right, or simply descriptive of what happens when a poet tries to write a novel without sacrificing his or her identity as poet? Laynie Browne's investigations over a period of several months at the online magazine *jacket2* sketch out the beginnings of an answer. Her subjects included Alice Notley, whose work is nearly always narrative and always in verse (I once had the opportunity to ask Notley what she thought of fiction writing: her response, simply, was "Poems are better"); H.D.'s autobiographical novel *HERmione*; Dan Beachy-Quick, the author of at least one novel but also an obsessive brooder over the fact of the Great American Novel as incarnated in Melville's *Moby-Dick*; Bhanu Kapil; Marguerite Duras (not a poet); the poet and visual artist Etel Adnan; Lydia Davis (not exactly a poet, not usually a novelist); Aaron Kunin, who has a second life as a Renaissance lit scholar); and Clarice Lispector (a prose writer much beloved by poets). I doubt it's a coincidence that most of the poets she's engaged are women: many of the most compelling women writers today feel the need to press up against, escape, or violate the strictures of genre (a word as close to gender as it is to *gendarme*); Maggie Nelson, Nathanaël, and Lisa Robertson come to mind as non-novelists doing edgy and urgent poetic work with prose. It may well be that the most flexible and hardest to define of forms, the essay, is what falls between the gap suggested by "poet's novel": a poet's sensibility coupled to the demands and resources of narrative.

I find the very phrase "poet's novel" to be transgressive, in a way that gives the genre/gender both its liveliness and its comparative invisibility (the obscure but real difference between a "poet-novelist" and "a poet who has written a novel"). It *queers*. Interviewed by Browne, Bhanu Kapil, the author of brilliant and unclassifiable works like *Incubation: A Space for Monsters* and *Ban en Banlieue* suggests that the poet's novel is peculiarly available to "writers of color, queer writers, writers who are thinking of the body in these other ways," and describes her fascination with "the lyric and textural scope of a novel-shaped space. The zone of impossible life."

One of the most prominent poets to have produced a poet's novel, defiantly self-labeled as such, is Eileen Myles; *Inferno (A Poet's Novel)* is a compelling recent example of the genre/gender. The parentheses are important for the way they suspend the claim as to the book's genre; the narrative it offers is that of the *Bildungsroman* or *Kunstlerroman,* more or less transparently based in the experiences of the author herself. The doubleness of Myles' parentheses inscribe the poet's generic transgression as well as the transgression of a "novel" whose claims to fiction are put in doubt.

Something similar happens with Ben Lerner's *Leaving the Atocha Station*; the protagonist, Adam Gordon, is transparently a version of Ben Lerner, and the novel's plot focuses, as Myles's does, on becoming a poet. Except for Lerner, it's the "becoming a poet" that should be in parentheses, since there is for his protagonist a fraudulence, an inescapable contaminating fiction, that penetrates the personae he inhabits: an American in Spain who speaks deliberately bad Spanish, the better to suggest by his incapacity his depth of thought and soul. He is a poet who only appreciates poems when they appear as quotations in prose and a grieving son whose father has not actually died. Gordon is a *manqué* version of his author, alternately comic and contemptible, fascinated by the musk of his own disingenuousness; Myles's Eileen, on the other hand, is earnest, questing, angry, and above all, desiring. Adam Gordon tries to be a poet because he thinks it *might* get him laid, but for Eileen sex and writing are almost indistinguishable, part of the continuum of intensities that is life itself. *Inferno* is more transgressive, more avant-garde than *Leaving the Atocha Station,* though the latter novel is arguably more entertaining, and less dependent on the reader's investment in the author's work a poet. *Inferno* puts the emphasis heavily on the *Bildung*; *Leaving the Atocha Station* is much more of a *Roman.*

If a poet's novel is not any sort of a *Bildungsroman,* is that when it ceases to be a poet's novel at all, and becomes instead a novel written by a poet? (Denis Johnson's story collection or novel-in-stories *Jesus' Son* strikes me as a kind of ironic anti-*Bildungsroman* that marks the transition point, in his career, from poet to novelist.) Or is what matters, what distinguishes the form, that sense of undomesticated queerness? That transgression?

Lisa Robertson speaks in an interview to the drama of the "discursive right" she feels, or rather fails to feel, regarding another genre, that of the philosophical essay, a discourse that "contains some of our most intensely gendered, authority-ridden constraints." Robertson continues:

> To claim a discursive right you have to engage intimately, and repeatedly, with that right's potential at the most intimate sites of your relationship to language. A right is not only given by a community or institution. It must be psychologically and intellectually confronted, even invented, in the privacy of cognition and composition. The fear has to do with that process itself. My relationship to philosophy has been that of a passionate life-long reader. Writing the *Nilling* essays I made a decision to enter this discourse, as an amateur.

I am a white male tenured professor, simply lousy with privilege, and yet I feel much of the same fear and trepidation when I begin to write a novel. It carries me away from the groove that Stevens speaks of in his letter to his future wife, the "railroading" that books might "shatter." But the question—it is still a question—is whether I am trying, as Robertson says about the essay, "to claim a discursive right" (which means claiming the identity of novelist) or whether for me what matters in in some way preserving or paying attention to that illicit quality, that fear. Remaining a poet: or as Robertson puts it, an amateur, which of course means both "non-professional," "dabbler," and "lover." Imagine if *Inferno* bore the parenthetical subtitle (*an amateur's novel*). Or even, more precisely, (*a lover's novel*). Would that capture even more precisely the transgression, the loosening of narrative imperatives (plot, etc.) that "poet's novel" always seems to imply?

Joshua Corey

Laynie Browne says, referencing Bhanu Kapil's work, that "Readers of poet's novels want our relation to the text to be released from the expected conventions of telling. We want instead, to be shown one of any manner of ways in which a text can behave." Release from "conventions of telling," from behavior. A release that can only be meaningful, of course, if one feels the force of those conventions in the first place: something that comes, as Robertson says, of being "a passionate life-long reader." I have long felt that novelists were the only "real" writers; everything else is either overly professionalized (journalism, scholarship) or incapable of professionalization, always already amateurized (poetry). But probably to be a writer of any sort is always to be participant, a not-so-secret sharer, in the unreal.

Novels are unique beasts, capable of negotiating, at least at times, the demands of the market and the more rigorous demands—the erotics—of reading. A poet's novel plays with the form, adopts it partially or wears it as deliberately ill-fitting mask. But if it does not actually take becoming a poet as its subject, then it walks a razor's edge: it becomes a novel, full-stop. Or it becomes something else, stained by its amateurism, its goofy passionate unrequited love, its fears, its queerness, its sojourn in a foreign land that remains, irreducibly, foreign.

The Poet's Novel: On Ben Lerner's Fiction

Some poets transition from poetry to novels rather in the spirit of an enlisted man joining the officer corps. Denis Johnson comes to mind as someone who turned from poems to novels without looking back; even more prominent is the case of Michael Ondaatje, whose best fiction, I think, still has a foot in poetry (*Coming Through Slaughter, The Collected Works of Billy the Kid*). Others, like Stuart Dybek and Charlie Smith, may continue to write poetry but nevertheless have moved on, having risen (or fallen) to the identity of the fiction writer.

The rarer and more interesting cases, to my mind, are those poets who write fiction but remain poets. Joyelle McSweeney has written two novels, *Flet* and *Nylund, the Sarcographer*, but because their prose is often strange, calling the sort of attention to itself that prose fiction rarely does, they don't sacrifice the eccentricity of poetry. Better known is the case of Roberto Bolaño, who began as a poet but became famous as a fiction writer. As far as I can tell from the one volume of his poetry that I've read, the world is entirely justified in esteeming him only for his fiction; yet he thought of himself as a poet (even a *poète maudit*), and I persist in thinking of him that way, for the strange anti-eloquence of his writing and his hilarious grim persistence in writing always only about poets and their rancid idealism.

I suppose that's really what I'm talking about here: those poets who write fiction as a bid to enter the center of literary attention that novels nominally occupy, versus those who, through temperament or incompetence, are destined to remain ex-centric.

Then there's Ben Lerner. A ferociously ambitious and successful younger poet from Topeka, Kansas, Lerner, a one-time recipient of a Fulbright fellowship to Spain and the author of three generally acclaimed books of poetry, turned himself into a novelist with *Leaving the Atocha Station,* originally published by Coffee House Press. It's about a ferociously ambitious and successful younger poet from Topeka, Kansas, albeit one who is not yet comfortable with or fully conscious of either his ambition or his success, on a Fulbright-like fellowship to Spain. His Adam Gordon is as transparently autobiographical as Bolaño's Arturo Belano, and at the same time both alter egos are presented to the reader through veils of irony and self-loathing.

In his first-person narration, Gordon presents himself to the reader as an almost entirely dysfunctional human being, preserving a semblance of autonomy through the use of various drugs, prescribed and otherwise. It is not at all clear whether we are supposed to respect his poetry or not—a few samples are presented that do nothing to defy Tony Hoagland's persistent denunciatory motto, "the skittery poem of our moment." Gordon himself doesn't respect it but Teresa, a Spanish translator and one of two attractive women that he finds himself entangled with, respects it enough to want to translate it and publish it in a handsome chapbook edition, a reading from which at a gallery in Madrid is the culminating event of the novel.

Lerner even goes so far as to give Gordon his own nonfictional thoughts; as a note on the copyright page tells us, "The novel includes, albeit in altered form, a reading of John Ashbery's poetry that first appeared in my essay, 'The Future Continuous: Ashbery's Lyric Mediacy,' published by *boundary 2*." He also does not fail to remind us that "Leaving the Atocha Station" is an Ashbery poem (one of his most obscure, which is saying something); Ashbery, and the world of poetry Ashbery has bequeathed to us, haunts the book. For much of the novel Gordon is preoccupied by his lack of fluency in Spanish and his attempts to use that lack of fluency "to preserve the possibility of misspeaking or being misunderstood, and to secure and amplify the mystery" that comes with language that fails to be fully communicative.

The consonance of this with poetry, in its deliberate obscurity, its refusal to be "about" anything, is entirely deliberate and forms the major theme of the book: the failure to be present to oneself or to others, in one's own life or in History writ large (the most significant event in the book is the 3/11 Madrid train bombings, the aftermath of which Gordon witnesses). Language, or rather language's failure, finds the pathos in this travesty of alienation, even as Lerner finds comedy in it; as Gordon reflects at a poetry reading he gives, "I told myself that no matter what I did, no matter what any poet did, the poems would constitute screens on which readers could project their own desperate belief in the possibility of poetic experience, whatever that might be, or afford them the opportunity to mourn its impossibility."

Gordon/Lerner may intend this as cynicism, but like any display of cynicism there's a bruised idealism at its center. "If I was a poet," he thinks later, "I had become one because poetry, more intensely than any other practice, could not evade its anachronism and marginality and so constituted a kind of acknowledgment of my own preposterousness, admitting my bad faith in good faith, so to speak." If one is a bad poet, a false poet, that does not injure Poetry's eidolon; much harder and more adult is to accept that poetry, like any art, can fail as often as it succeeds, and as a human being one can be part of that success or failure and bears the responsibility for trying.

So we have here again another portrait of the artist as a young man, which like Joyce's novel displays a good deal of irony toward its protagonist without completely disowning either his idealism or the writer's own ambitions, albeit in a negative, almost Gnostic form.

I can't decide yet whether this novel constitutes a bid for centrality—if Lerner will now be leaving the Atocha Station of poetry for the maculate shores of fiction—or if its obsessive focus on poetry and failure will consign it to eccentric status. It's quite funny, I should say—in his self-inflicted humiliations the protagonist reminds me of nothing so much as an intellectual Larry David—and there's some interesting if lightly milled grist for considering Gordon as an archetypal self-involved radical artist from "the United States of Bush." How archaic already that designation seems, another sign of American innocence as inexhaustible destructive resource; as Gordon remarks in one of his endless attempts to sound deep without actually committing himself, "The proper names of leaders are distractions from concrete economic models." The fatuousness of this, even in its truth, damns the helpless self-regard of the beautiful-souled American Left with withering effectiveness.

In an interview with his friend Cyrus Console (who also turns up as a character in the book), Lerner speaks of Adam's predicament in terms of aesthetic position: "the virtual possibilities of art are always in a sense betrayed by actual artworks." What fascinates me is how the positions *virtual* and *actual* (terms, Lerner tells us, taken from the critical writing of the poet Allen Grossman) roughly correspond to the two genres under consideration here. Poetry, at least modern poetry, in its fragmentation, its gesturality, is the quintessential art of the virtual: it suggests, Gnostically, the withdrawal of the numinous from the space of the poem. The novel is a creature of the actual, even in its greater physicality as object (a distinction rapidly eroding); as young man, I thought to write a novel, like reading one, was in some way to participate the real. (Fantasy novels, oddly, for me always bridged the gap: their worlds were not real but painstakingly actualized, even as their endlessness, their tendency to trilogize or series-ize, dovetailed back into the virtuality of the always-incomplete. This is why I halfway hope that George R. R. Martin *doesn't* finish *A Song of Ice and Fire,* to preserve some speck of the virtuality the TV series had devoted itself to shredding. End of digression.)

"I promised myself, I would never write a novel," Lerner's protagonist says—or is his promise really a dare? Poetry perpetuates adolescence through its refusal to actualize: a poem in itself is like a young man dawdling his way through college, refusing to declare a major or propose to his girlfriend, refusing to commit, to be engagé. This is the pathos of poetry, even to the point of "Pathetic!" But it's also the source of poetry's great reserve of utopianism and hopefulness, even when, tonally, it despairs. Oh I'm sure there's a poetry of the actual as well, akin to what Robert Van Hallberg calls "civic" poetry so as to distinguish it from the Orphic. But if the former is more grown-up, more resigned, it lacks I think the power to shake the heart that comes with the Orphic. The tragicomic valley of hesitation between them is where Lerner's novel is located.

Lerner's second novel, *10:04,* was published by Picador, an imprint of Macmillan, and made it onto some bestseller lists. He followed it up with a short critical book, *The Hatred of Poetry,* which tries to present in a theoretical mode the ambivalence toward poetry that both of his novels dramatize. Lerner's mixed, Mariane Mooreish feeling ("I too dislike it") for his home genre seems inseparable from the way in which he has ridden that ambivalence to mainstream visibility and success; he joins the contemporary pantheon of writers like Karl Ove Knausgaard, Sheila Heti, Jenny Offill, and Rachel Cusk, all of whom in different ways challenge traditional literary values with their sometimes deliberately awkward styles while insisting on a degree of autobiographical content that challenges the validity of the label *fiction*. In these auto- or metafictional novels, what is normally part of the subtext of a work of fiction—the relation of the narrative to the author's own life and times—becomes text; the subtext, in essence, disappears, replaced by whatever political or historical context the reader is able and willing to bring to bear. (Bolaño's fiction, for example, gets a great deal of resonance from its implicitly political character, leaving implicit for example the connections between Nazi ideology and the political apathy that has permitted the murders of hundreds of women and girls in Ciudad Juarez to go unsolved.)

The narrow, poorly policed zone between fiction and autobiography has long been lyric poetry's beat. Poetry, in fiction as sometimes in life, serves as a destabilizing force, a challenge to what makes prose *prose*, as in the sense of, to use another Moore-ism, "plain American that dogs and cats can read." It thickens the fictional plot, in a precarious, pretentious, occasionally thrilling way, by foregrounding the self as factory floor for the production of meaning, a guarantee of what mere fictional sequence—*The king died, then the queen died*—can no longer authenticate. As a card-carrying poet, Lerner's work makes this explicit, but so does the writing of his hero John Ashbery, who has rarely cared to call his works anything other than poems, including his 1972 prose book Three Poems. As Ashbery writes at the opening of "The New Spirit":

> I thought that if I could put it all down, that would be one way. And next the thought came to me that to leave all out would be another, and truer, way.

Joshua Corey

      clean-washed sea
                                  The flowers were.

These are examples of leaving out. But, forget as we will, something soon comes to stand in their place. Not the truth, perhaps—but yourself. It is you who made this, therefore you are true. But the truth has passed on

                                          to divide all.

Horizontal Hold: Poetry and Narrative

The means of narrative are as fundamentally different from those of lyric as its goals. To adapt Bakhtin, they are fundamentally different chronotopes: one is vertical and simultaneous, the other horizontal and chronological. Writing my first novel, as a poet, I encounter and even encourage friction between these modes.

The pleasures of poetry are the pleasures of simultaneity. I read a line of verse, and it's like a chain reaction of little detonations: the sound play, the layers of reference (in the line's structure, diction, proper names, etc.), the manifestation of images, and the instantaneous revisions of the preceding lines created by the double-jointed syntax made possible by line breaks. It's an intensely vertical experience, though this feels less the verticality of the words themselves (most poems, of course, are narrower than the page they're printed on, unless they're very long-lined) than the vertical layering of a palimpsest or of one of those old biology textbooks with overlays for the skin, musculature, circulatory system, and skeleton (often these depths are presented unequally and with simultaneity, so that even on the first page you can see the bones of the hand, the red fist of the heart, the striations of the quadriceps, etc.).

With narrative prose on the other hand it is truly one damn thing after another. Words and details accumulate like grains of sand in an hourglass; though you'll never remember all of them, though many of these details are all but designed to be forgotten, they nevertheless heap up into the foundations of characters, places, plots, themes, weathers, worlds. In one of my chapters (though I hesitate to call my units of composition chapters—they're more like sections, or threads), one of my several narrators is about to meet the woman who will change his life. That's the decisive moment: if I were writing a poem, I might present it directly, or even more likely ellipsize it and present the aftermath through a few coordinated details.

But because I'm telling a story I write toward the event, filling in the moments of a character's lonely life in an overheated studio apartment in Washington Heights in 1971, conscious of growing suspense each page the woman's presence is intimated without her actually manifesting. Every night I sit down to write thinking Now, now she will appear, and yet she never quite appears. And yet none of what I'm writing is filler: the words are grains of salt or sand for the event to stand on, but also I hope savory in themselves, and they work to evoke what I find most attractive about novels (and rare in poems): the feeling of immersion in a world.

But I no longer seek complete immersion; the "vivid, continuous dream" that John Gardner said it was a novelist's duty to conjure. I don't want the words to disappear as easily as they once did. But neither do I want them, as I usually do with poems, to remain primarily words, striking upon the eardrum and memory, vivid morsels like Proust's madeleine, which must shed its present-tense existence in the moment of recollection. Instead I seek a kind of flicker effect, a sense of the grain of the form, as might a filmmaker who simulates scratches on the emulsion or chooses black-and-white so as to make the film's filmness part of its content. I want my readers sweltering in that room full of fug and flaking leaded paint, high above February streets dusted with the dry, fine snow that real cold can bring; but I also want them caught in the coils of my sentences (my narrator's sentences), feeling in their unfolding syntax his characteristic mix of melancholia, hopefulness, and delirium.

And so narrative ceases to be a single line and becomes dual, parallel, multiple, a train track the reader straddles or hops between on her ride toward some sort of climax of the story and the language in which it is told.

POETIC FICTIONS AND FICTIONAL POETS

"The difference," wrote the nineteenth-century English poet Randolph Henry Ash, "between poets and novelists is this, that the former write for the life of the language—and the latter write for the betterment of the world." This eminently Victorian sentiment is scarcely compromised by the fact that its utterer is entirely fictional, a character from A.S. Byatt's novel's *Possession*; the fictional poet's claim has been recycled as the opening sentence of an essay by Brian Phillips on novels by poets called "Fortune-tellers and Pharmacists" that appeared in the May 2009 issue of *Poetry*. Phillips doesn't quite take this fictional poet's assertion at face value—he'd rather read the novelist's preoccupation with "the world" as fundamentally one of interest rather than activism—but he does seem to accept the fundamental dichotomy it offers. It seems to me that this dichotomy falls apart as soon as it is scrutinized: what are Shelley's unacknowledged legislating poets, in the Romantic view which I think still dominates our poetic discourse, if not imaginary betterers of the world? And it would be obtuse to assert that the likes of Joyce and Nabokov weren't writing "for the life of the language." Nevertheless, Ash's/Byatt's/Phillips' assertion makes for a useful jumping-off point, a view of writing, whether you call it poetry or fiction, as divided into writing *about* something versus simply *writing*.

This dichotomy tends to be dialectical in actual practice, but it seems to me to be something of an uneven one: even the most abstract of poets never fully escape subject matter, and most poets scarcely wish to; but there are plenty of novels and stories out there which, while of course not escaping language, nevertheless express a powerful will to escape it in the least progressive of ways, either as the "vivid continuous dream" John Gardner describes or, more baldly and profitably, as a film. Even novelists acclaimed for their sophistication such as Ian McEwan seem sometimes to be writing film treatments as opposed to producing a work with its life centered in language.

For such a text, the question "what's it about?" becomes a mere pretext, a means of organizing and facilitating, virus-like, the progress of writing itself. *Story* is, essentially, syntax. Prose may be better suited to such a program than verse, since in verse the line as unit of utterance constantly recalls the reader's attention to questions of form. I am essentially recapitulating Charles Bernstein's argument in his verse essay "Artifice of Absorption," but I am also thinking of a 2007 interview with the poet John Olson, in which he speaks of how, in the prose of writers like Virginia Woolf of Gertrude Stein, "Words burst and burble in incessant association.... The disruption of syntax is similar to what happens in a thunder cloud. Lighting and thunder are products of volatility and friction. Conflict brings everything alive." Olson's novel, *Souls of Wind,* brings Arthur Rimbaud to the American West, on a collision course with his American doppleganger, Billy the Kid, which makes it fit my minimal definition of a poet's novel: it must be written by a poet and about a poet; the gap between author and character is indeed filled, or out to be, with volatility and friction. The writer who has achieved the most success and attention with this strategy is of course Roberto Bolaño, who produced great fiction writing about poets and their inevitably doomed attempts to take total refuge in the life of language, forsaking every "about." *By Night in Chile* shows us the doom of a poet of the right that attempts this, while *The Savage Detectives* focuses, if that's the word, on the disappearance of two poets of the Left; Bolaño's staggering opus *2666* encompasses all this terrain and more. The tremendous sensation of liberation I experience reading Bolaño derives in part from the permission he seems to offer to, well, write what I know. (Though what I know as a poet is a lot less glamorous, and dangerous, than the dissolute post-Beat landscape traveled by Bolaño's visceral realists.)

Phillips discusses novels by Laura Kasischke (*Be Mine,* "a ceremoniously plotted gothic thriller"); Carol Muske-Dukes (*Channeling Mark Twain,* about a young woman "who teaches a poetry workshop in the women's prison at Rikers Island in the early seventies"); a collection of short stories by Mary Ruefle (*The Most of It,* "a book of vivid, funny, and unpredictable palm-of-the-hand stories, many of them under a page in length"); and Forrest Gander's first novel, *As a Friend*. Of this group, Gander's book seems the closest to a true poet's novel, as from a plot perspective it couldn't sound less promising: it's a short and elliptical narrative about the sort of Byronically charismatic poet who, in the abstract, sounds like a completely insufferable human being. The hero is the sort of fellow invariably described as "smoldering" (or in Phillips' wonderfully overripe phrase, a guy that "seems to exist in some kind of sweaty harmony with the axial lean of the Earth"), captaining a story suffused with the Gothic, sex, and suicide. To some people that no doubt sounds like a heady stew, but my first reaction, at least to Philips' representation, is to say no thanks, I'd rather just read the original Faulkner.

But Philips draws me in with his claim that Gander's novel, and the fatally attractive character of the hero, is "explicitly about poetry." The compelling center of gravity that is the book's hero, Les (my guess is that he's based on Frank Stanford), is a representation of the potential power of poetry to be, as Phillips puts it, "a form of supercharged awareness that cultivates the same ethical attention as human relationships." That awareness is extended democratically, one assumes, to people, things, and words; and in Gander's novel, it proves to be more openness than Les can sustain, to judge by his suicide.

Some might judge Gander's focus on the life of a poet to be a severe limitation upon his fiction; if Bolaño escapes similar censure, it probably has to do with the increasingly epic sweep of his works, plus their political content, never separable from the author himself and the legend of his exile from Chile after Pinochet (this is because, not in spite of, the fact that the often-told tale of his brief imprisonment in the days after the September 11, 1973 coup have been pretty consistently debunked. But I see it as an opening, at least potentially (we'll see what I make of Gander's hothouse prose when I encounter it directly), a way to make writing its own "about," while at the same time inviting in enough narrative world (characters, setting, events) to allow the language its range, its fuller life. It suggests to me a possible path for my own writing, for accommodations beyond the lyric or even the prose poem. And if Gander has done it right, there will be enough "about" there to interest readers of traditional fiction as well. Because I'd be lying, as I imagine the poets Phillips talks about would be, if I didn't admit that part of my interest in fiction lies in the somewhat wider readership it can achieve.

What interests me most is the testing of genre; from Phillips's description it sounds like Mary Ruefle is up to that in some of her short-short stories, many of which "tilt toward some distinct fictional genre, functioning at times almost as novels in the act of suppressing themselves." That's a fascinating turn of phrase, suggesting that self-suppression is something intrinsic to the novel form, or at least to the form as practiced by poets. A mutilated novel, as any short story must be, is maybe more intrinsically poetic than either of the novels Gander has published (the publication of a second novel, *The Trace,* suggests that he too is under narrative's spell, though I can't imagine him giving up on his poet's identity).

Milan Kundera says that each novel must follow its own law, be its own model. This applies to poems too, of course, and stands behind the long conflict between the adherents of traditional forms and those who stand and shout with Creeley and Olson that FORM IS NEVER MORE THAN AN EXTENSION OF CONTENT. What to call a form supple enough to include characters and events and essayistic digressions, shards and skeins of beautiful language, autobiography and the totally made-up, surrealism and satire and realism? Is the novel after all a sort of anti-form, a flexible container that assumes the shape of its contents? Or does it offer, tantalizingly, an outside to modes of syntax exhausted in both the lyric poem and the realist novel—a means of thinking, along the axis of "plot," toward the intersection of meaning and the meaningless as they collide in language? If I follow that lawless law, I will write a novel, without ever fully departing from the poet's natural domain.

Ambience, Consecution, the Open: Poetry as Fiction

Here is a blindingly obvious assertion: poems are written in lines, prose is written in sentences. And it is this distinction I follow as a poet-turned-novelist, beguiled as I've become by the logic of sentences. Very long sentences, as it happens, with enough comma splices to risk revocation of my license as an English professor. A poet works in phrases, clauses, in syntax detonated by each line break; to a poet, sentences are exotic where they are not simply awkward and unruly. Nearly as seductive and strange are paragraphs, very long paragraphs, the sort of long paragraphs one encounters reading Proust and Adorno and Saramago and Thomas Bernhard, the kind with scarcely an indentation to mark each one from another. Stanzas and strophes have nothing on paragraphs for their elasticity, their infinite yet tensile capacity. "Sentences are not emotional but paragraphs are," says Gertrude Stein. But the problem with sentences and paragraphs is not that they are emotional or unemotional. It's that they *say* things. And saying things, as I like to remind my writing students, is not what poetry is for.

Mallarmé: "I say: a flower! and, out of the oblivion into which my voice consigns any real shape, as something other than petals known to man, there rises, harmoniously and gently, the ideal flower itself, the one that is absent from all earthly bouquets." Poetic voicing is inseparable from oblivion, from the invisible. But fictive voicing is all too mimetic, all too obliterative of oblivion. It is difficult for fiction to foreground the fundamental rhetoricity of its language; it is difficult not to lapse completely into what John Gardner's "fictive dream" in which "the writer forgets the words he has written on the page and sees, instead, his characters moving around their rooms, hunting through cupboards, glancing irritably through their mail, setting mousetraps, loading pistols." The reader forgets too. It's like Eliot's objective correlative, only without the objective part. It's language idealized, all spirit and no letter.

Fictive sentences don't have to work this way. Gordon Lish offers his theory of "consecution," as explained in "The Sentence Is a Lonely Place," an essay by one of Lish's former students, Gary Lutz. Lutz writes that consecution is "a recursive procedure by which one word pursues itself into its successor by discharging something from deep within itself into what follows." The writer reacts to the material properties of constellated words and letters, and proceeds by association from one sentence to the next. In a manner somewhat akin to Ron Silliman's "new sentence," each sentence exists in its own torqued bubble, generative of and yet separate from the sentence that follows it (Lutz calls his article on consecution, "The Sentence Is a Lonely Place"). In a review of one of Lish's novels, *Peru,* David Winters claims that for Lish, "*composition cuts across ontology,* not only aesthetics."

Winters goes on to compare the "cut" of consecution to, of all things, the *clinamen* of Lucretius: "consecution may be less a methodology than a metaphysic; a miraculating agent; an instance of spirit or pneuma submerged in the world. In Lucretius, the force of composition is described as a clinamen—our world is born from a 'swerving of atoms in their fall from heaven. Such is the purpose served by *Peru*'s perpetual swerving, rhyming and recursion. Each consecutive swerve steps closer toward a total curvature, an arc that delimits the work as a world apart." Each Lishian sentence is its own world, its own monad, in which the universe of the story is *contained* without being merely *represented.* It's a mimesis beyond mimesis; the immanent transcendence of representation. The reader encounters the story as a sufficiency, as a world to be explored rather than as something presented. It's an essentially Modernist rather than postmodernist technique.

The Lishian "cut," the Lucretian "swerve": these are comfortably poetic concepts for me, reminiscent as they are of the *volta* or turn that is central to the operations of verse. The more-than-semantic, physical cut-in-language of the *volta* is what charges a poem with energy unsupplied by subject matter. Poems cannot completely evade subject matter; words never can. But they come much closer to such evasions, and can entangle a reader in themselves, with a more intensively minimal mimesis than can fiction. And this perhaps is why

Yeats can say that poetry makes nothing happen but rather "survives, / A way of happening, a mouth."

Fiction is also a way of happening. And yet to be fiction, *something has to happen*. To write it, there has to be story. But there's a problem with the Lishian ontological sentence: it's too definitive and determinate. It *says things*.

A happening is an *event*. Critic Cooper Levey-Baker's essay "Where To?" traces the possibility of the novel as event, though he seem to mean something more like the scene or environment in which events take place. A way of happening: something like architecture or ambient music. Touchstones for his piece include an artwork by Anish Kapoor (creator of Chicago's beloved Bean, aka Cloud Gate) and the collaborations of filmmaker Béla Tarr and novelist László Krasznahorkai. Levey-Baker seems interested in recapturing a particular dimension of Modernism: the challenge to the reader or viewer to encounter the artwork (a film or a novel) so as to make its silence audible, often to the point of discomfort: the unpleasures of *boredom*. The very long shots without cuts in Tarr's film version of Krasznahorkai's *Satantango* are the equivalent of the novel's very long sentences, which endlessly defer answers to the audience's questions about what exactly is going on. As at a poetry reading, or leafing through one of Ashbery's longer works, one's mind wanders without ever losing the sense of being in the *presence* of something, an environment in which the figure-ground relation is rendered ambiguous, if not threatening.

Boredom, Levey-Baker claims, is the last refuge of the avant-garde, the one affect that cannot be recuperated by the entertainment-industrial complex. Long sentences, in their excessiveness, their accumulation and angular momentum, do not have to be boring; but they do tend to be far more *open* than short sentences. In their attenuated hypotaxis, the extension and interaction of dependent and independent clauses begin to overwrite each other, to introduce a dubiety, room for interpretation.

The past master of this is of course the Master himself, Henry James. Here's a sentence, chosen more or less at random, from *The*

Joshua Corey

Golden Bowl: "He remembered to have read, as a boy, a wonderful tale by Allan Poe, his prospective wife's countryman—which was a thing to show, by the way, what imagination Americans COULD have: the story of the shipwrecked Gordon Pym, who, drifting in a small boat further toward the North Pole—or was it the South?—than anyone had ever done, found at a given moment before him a thickness of white air that was like a dazzling curtain of light, concealing as darkness conceals, yet of the colour of milk or of snow." This is not unstraightforward; and yet its dart backward toward an impugnation of the American imagination, its dart sideways into Poe, and its ambiguous image of the white mist of others' motivations (concealing the future of our hero) lend an astonishing multiplicity to the sentence's mimesis of what is supposedly happening in Prince Amerigo's mind. James is famous for his psychology, but thanks to his brother William's work we know how close psychology is to philosophy, which is to say the art of disclosing the real. Reality, as William James teaches us, is perspectival. The activity required of the reader of a Jamesian sentence sends her grasping in and through language for a meaning one cannot help but be conscious of creating.

James is also capable of Lishian sentence pairs, as in the following beautifully asymmetrical chiasmus: "He was taken seriously. Lost there in the white mist was the seriousness in them that made them so take him." The reader leaps from stone to stone. The cut is there. But it's the longer sentences that make James James, and that suggest, for me, a possible fiction, an immanent mimesis, the paragraph-environment, story in language. The poem as scene of possibility, from which prose takes flight, realizing one possibility but never entirely discarding what might have been—something akin, maybe, to Walter Benjamin's concept of the dialectical image, a presence in the present that recalls, critically, to our minds, the presence of the past and its unrealized potential for other worlds than these.

A Little Endarkenment: Poetry's Outside

I wanted to find an outside to poetry. Not an escape, exactly, though there are times I wish that I could escape from poetry, which exerts its gravity on culture invisibly, like dark matter. Call it dark culture, which can be referenced by the grid but must be experienced off of it. (The grid can refer to poetry, etc., but when you experience poetry on the grid, what you really experience is: the grid.) Reading is a vanishing experience and the weight of all those books, more of them every year, is something perceived ever more lightly, something inexperienced. And yet it is possible to set the grid aside, or to use the grid still as reference or double to life rather than life itself, though we are fast forgetting how.

Poetry is off the grid and as dark culture its existence is untimely, precisely because of the ways in which it marks time. In writing a novel I could hardly expect to transcend these things. Instead I wrote myself more deeply into poetry, into my own line. The line simply expanded and extenuated, trembling on the brink of the sentence stretched to its limit. The sentence would not stay put. Its only satisfaction was the next sentence.

"Limits / are what any of us / are inside of," says Charles Olson.

Poetry is tasked for its irrelevance, its refusal to operate as an amplifier of tendencies already adequately represented by and on the grid. The grid, that endless surface the first world skates on—that this text skates upon—claims to offer us an adequate representation. The grid claims to be Borges's "Map of the Empire whose size [is] that of the Empire, and which coincided point for point with it." In fact the grid is the Empire itself. We feed it our existence and so feed its existence, compulsively and continually. Ungridded experience, itself merely a reference point, is "Useless, and without without some pitilessness was it, that they delivered it up to the Inclemencies of Sun and Winters." IRL.

Culture is a multiphasic field in which we negotiate personhood: our appearances to each other, as individuals and as members of collectives. If you are a laborer in the fields of dark culture your work stands in an uncertain relation to your appearance or invisibility on the grid. The valuelessness of poetry is a commonplace, but so also is the ineradicable minimal value of being a poet. The grid is haunted by the specter of being-a-poet, which is a claim to personhood without authorization.

"I am unbaptized, uninitated, ungraduated, unanalyzed. I had in mind that my worship belonged to no church, that my mysteries belonged to no cult, that my learning belonged to no institution, that my imagination of my self belonged to no philosophical system. My thought must be without sanction." Robert Duncan, *The H.D. Book*.

We are back in Shelley's territory of the unacknoweldged legislator. But my desire to find the outside of poetry, the skin of its dark matter, is not entirely Romantic. It's an intutition that poetry does not represent experience but is an imitation of the action of experiencing. Poetry presents an image of what Alfred North Whitehead calls "prehension" in action.

I wrote a novel because I wanted a large prose field for prehension, which is both positive and negative. Positive in its selection of details or data in pursuit of a vector of cumulative experience—the past that composes me. Negative in its vast unselection, everything I don't write about, whose pressure poetry can make felt. I don't know if prose can. There is a horror at the center of my novel that to my horror has become part of the grid. What ought to bend or break the grid and put its thoughtless apparatus of representation has become integral to that representation.

Prose and poetry fall into dark culture when they are too insistently evental. The grid can only reproduce objects; it objectizes events. History vanishes into the twilight of my timeline; in the meantime, I can respond to it only affectively: I like it, I favorite it. Without analysis, almost without meaning, it passes by.

They say you should write the kind of book you yourself would want to read. But what I wanted to write was: reading.

Reading is in the dark. I see your shadow there.

"In the Deserts of the West, still today, there are Tattered Ruins of that Map, inhabited by Animals and Beggars...."

The grid tears easily when stressed. It is ill-equipped to represent without rupture or distortion the personhood of the non-normative, "Animals and Beggars," the feminine, the queer, the non-white, the poor.

Dark culture pours through tears in the grid for moments surrounded by incessant and ceaseless repairs. Converting time back into space, history into Empire.

Minions of the grid, bent and badly mirrored, only recognizable as human in the anamorphosis of dark culture.

The outside to poetry is time as it is lived. Poetry, like life—

Is mortal. In the line. I feel, enjambed—

"... in all the Land there is no Relic of the Disciplines of Geography."

Nekuia: The Novel

That first-page feeling. Imbricated in an uncreated network. A context for loving life. The I appears like an effect of a record's rotation, upright silver spindle surrounded by gently bruised silence. Static. It's analog, this notion of a surface that's simultaneous with the infinity of depth. Pearls, nutshells. You bury the changes or hide them in a landscape. Pretending not to breathe. I was looking for an *appropriate* unit of syntax: the root of appropriate is property, or as Locke said, that in which you mix your hands. What's the smallest pinhead and the largest number of angels. If it keeps moving a character may occur. *Stimmung* between the lines. Grain of the voice. Prose makes for betweens like that record (*The Yes Album*): another obsolete technology of the word is captured for the Queen to use. You must restart your system to complete installation of updates. Which come from nowhere, like all data, mine or nobody's, holding out a key, a tiny glass heart, or just pointing out of the frame. Writing is not productive; it only stokes the means of production, a steam engine spinning its wheels. Context, within text, warp and woof, the seamy side that shows you how it's done. The man who'd accept a coin in his cup and crinkle his eyes to assure me that whatever it is it's not my fault. He had a white beard and a yellow mustache. He's dead now for all intents and purposes. To. The needle rides the grooves like a surfer aping transcendence, I mean a really little one, a tiny surfer on an endless black sea, he isn't bothering anybody. Wised up. The record is an image of the underworld, like the feeling of paper sliding under my pen hand, skin of bent fourth and fifth fingers, the fetal curl. That's for righties; lefties, like elephants, never forget: the blank page is always before them. I'm not trying to escape determination, not really. When this session ends it will simply stop and you can assume a complete stop. Not a paratactic gesture toward the numinous, or to the force of capital exerting its gravity on molecules like the supermoon touching what passes for the sea around here. I'm done challenging texts to pistols at dawn. I go to bed early and get up the same. Keep shoveling.

I'm driving this car as far as it will go; when it breaks down I'll run, after that I'll walk, after that I'll stand for I'll have come to the end. It's good to be at home.

I am just a sentence in this badly translated prophecy. I am just a needle dragged raggedly off the turntable. I need to believe in a world that believes in me. I like it, like liking. There is a glacier somewhere acting exactly like the sky. Wind. High blue pressure of the thinkable. Best felt by spread fingers, by long hair, closed eyes.

I seek from reading and writing two complementary yet contrary things: the sense of a world in which my personhood (as hero, citizen, even as victim) becomes possible. And to surrender the self in intellectual or spiritual communion with another, him or herself a world in and through which connections come to light, myself only a node or synaptic gap across which these connections must leap.

This is a ghost story. Story of a ghost, of course, but also the story itself is ghostlike, doubtful yet insistent, recurring without coherence, insisting on a moment of recognition that can never arrive while you yourself are living. *He held back his mother with the naked blade until the prophet could drink his fill.* A story told and retold becomes myth and myth is nothing but a texture, a backdrop to life as it is lived, every day, with a sense of something behind the ordinary. Working walking talking sleeping. Of course, backgrounds are fatal to their foregrounds. When myth becomes the story, when it overtakes the everyday, both stories vanish. We are in the gray light that succeeds narrative and the word *afterbirth* is horribly appropriate. Bury the thing that feasted this life, for myth is deoxygenated blood. Dark and darker on the snow, in it. She is stargazing blind, hands outstretched, masked in bandages: her hands, I mean. Mummy in the snow, white on white.

The record, that lustrous boundary of a room's tone. Songs are not data. Inscribe that space with listening's effort. A man asleep on the sofa with an open book on his chest. Sun on the window, rain. Snow muffles the unheard. Only lifting the needle can wake him. The book slides to the floor: an event, almost. Begin playing it again— the outermost track of anticipation. Lossless. The audiophiles call it warmth, dimensionality. A lunar feeling. Placed in orbit, we infer a center. But we don't need a center. We have the song.

I disappears into the telling. Or I strike a stone and new voices appear, voices with one haunted face, telling stories that culminate in the only invisibility that matters. Catch it by the tail, that old story, before it freezes. Unwrap her gently, with reverence. Of course there's nothing there, there never was, except before the time of telling, of narrative, just the glide of an empty hand over paper. I am a baby in my bath, and she is near me. I am a grown man and she is gone. That is not a story, but this is: One morning, I awoke and felt a presence. A made thing. I spoke to, wrote toward, that presence, until it crossed back from Lethe, until the death mask spoke, until it disappeared forever.

VI
NOTES AND THOUGHTS ON VISION

Elegy, Arcadia, Apostrophe

Elegy and Arcadia: two poles of my imagination, united by the poetic trope of apostrophe: the address to someone or something not there.

The void in the vocative O!

Arcadia is the past, the lost paradise whose imaginary function is inseparable from its pastness, its lostness. But Arcadia, ironized, can also be of the future. And when I think of the future, I think of elegy: seeking after consolation for what has been irretrievably lost.

The French prose poet Francis Ponge, whose first book I translated in partnership with Jean-Luc Garneau as *Partisan of Things*, accomplishes an Arcadia of the present in a series of near-apostrophes to common everyday objects. The oyster, the orange, the cigarette, they may very well have been, probably were, *there*. But were they, are they, capable of reciprocating the poet's attention, his address? Here's our version of "L'huître":

OYSTER

The oyster, though the size of an average pebble, has a more rugged appearance, with less uniformity to its brilliant whitishness. It is a world obstinately closed. All the same it can be opened: grip it with a rag, use a serrated knife that's not too sharp, and work at it doggedly. Curious fingers will cut themselves and break their nails; it's dirty work. The blows administered to the shell sheath it in white circles, sort of like halos.

Inside one finds an entire world to be eaten and drunk, underneath a firmament (to speak precisely) of mother-of-pearl. The heavens above collapse into the heavens below, forming a pond, a viscous little green bag, ebbing and flowing in our smell and sight, fringed with a blackish lace.

On very rare occasions a little phrase pearls in its nacreous throat, which we immediately seize for a decoration.

The oyster is not so much addressed as described, and yet that description contains a kind of deification, a spiritualization achieved paradoxically through Ponge's dry, pseudo-scientific attention to such physical details as the ruggedness of the shell's exterior and the pearliness of its interior. The oyster takes on a spiritual life as it becomes unstable in the poet's eye, shifting unpredictably from object to metaphor and back again. All of Ponge's things are constantly changing into language and back again, and our attitude toward them, as toward language, can be affected by our humanism or merely rapacious, as when we "seize for a decoration" the "little phrase [that] pearls in its nacreous throat."

Ponge's original for "phrase" is "*une formule*"; my translation as "the little phrase" alludes to the little phrase of Vinteuil's sonata in *Swann's Way*, a snatch of music that becomes, for Swann, the metonymic emblem of his passion for Odette. As Proust writes, the phrase changes as Swann listens to it; at first he appreciates "only the material quality of the sounds which those instruments secreted"; then the notes of the phrase "substituted (for his mind's convenience) for the mysterious entity" he began to perceive after hearing it repeatedly; finally it is played, again and again, inexpertly, by the fingers of Odette for Swann's pleasure; it becomes symbolic and debased, just as Odette herself is the debased and inadqate vessel for the finest and strongest emotions that Swann will ever be capable of feeling. She is there; he even marries her; but the marriage itself is a kind of apostrophe or elegy to the dead feelings the real Odette has come to represent.

Everything I write seems to take this form—of course writing itself represents what is not there, presents nothing other than itself. It's been fascinating to write fiction, to tell stories, because it throws into sharper relief language's poetic function. When I write a poem, the language is primary; when I write a story, representation of an imaginary world takes precedence, though the most vivid representations, or images, are those that pull some participatory impulse out of the reader to make them real. Poetry, by comparison, is weirdly self-sufficient, or so it can seem. The reader's encounter with it doesn't complete the poem; if anything, poems are repellent, experiences on the page that fling the reader back out into the moment. They are the absolute opposite of stories, or social media posts; they don't absorb the reader but confront him in vivid strangeness, like Ponge's oyster.

Most readers are impervious to the poem's all-but-mute appeal; it requires a certain perversity (pun intended) to have a taste for language being itself. The rest must be lured by the sop of story, the bones of meaning, as in T.S. Eliot's famous analogy: "The chief use of the 'meaning' of a poem, in the ordinary sense, may be (for here again I am speaking of some kinds of poetry and not all) to satisfy one habit of the reader, to keep his mind diverted and quiet, while the poem does its work upon him: much as the imaginary burglar is always provided with a nice piece of meat for the house-dog."

The words, the apostrophe, are really *there*: on the page, in your ear. The lost person, or yet-to-be place, cannot be. These are the rules of the game, but they are played differently in poetry, in translation, and in fiction. I am learning these rules. In the new novel that I have just finished, an artificial Arcadia is the scene of elegy: the survivor of a disaster, living in relative comfort, mourns the woman who did not, chose not, to survive with him. He apostrophizes her, addresses her, throughout: she is the muse of the story that he tells of his survival and his community. But it is a novel and not a poem; canny, I hope, about the poetic difference, another test of the dialectic of presence and absence that defines the written word.

Notes Toward the Dramatic Lyric

This riddle is the riddle of our century's philosophical investigations. Husserl's phenomenology and Einstein's relativity offer much the same revelation as Cubism: we exist not in g-d's green meadows but within our own perceptive boundaries. Language proposes and vows to bear experience across such thresholds, but this solves nothing; if we're not trapped within ourselves, we're still trapped within language itself.[1]

The Language poets have made, in their work, a declaration of equivalency between the words they use and the objects in the world those words usually refer to. They follow Gertrude Stein's famous proposition: a "rose" (letter R, letter O, letter S, letter E) is an object equivalent to a "rose" (a thorny flower of the genus *Rosa* colored on a spectrum from aspirin white to arterial red) which is an object equivalent to a "rose" (symbol of passion, of romance, of clichés about romance, of the ephemeral) which for that matter is an object equivalent to "rose" (past tense of "rise," to move from a lower to a higher position, to get out of bed, to come into existence). Language poets wrestle with, bemoan, and celebrate the Word's tangible mutability or Protean concreteness. A Language poet, or any poet who writes in full consciousness of what the 20th century's disasters and innovations have made possible and necessary, sees the Word as being like the thin wall between rooms at a cheap motel. Through the wall comes the unignorable, obscure sound of the Big Other: muttering, squabbling, making love. The wall prevents us from a complete experience of the Other's subjectivity, but it is also the agent, the connector, the transmitter that makes it possible for us to recognize the reality of the Other's subjectivity in the first place. We can't get out of L=A=N=G=U=A=G=E, but we can at least put our ear to the wall.

---

1 Joshua Clover, "The Rose of the Name," published in *Fence*, v. 1 n.1., Spring 1998. http://www.fenceportal.org/?page_id=731

The yearning for contact with others, for intersubjectivity, is identical with the yearning for unmediated contact with reality, for what Emerson called an original relation with the universe. This rootedness in the subjective leads us to the other dominant strand in Language poetry: viewing the traditional unified self posited by lyric as an untrustworthy vehicle for speech. These poets contradict the assumption made about the self in mainstream lyric poetry: that the self is an integrated whole in the world, capable of addressing reality within the hearing of a listener. That the self is not an integrated one is something we've known since Freud (though today's conventional lyric flouts that knowledge in its evocation of a singular speaker as if Modernism, much less postmodernism, never happened). I have already discussed the impossibility of unproblematized speaking; the Language poets have set out to write in full awareness of the paradoxical implications of Wittgenstein's notorious tautology, "Whereof one cannot speak, thereof one must be silent." Finally, and for me most admirably, the Language poets are suspicious of the monocultured self as a necessary precondition for speaking. Where mainstream narrative lyricists imagine they enjoy unquestioned the American creed of individualism (as if the extra-linguistic Real were achieveable without struggle), the Language poets see a solipsist without any metaphysically secure home in the world. They recognize that narrative lyric, in its relentless representation of the poet-self's experience, resists intersubjectivity or any sympathetic identification with others that is more than fleeting or sentimental. Even Elizabeth Bishop, hardly a Language poet, felt the poignancy of this, as in these lines from "In the Waiting Room":

> But I felt: you are an *I*,
> you are an *Elizabeth*,
> you are one of *them*.
> *Why* should you be one too?
> I scarcely dared to look
> to see what it was I was.

Such suspicions have shaped much of the avant-garde work produced in the post-Language era, and I find their intellectual adventures, informed by Marxism, feminism, postcolonialism, Lacanian psychoanalysis, and Derridean deconstruction exciting, at least in theory. It is in fact that "in theory" that is so gratifying—the willful ignorance of theory (part and parcel of the generally rampant anti-intellectualism) prevalent in creative writing programs is utterly disheartening, a spectacle of so many ostriches smothering the potential of otherwise fine verbal gifts in the sand. But the manifold pleasures of avant-garde poetry can sometimes fall into the same solipsistic trap as mainstream poetry, with only this slight improvement: the poet is fully aware of the situation. Worse, their sense of language as tangible can fail to produce tangible language—the conversion of theory into praxis overrides the poem's need to become itself through following the paths of music and association.[2] Hewing to a particular party line, as many self-conscious experimentalists do, can result in language that is so abstract, convoluted, and divorced from verbal pleasure that one can scarcely locate the thought, much less the feeling, that was the occasion of the poem's cry. I'm not speaking of the kind of pregnant mystery that delights and instructs in a nonlinear, nondiscursive fashion here, but rather of the kind of flat obscurantism that is every bit as dull to read as the heartfelt banalities of conventional lyricists. Poetry *should* create a state like dreaming in the reader, but if at all possible it should not put the reader to sleep first.

---

2 Clayton Eshleman has recognized, in Harold Bloom's schematic of the agon between a strong poet and his (always *his*) forebear, something more useful: a schematic of the creative process. In that process he identifies the stage Bloom calls Kenosis, or Emptying, as the moment where the poet clears away the conventional (received) ideas as to how the poem's theme should be completed. He calls this Emptying the "willingness to introduce contradiction and/or obscurity *via sound-oriented or associational veers*" (emphasis mine). When I find Language poetry unsatisfying, I can usually attribute it to a failure of Kenosis: the contradiction and obscurity that the poet introduces derives not from music (tangible word as phoneme) or association (word as node in a web of both linguistic and referential associations) but from some received theory, however interesting, that the poet is force-marching his or her lines out of. Quotation from Eshleman, *Novices: A Study of Poetic Apprenticeship* (Los Angeles: Mercer & Aitchison, 1989), p. 24.

Lyric poetry in English has been midwife to the creation of the modern self. It has traditionally been an individualistic and Cartesian mode (though efforts to resist individualism and dualism within lyric have been productive). I do not really expect that any kind of communitarian lyric is possible or even desirable. Insofar as genre distinctions are useful, I expect that writers will continue to be drawn to the lyric because it is produced by an individual's voice. But that doesn't mean that there is such a thing as *the* individual voice; nor is it necessary for the speaker of a poem to be identified with the poet's "I" in order to reflect his or her subjectivity. The subjective remains the ultimate and exclusive territory of the lyric: it enacts a human voice's attempt to create a relation to the world outside him or herself through the hopelessly flawed, exhilaratingly concrete medium of language. That human voice usually belongs to an individual; in the lost genre of epic poetry it belongs to a culture; in religious scripture it is institutionalized and lies waiting for those willing to break open the tomb and give new life to it with their own living voices.

It is difficult for the pure lyric to escape the trap of solipsism, and almost impossible for the narrative. One possibility for lyric subjectivity today is what I'll call the dramatic lyric, which originates within the Shakespearean soliloquy. In these soliloquies, as Harold Bloom observes, a kind of self-overhearing takes place: the Shakespearean hero speaks from the heart only to hear his heart being changed by what he speaks. There is a sense of discovery and exhilaration in the representation of this kind of thought, even when that thought leads to frustrating or frustrated conclusions. This kind of poetry, which is as critical of self as it is revelatory, strikes me as being a brand of lyric that needs to be revived. Its vitality seems in part to stem from the genre paradox of "lyric" statement within the framework of dramatic poetry. The speaking self gets a valuable shot in the arm from being a player in a larger dramatic community, conscious of his or her place as one voice in the simultaneous babble of poetry from *Beowulf* to *The Tennis Court Oath*: the speaker is one character among several who also get to speak (and transform) their minds. This mode refuses, or at other times directly engages, the solipsism that encumbers most contemporary lyric poems. It is a mode of self-declaration that manages to be other-aware, if not other-directed. Most compelling for me is this mode's engagement with matters of the heart: in the speeches of characters like Lady Macbeth, Lear, Cleopatra, Gloucester's sons Edgar and Edmund, and above all Hamlet, we are privileged to hear powerful intellects applying all their verbal cunning to the task of baring, even transforming, a complex heart. ("Some good I mean to do," rasps the dying bastard Edmund, "Despite of mine own nature"—a haunting mirror image to Iago's declaration, "Demand me nothing: what you know, you know: / From this time forth I never will speak word.") There is a richness of feeling here that I don't find in the transparent, sentimental, "authentic" language of the narrative lyricists.

Of course I'm not making a bid for the resuscitation of iambic pentameter.[3] I am only suggesting that the richest and strangest poetry being written today comes out of an awareness of all that both Bloom's canon and the canon of the postmodernists (vividly represented by the New York School, the Black Mountain Poets, the San Francisco Renaissance, the Language poets, Flarf, the Ellipticals) have done to make it possible for us to confront our 21st-century predicaments. Within the locked room of language the self fragments and re-coalesces in the presence of the world, achieving, against tremendous odds, an original relationship with the universe.

The camaraderie of a university workshop, however valuable, is only a synthetic gesture toward the free and elective communities artists were forced to create before the institutionalization of creative writing. It is not too exaggerated to say that the atomized individual poet, flitting from teaching job to teaching job, publication to

---

3 The New Formalist approach is neither here nor there in this discussion; it is merely the most dogmatic and conservative strain of the mainstream poetry I've criticized. Whatever credit they get for their rigorous study of the tradition (as opposed to the slack ignorance of many free verse lyricists) dissolves in the narrowness of their conception of that tradition (it seems to begin and end with late Auden) and by the poverty of the sentiments they enclose in their received formal straitjackets. I am not opposed to traditional forms, but they only make sense to me when the form becomes as tangible an object in the world as individual words, phrases, and lines.

publication, is forced into what György Lukács called "the realm of abstraction" where his or her autarchy is diminished, leaving the poet with nothing beside "formalistic experimentation" and *Angst*. All we have with which to fight this trend is each other. We can create a space outside the university, well outside state sponsorship, where real interaction and intersubjectivity becomes possible. We need to create our own magazines and small presses and nonhierarchical writing workshops. We need to fight boring poetry. There's a criticism abroad today that says poets write only for other poets. I say turn that on its head by finding a way to turn more readers into poets—to somehow lend readers our negative capability, our freedom to play, our secret judo holds. We need to create what Oscar Wilde, in "The Soul of Man Under Socialism," called "the temperament of receptivity" in our readers: the reader or playgoer "is to go to the play to gain an artistic temperament."

Poetry isn't "difficult." Poetry exerts pressure on the language (of politicians, of advertisers, of churches, of power) that otherwise obscures experience of the Other and the Real. If we can't create readers willing to apply that same pressure, it's not poetry that's doomed. It's our whole sense of reality. As Wordsworth wanted a poetics of "a man speaking to men," I want a humanism of poets creating poets.

Notes Toward the Postmodern Baroque

The baroque is a major mode of contemporary American poetry—a mode of early modernity particularly well adapted to a postmodern era which has seen an acceleration of the modern tendency to break down experience into fragments. It is peculiarly well-suited to a poetics of resistance—not in a nostalgic re-creation of some lost lifeworld, but through a radical materialism that paradoxically creates a new aperture for subjective, even spiritual, experience.

A product of the Counter-Reformation, the historical baroque was a response to the assault on the Catholic church being led by Protestantism. The baroque style in art was born in the same period as the Inquisition and the Society of Jesus—institutions designed to combat heresy and compel orthodoxy. But where its siblings are repressive or disciplinary, the baroque was intended to attract the allegiance of the common people. Through painting, music, and architecture, what had become a rigid and corrupt administrative structure sought to present its doctrines in a more fresh and appealing way; we might nowadays call it, "Catholicism with a human face." As a style, the baroque "establishes a total art or a unity of the arts" (Deleuze)—an untimely manifestation of the modernist urge toward the *Gesamtkunstwerk* or "total artwork" that dissolves the boundaries between the arts as it dissolves the ground between artwork and spectator. Gilles Deleuze's reading of the baroque in *The Fold* stresses its spatial and architectural qualities: "the painting exceeds its frame … sculpture goes beyond itself by being achieved in architecture," so that "the painter has become an urban designer" and "The sum of the arts becomes the Socius, the public social space inhabited by Baroque dancers." Such an aestheticization of public space reminds us of the aestheticization of politics characteristic of Fascism and its spectacles: one thinks of the soaring forms and innumerable torches defining the seemingly limitless space of the Luitpold Arena in Leni Riefenstahl's *Triumph of the Will*. And yet the baroque also refers us to the sculpture of Bernini and the paintings of Caravaggio, which convey the spiritual through its impact on solid matter. Caravaggio turned street people into saints and back again, while Bernini's sculpture of Teresa of Avila captures an ecstasy that transcends and returns us to the saint's transported body. There is a monumental baroque and a baroque of intimacy. There is a blurring of the bounds between the sacred and profane, even as the ruling ideology that the baroque artists served was struggling to enforce the distinction. In their work, the spirit becomes a special effect of the ecstatic and suffering body. Catholic ideology is the detached superstructure of the too too solid flesh whose nakedness compels our attention.

Today we are living through another legitimation crisis, or to speak more accurately, a crisis of legitimation. The right-wing reaction to the liberation movements of the 1960s has pulsed like a shockwave through our society, opening an unprecedented rift between politics and culture that continues to widen. As Andrew Joron has remarked, "Here in America … 'culture' has been reduced to a simple play of intensities, to the simultaneously brutal and sentimental pulsions of mass media. Any 'legitimation function' would be superfluous: the American machine, with its proudly exposed components of Accumulation and Repression, has no need for such a carapace." Increasingly, it seems that the forces of capitalism no longer even need the carapace of politics, let alone culture. For confirmation of this we need only glance at the Riefenstahlian spectacle of George W. Bush's infamous "Mission Accomplished" speech, which the speed of events transformed almost overnight into a dialectical image of the man's hubris and haplessness. And yet the war machine marches on unfazed, sustained as it is by a subtly self-distributed myth of accumulation and enclosure that retains all the mystification of myth while discarding its traditional forms.

In a time when even the acknowledged legislators appear helpless to do anything other than ride the tiger of accumulation, what are the unacknowledged ones to do? The blue pill of ideological critique offered up by the Language poets seems to have lost some of its kick, while the "I do this, I do that" of the New York School has come to seem merely descriptive of how most of us behave in the residual shopping mall of culture. My heart is no longer in my pocket with my copy of Pierre Reverdy—it has been broken up and distributed along innumerable lines of socio-economic flight—a part of the larger reality that must, in Paul Celan's words, be searched for and won. The baroque comes to my aid by foregrounding the tenuousness of the connection between ideology and materialism, cultural politics and the means of production, the spirit and the letter. To quote Deleuze once again, "In the Baroque the soul entertains a complex relation with the body. Forever indissociable from the body, it discovers a vertiginous animality that gets it tangled in the pleats of matter, but also an organic or cerebral humanity (the degree of development) that allows it to rise up, and that will make it ascend over all other folds."

What Deleuze describes, I believe, is nothing less than a new way of thinking about those aspects of reality that resist representation, whether speaking of the soul and subjectivity of the individual or the social as a whole. And it suggests an approach to poetry that, in its foregrounding of folding interplay of the sensuous signifier, anchors truth-content in bodily experience. It seems to me today that we have a very strong poetry of "vertiginous animality," whose radical materialism serves to ironize and corrode the myths of accumulation. I refer of course to flarf, which in the words of Stan Apps is a poetics that "consists of decisively rejecting mysterious theatricality, and thereby creating an aesthetic of material accountability." Flarf's loony, goony, and aggressive repurposing of discourse—from the boardroom to the porn movie, from Silliman's Blog to the *New York Times*—punctures the balloon of mystification that poetry, of all the arts, is the most prone to conjuring. At the same time, flarf poetry is hardly untheatrical: it is a shadow play of discourses and unattributed voices, played out on a skewed soundstage's version of the American totality: psychiatric regulation of subjectivity in Katie Degentesh's *The Anger Scale*, normative gender stances in Drew Gardner's "Chicks Dig War," patriotic road rage in Kasey Mohammed's *Deer Head Nation*. The title of Michael Magee's *Mainstream* says it all: this toxic, mortally funny spewage of language arranged in lines, superficially at home in any anthology of verse, is our new mainstream, visible to anyone who will open their eyes to the ways in which we actually think, write, and speak. The comfortable mythology of the stable subject in the scenic mode has been left long behind, of course. But also rejected is the very notion of a subject able to rise above his or her very bodily immersion in the material gunk of discourse—there is no higher ground.

Here is where I part ways with the flarfists in my own ambitions for poetry. To supplement their corrosive irony and the necessary "inappropriateness" of their "vertiginous animality," I look for a baroque that feels its way back toward something like spiritual experience and knowledge—what Deleuze calls "organic and cerebral humanity." The combination of "cerebral" with "organic" is key: we are speaking of a conceptuality or subjectivity that cannot be divorced from bodily experience, that accepts the body as its ground. As a mode of the baroque, this speaks to the reality of St. Teresa's ecstasy before the church fathers found ways of assimilating it to doctrine; it speaks to the warm flesh of Caravaggio's painting of John the Baptist as the saint grapples with a ram while directly, erotically engaging our gaze: by being so sensuously enfleshed, we feel more acutely the possibility that he is a forerunner of the divine. To speak in more materialist terms, I believe it is through the folds, ornaments, and patterns of sensuously folded and patterned language that we discover the truth of our subjective relation to the sociolinguistic whole.

In the space permitting I can only hastily allude to two of the most remarkable examples of this mode of the baroque, Jo Anne Wasserman's *The Escape* and Shanxing Wang's *Mad Science in Imperial City*, both published by Futurepoem Books. Both of these books press hard against the usual genre distinctions of poetry, alternating prose with verse and, in Wang's case, incorporating copious scientific terms and diagrams. Both are highly inventive in their use of form—Wasserman's book is distinguished by its narrative sestinas (the combination of "narrative" with "sestina" into a single phrase seems thoroughly baroque in itself), while Wang pursues writing itself like the ourobotous of legend, searching and never finding the correct English for his tumultuous experience as a ambivalent subject-object of recent Chinese and American history. Both draw strongly on autobiography, but also on innumerable other discourses and social texts to produce the unmistakable effect of spirit. You read these books for cognitive maps of the world that the normative discourses of enclosure conceal. You read these books to rediscover what's still possible for subjectivity within the body of what's written, said, and done in the name of a history that is under no institution's control, or author's agency. The work of these poets hints at a continuing role for both major modes of the baroque in our poetry—a dialectic of destruction and construction that keeps us in touch with the body of the word, and reminds us of the possibilities of spirit.

Notes Toward a Cosmological Realism

"The Great Outdoors" is Quentin Meillassoux's term (*le grand dehors*) for the objective universe, as described in his book *After Finitude*: "the absolute *outside* of pre-critical thinkers ... that outside which thought could explore with the legitimate feeling of being on foreign territory." We have lost the Great Outdoors, Meillassoux argues, to post-Kantian "correlationism": "the idea according to which we only ever have access to the correlation between thinking, and being, and never to either term considered apart from the other." Kantian critique, which defines what can and cannot be accessed by the thinker (phenomenon and noumenon) is the archetype of the post-structuralist position summarized by Jacques Derrida's notorious claim that "*There is nothing outside of the text* [there is no outside-text; *il n'y a pas de hors-texte*]." In *Science and the Modern World*, Alfred North Whitehead refers to this as the "subjectivist" posture:

> By a subjectivist basis I mean the belief that the nature of our immediate experience is the outcome of the perceptive peculiarities of the subject enjoying the experience. In other words, I mean that for this theory what is perceived is not a partial vision of a complex of things generally independent of the act of cognition; but that it merely is the expression of the individual peculiarities of the cognitive act. Accordingly what is common to the multiplicity of cognitive acts is the ratiocination connected with them. Thus, though there is a common world of thought associated with our sense-perceptions, there is no common world to think about.

Whitehead goes on to describe the epistemological "half-way house of those who believe that our perceptual experience does tell us of a common objective world; but that the things perceived are merely the outcome for us of this world, and are not *in themselves* elements in the common world itself." For Meillassoux, I suspect that this would still read as correlationism: the stance described corresponds to Kant's division of the aspects of things into perceptible phenomena and concealed, inaccessible noumena. But Whitehead's goal is to develop a consistently "objectivist" philosophy, a speculative yet rigorous extension of the naive realism that takes the reality of things for granted. "This creed is that the actual elements perceived by our senses are *in themselves* the elements of a common world; and that this world is a complex of things, including indeed our acts of cognition, but transcending them. According to this point of view the things themselves are to be distinguished from our knowledge of them."

Whitehead criticizes what he sees as the incoherent modern division of two modes of knowledge or science that deny our access to Meillassoux's "great outdoors" or Whitehead's "common world": "A scientific realism, based on mechanism, is conjoined with an unwavering belief in the world of men and of the higher animals as being composed of self-determining organisms. This radical inconsistency at the basis of modern thought accounts for much that is half-hearted and wavering in our civilization." In *The Concept of Nature*, Whitehead names this inconsistency, "the bifurcation of nature":

> What I am essentially protesting against is the bifurcation of nature into two systems of reality which, in so far as they are real, are real in different senses. One reality would be the entities such as electrons which are the study of speculative physics. This would be the reality that is there for knowledge; although on this theory it is never known. For what is known is the other sort of reality, which is the byplay of the mind. Thus there would be two natures, one is the conjecture and the other is the dream.

On the one side we have a nature conditioned and glimpsed only by theoretical science; as Whitehead says, primarily "*there* for knowledge," the cause of knowledge, inaccessible to the unaided mind. On the other side we have an acculturated "dream" of nature, the nature that is there to be perceived. As Whitehead explains:

> The nature which is the fact apprehended in awareness holds within it the greenness of the trees, the song of the birds, the warmth of the

sun, the hardness of the chairs, and the softness of the velvet. The nature which is the cause of awareness is the conjectured system of molecules and electrons which so affects the mind as to produce the awareness of apparent nature.

Fact in awareness versus *cause of* awareness: these two versions of nature, second-order and first-order, are mutually exclusive. The division is structurally parallel to, though perhaps not identical with, the bifurcation of our world into nature and culture, or what Bruno Latour has called "the modern constitution": the modern practice of severing scientific investigation in the laboratory from the dimension of political determination, as though scientific discoveries of the structures of the natural world had nothing to do with the manifestation of social and political structures. Science/nature is the transcendent boundary to culture/politics, and vice-versa: they are incommensurable modes of thought, an intensification of C.P. Snow's famous division of western society into "the two cultures." Latour seeks an end of this division and a restoration of what he dubs, "the Middle Kingdom," the hidden empire of hybrids of the social and natural:

> Nature does revolve, but not around the Subject/Society. It revolves around the collective out of which people and things are generated. At last the Middle Kingdom is represented. Natures and societies are its satellites.

Latour's Middle Kingdom is akin to what Whitehead calls "a common world which transcends knowledge, though it includes knowledge": the matrix that produces things *and* ideas about things. From my position as a writer and scholar of poetry that has been deeply informed and conditioned by post-structuralist thinkers who tend to reduce phenomena to social constructs, it feels urgent to inscribe a path by which poetic thought can re-establish *contact* with the world, in the sublime and terrifying sense with which Thoreau uses that word in *The Maine Woods*. But it feels equally urgent, or necessary, to me as a writer to take words seriously as things. Contact with language *is* a form of contact with "the things themselves" and "the common world."

These are the foundations of a realist if not materialist cosmology to be inscribed in and through poetry: a map of the universe that is wholly immanent, a Middle Kingdom. Is it more accurate to write this cosmology as a form of materialism (Jane Bennett's vital materialism), by which entities and societies on every scale (electrons and cells and mica and ferns and mongooses and cities and opera companies and rainforests and tectonic plates and dwarf stars and nebulae) are all equally real, composing and recomposing climates that alter the trajectories of their component parts? Or is it more correct to project a speculative realism for which ideas, fictions, and fantasies are as real as these material entities? Whitehead's philosophy of organism best accommodates that thinking in his own division of the world's quanta into "actual entities" and "eternal objects"—the latter seeming to mean percepts such as color (available to many different kinds of entity) but also concepts (belonging to humans and to "God").

Perhaps one more division—between materialism and realism—is unnecessary and against the grain of the movement of thought that I am here exploring. But there is a poetic legacy, extending as far back as Lucretius and forward in the Anglo-American tradition through Wordsworth, Shelley, Thoreau, Dickinson, Whitman, Stevens, Williams, the Black Mountain poets, up through John Ashbery, that one might map onto this generative cosmology, enabling a realism capable of presenting the mutual dependencies—poetic hybrids—of experience, language, and knowledge.

Poetry and Silence

1.
Why write poetry, why read it? Because it makes silence audible. What do I mean by that? First of all, that poetry addresses what otherwise goes unheard. We live in a time when it seems all but impossible to imagine *otherwise*: a life different from the lives we spend rushing around, our attention chopped into slivers by screens, always fleeing from solitude and our own thoughts; lives spent getting and spending, working too many hours at increasingly precarious jobs, buying things we don't need, trying not to think too hard about the trash spiraling into our oceans or the carbon accumulating in our air. Other kinds of lives, lived in solidarity with others and with ourselves, in greater harmony with our environment, with time for contemplation and being present with the ones we love: these are possibilities that have been all but silenced. Poetry is a place to find them again, to give voice to possibility.

2.
There are many kinds of silence: the silence of injustice, the silence of oppression, the silence of sexual and racial difference, the silence of ableism, the silence of people living and suffering in languages other than English. I try not to mistake poetry for politics, but it's nonetheless true that poetry can open a space in which these silences might speak.

3.
There is silence inside myself, when I pause long enough to hear it. There's a part of me that disagrees with almost everything I say, that answers every statement I make with a silent question of its own. It's that silence, that struggle with always having to *say something*, that drives me to make poems. I want the *saying* without the *something*.

4.
William Butler Yeats said, "Out of the quarrel with others we make rhetoric; out of the quarrel with ourselves we make poetry." I haven't found a better explanation for why poetry is central to my life: it's a way of communicating with and bringing together different selves, different parts of my experience, that are otherwise estranged from each other, that are otherwise silent. A part of me disagrees with almost everything I say. In a poem, by putting language under pressure, so that the syntax that makes the sentence rubs against itself like the rubbing of tectonic plates, I can break out and through silence. I can be present with what otherwise goes unsaid.

5.
God of course is the most silent of all. Maybe poetry is a way of making the god-shaped hole in things more visible, more present.

6.
I started writing poems because my mother wrote poems and it was a place where we could meet. I am still trying to fill the empty place she left in my life with words.

7.
Offering many answers to a question might be a way to avoid answering it.

8.
Christopher Marlowe, William Shakespeare, John Donne, George Herbert, Andrew Marvell, John Milton, William Blake, William Wordsworth, Samuel Taylor Coleridge, John Keats, Percy Bysshe Shelley, Emily Dickinson, Walt Whitman, Ezra Pound, T.S. Eliot, Gertrude Stein, H.D., Wallace Stevens, Langston Hughes, William Carlos Williams, Louis Zukofsky, George Oppen, Allen Ginsberg, Robert Duncan, Charles Olson, Adrienne Rich, Frank O'Hara, John Ashbery, James Schuyler, Susan Howe, Fanny Howe, Jennifer Moxley, Lisa Robertson.

They are not all religious poets but they have all brought me religious moments. They are glorious company, to be plucked at any moment out of memory or off the shelf, out of silence.

9.
Poetry is conversation.

10.
Poetry is a job. I teach poetry, how to write it and how to read it. Alas, more people are interested in writing it than reading it, though the two should be inseparable. I publish my poems in magazines and books, I help to publish other poets through my editorial work as an anthologist and publisher. They say that poetry is dead, they say that poetry is dying, they say that no one reads anymore, they say it's too difficult, they say it's not relevant, they quote Auden snidely, "poetry makes nothing happen," leaving out the last part of the stanza: "it survives, / A way of happening, a mouth."

Maybe the most spiritual thing I do is to answer these provocations with a shrug, and carry on.

11.
Ten is a nice number.

A Lyric Cosmology

Two lyric traditions: direct expression of subjectivity (Romanticism) vs. the persona (Modernism). The first is cosmological because it presents the self in passionate negotiation with a universe it takes to be natural. As Nature withers away as a source of meaning, the fundamentally mimetic and narratological persona lyric takes over: wearing a mask it seeks to expose the masks of social meaning. After 1989 the postmodern lyric goes even farther into the capitalist abandonment of political subjectivity, leaving us with a pure consumerist poetics in which the absence of value is no longer a scandal, but the void we swim in, untouched and untouchable by others.

To resuscitate the subjective lyric cannot mean yielding to a regressive dream of a unified Nature. Instead, subjectivity must be pluralized: the speaking self of the poet encounters and responds to other speaking selves, not all of them human, none of them "primitive" (there can be no more leech-gatherers seen as "closer" to the universal Nature and subjected to the social poet's interrogations). The practitioner of subjective lyric may borrow techniques from ethnography, as Charles Olson does, but must operate less as anthropologist than "archaeologist of morning": that is, as co-active and cooperative with the more-than-human socius he poetically encounters, and not writing as the bearer of an imperial universalizing "scientific" objectivity.

What is most valuable and unique to the lyric, I believe—a value coextensive with capitalist propaganda about lyric's valuelessness—is its built-in refusal of anything resembling an "objective" stance. Lyric offers a form of diplomacy: it presents a speaking self in productive tension with the real and potential subjectivities of others. The lyric speaker has a passion for the other, in every sense of that word: suffering, ecstasy, eroticism, sacrifice.

In the present postmodern environment the self as bearer of value has been almost obliterated. People of color, LGBTQ folk, disabled people, and women are at best tolerated by the regime, largely if not exclusively for their value as consumers and as markets (capitalism trumps, barely, the white-supremacist patriarchy that predates it, and this is the true meaning of "liberalism"). But the selves of white males are also empty, non-sites of the vast privilege accumulated on their behalf, lashing out reflexively whenever that privilege are challenged, treating every presentation of subjectivity—perhaps even their own, since subjectivity is inherently messy, contradictory, and emergent from relations with others—as an existential threat.

The value of the self, as more than a counter in the lyric game, is yet to be (re)discovered. Even more deeply suppressed is the possibility of collective subjectivities. And there is, after all, a real danger that outside the regime of tolerance, without developing the passion for otherness that is intrinsic to lyric, we will find ourselves in a state of total war. (As opposed to the war that, to paraphrase William Gibson, is already here, but unevenly distributed.)

I return to the poetry of Olson and Duncan because in their passion for cosmos and polis as emergent territories (as opposed to what's supposedly simply stable and already there) they have kept the flame of subjectivity—as something to be ventured, tested, and risked—alive. Contemporary poets who come out of that tradition often come armed with the experience of a passionate collectivity behind them: I think of Lisa Robertson's feminism or Peter O'Leary's Catholicism or Nathaniel Mackey's deep engagements with jazz, Dogon mythology, and the Black Arts Movement. It may be much harder for those of us who do not have such backgrounds to wager everything on the subjective lyric, rather than hiding behind masks of irony or dictate faux-objective political critiques. Well, begin from that ground where you are already most engaged, most implicated. It might be the workplace, or the family, or the university, or the military. We are none of us isolatos when we speak from the "I."

Stay-Puft: On Secret Knowledge

> *Perhaps when one makes something one affirms, and when one tries to make and knows they cannot (another kind of making) one determines. One determines that they cannot, one determines this by endlessly attempting.*
> —Mary Ruefle, "Madness, Rack, and Honey"

A number of truths on display here. One truth is akin to Walter Benjamin's thesis that "The work is the death mask of its conception." That is, the actual work is a thin and dead reflection of what was quick and living in the author's mind. One tries to grasp the conception, to capture it alive and in motion, but like the philosopher in Kafka's parable of the top, it is oneself that ends up spinning: the top is dead or undead, like Odradek.

But there are two opposed stances toward making here. To make a work, Ruefle says, "affirms one's relation to the incomprehensible condition of existence." And for a long time, I thought of my poetry as such a work, going back to the claim that Ruefle amends, that it is "the nature of poetry to assert individual identity." My ego demanded so many Mini-Me's, so many poems that, like Duncan's meadow in one quicksilver mood, were "a made place, / that is mine." The poems were objects, more or less exquisite, ends in themselves as people should be, themselves, ends.

But there are times when one cannot make a work. When working or trying to work ends in frustration and fragments; or (it is almost the same thing) when what one writes refuses to be a work like other works, like what one had faintly in mind. In short, one fails, and falls, into text. There is no work, like there is no Dana in *Ghostbusters*; there is only Zuul, minion of Gozer the Destroyer, who comes to the work of destruction indifferent to his form.

In the destruction of the work there is nothing to affirm. There is only the adventure of "crossing the streams," doing the unreasonable thing (as Charles Bernstein remarks in "A Defence of Poetry," "ratio ... DOES NOT EQUAL / sense!"). To destroy the Destructor is not to affirm one's identity, or even "one's relation to the incomprehensible condition of existence." It means to roll the dice (which never will abolish chance) which will determine—for the moment—that relation. And we must roll the dice again and again. (Even if *Ghostbusters III* never comes to fruition; especially then).

Ruefle quotes Alberto Giacometti: "I do not know whether I work in order to make something or in order to know why I cannot make what I would like to make." This suggests making as a process of education, nicely suggested by the German word *Bildung*. In failing to make "what I would like to make," you learn a little more about what it is you would really like, and perhaps edge closer to the affirmation of actual making, of creation. Or you can look at it in the mirror and affirm negatively with Beckett: "Fail. Fail again. Fail better." But I am a little suspicious of these aphorisms, which get passed hand to hand around the Internet until all the context—all the difficulty—has been rubbed away.

I am a little tongue-in-cheek with the Stay-Puft Marshmallow Man, but my intention is a serious one. *Ghostbusters* plays with occult knowledge in order to make us laugh, but there is something more than a little sublime and terrifying about the form Dan Ackroyd's Ray chooses for Gozer, particularly after the crossed streams of their "unlicensed nuclear accelerators" have set him aflame. Ray tries to make knowledge harmless, to package it in the form of the friendliest possible commodity, and fails. "Poetry is the scholar's art" says Stevens, deriving from a vision of the imagination as "the sum of our faculties." It animates knowledge, and demonstrates the occultness of knowledge by giving it a sweet, tumultuous, and flammable body.

Knowing conjures; knowing is a summoning. Knowledge is made present by metaphor, and metaphor, as Ruefle reminds us, "is not, and never has been, a mere literary term. It is an event. *A poem must rival a physical experience* and metaphor is, simply, an exchange of energy between two things." Which echoes Olson: "A poem is energy transferred from where the poet got it (he shall have some several causations) by way of the poem itself to, all the way over to, the reader." *Energeia*: within work. *Eventus, evenire*: to come out of something. The event comes out of the energy that is within the work, that must be conducted with as little resistance as possible from the poet's knowledge (always occult and hidden: knowledge of the body, of history, of myth). It "rivals" a physical experience; it *is* a physical experience. It burns on the way out, and on the way in.

I am trying to understand the importance of the occult and the hidden; of the text as paradoxical fragment of the work (the energy) it contains; of the ghost in the small or large machine made of words. I am trying to understand the role of the occult and made-up, of the metaphors. Ruefle: "To conceive of things that don't exist is a *natural* act for a human being." What is the nature of making and of making-up? What happens when we answer the destruction of a known reality with the destruction of the unknown?

I ain't afraid of no ghost. Oh, but I am. And I am.

Six Dimensions

VOLTA

The turn, the break, "This Be the Verse." The clinamen, the swerve:

> The atoms, as their own weight bears them down
> Plumb through the void, at scarce determined times,
> In scarce determined places, from their course
> Decline a little—call it, so to speak,
> Mere changed trend. For were it not their wont
> Thuswise to swerve, down would they fall, each one,
> Like drops of rain, through the unbottomed void;
> And then collisions ne'er could be nor blows
> Among the primal elements; and thus
> Nature would never have created aught.
>
> Lucretius, *The Nature of Things*, trans. William Ellery Leonard

Heidegger says that only a god can save us. But Lucretius says we have no gods. Only the volta.

DOUBLING

"*I* is another," says Rimbaud, castigating "the false significance of Self." The pronoun in the poem is the mask. The poem is the impossible touch of the other in the mirror. And the poem works by doubling: call it rhyme, call it repetition. How many flowers? "A rose is a rose is a rose is a rose is a rose."

A dimension is a question of *structure*.

Joshua Corey

CADENCE

The quality of time in the body (of the speaker, of the listener, of the line, of the poem).

SILENCE

Language is not identical with itself. Attentiveness to this.

Each dimension midwifes the emergence of the others.

THINGS

Language is not identical with itself. Forgetfulness of this.

The rhythmic emergence and submergence of the referent. Immanent mimesis of the poem, which does not describe things, which is a thing in relation to the other things it does not describe.

OUTSIDE

What the volta admits, what the language doubles, what the cadence remarks, what silence acknowledges, what cherishes the things.

The spirituality of the Möbius strip, which is a thing any child can make with a strip of paper and some tape.

The activeness of creatures without a creator.

What Hopkins calls "Christ." What Jews call

The Law. "There are no / final orders."

No home.

Theses on Visionary Materialism

1
That poetry is a mode by which words are made present as things without ceasing to refer.

1.1
The rivalry between signifier and signified, the reader's being brought to that boundary, is a poem's happening.

2
That poetry is a subset of imaginative literature, in which the operations of the reader's imagination are brought to bear on the rivalry between mimesis and rhetoric, thingness and speech.

2.1
A subset of the beloved, stand-in for the desired.

3
That there is reading and there is beholding or apprehending, and prior to both is judgment or a question: what kind is it?

3.1
What kind is writing?

3.11
Men judge of things according to their mental disposition, and rather imagine than understand (Spinoza).

3.2
Reading or apprehending, what belongs to the reader has the name of an action: there is creative reading (Emerson).

3.3
Concealment and revelation: the false dialectic.

4
That the boundary between word and thing, signifier and signified, rhetoric and mimesis is not a boundary in the sense that it indicates the divison of a whole.

4.1
For these seeming binaries are two halves of the word, or the sign, or the poem, that is itself multiple, more than halves/halved.

4.2
The boundary that makes a binary is itself an unbounded territory, a Möbius strip along which the reader travels.

4.21
The reader cuts the strip, cutting the Gordian knot, like Alexander, denying that problems are problems.

4.22
Another reader cuts himself, an abject if not resentful abdication of interpretation to the mute power of things.

4.221
The body is marked but the eye forgives.

4.3
The boundary as Möbius territory is the monism of reading. Spirit and letter, flesh and decay, are not in dialectical tension but simultaneous on the strip. Line by line, word by word, the preponderance of spirit or of letter in the reader's experience is purely local and momentary.

4.4
Poetry's monism does not predicate a holistic or organic relation between signifier and signified, poet and poem, word and Word, man and nature. It is possible to be visionary without believing in the unseen. This ought to be the definition of vision but it is not.

4.41
There are men lunatic enough to believe that even God himself takes pleasure in harmony (Spinoza).

5
That poetry is vision.

5.1
But vision is not the whole. The whole is the untrue (Adorno).

5.2
Vision bears the possibility of contact with the real.

5.21
Not in the sense that vision pierces the cloud of unknowingness, the cloud of ideology, that we see into the life of things (Wordsworth).

5.22
Not in the sense that vision splits the world into real and unreal, or the phenomenal and noumenal, or the real and the imaginary, or earth and heaven, or earth and world.

5.23
Not man and man or woman and woman or woman and man.

5.3
Vision is in history and is partly conditioned by it. A condition of its truth.

5.31
Vision does not mystify.

5.32
Vision does not unify.

5.321
Vision is sexed. The eyes of Robert Duncan did not focus on a single object.

5.33
Vision is local and material and historical. Thus:

5.34
Vision is a traveler.

5.4
Vision is natural insofar as nature is historical (Darwin).

5.41
"If it's hysterical it's historical."

5.5
Vision binds the two halves of the Möbius strip. But in this case, two halves do not make a whole.

5.51
The two halves are like a whole in the sense that they offer the completest possible range of poetic action. In reading.

5.512
But see 5.1, above.

5.6
The two halves make up a "whole" that is multiple. More and less like a woman or a man.

5.61
Less is also more. My womb is wandering.

5.7
Truth is in the eye that measures this excess.

5.71
The eye that follows the line.

6
That vision is cognition, peculiar to poetry, or to any mode that presents an only apparent singularity, like a body.

6.1
A singularity of which we ask, What kind is writing? (A little more than kin.)

6.2
Or which asks of us, What do you want from me? (A little less than kind.)

6.21
Poetry is supposed to know, like the discourse of the master. But the poem is not even a shard of poetry. The poem is NO THING.

6.3
Reading interrogates its own demand. That the poem be a whole.

6.31
It tarries, not just with the negative, but with the "more" a poem is or indicates.

Joshua Corey

6.4
Vision splits the poem, or is split by it. But is whole on the other side.

6.5
There are no hierarchies, no infinite, no such / many as a mass, there are only / eyes in all heads, / to be looked out of (Olson).

6.6
But the impasse is this: poetry is only partly rhetoric, only partly mimetic. It wants to be part of the world yet exceeds it, quite literally, by halves.

7
That vision exceeds, by its nature, vision is excessive. The more than whole is the true.

7.1
The truest poetry is the most visionary, the most excessive.

7.11
This includes the excessively impoverished.

7.2
The baroque and multiple / the abject less-than-one: these are the modes of vision (of excess) of the age of the poets (Badiou).

7.21
Poetry exceeds (succeeds) silence. It is almost prose.

7.22
Poetry succeeds (exceeds) its speaker.

7.3
A climate of vision includes poem, poet, reader, and world. All instances of the local and historical in a relation that exceeds, without transcending, the local and historical. Like a body, and the shame in it.

7.4
A climate of vision is impure, may blur and mislead, must not depend on the esoteric, must speak the shibboleth on demand.

7.41
The esoteric mistaken for excess; the former at best a mode of the latter. The esoteric tries to put an end to sex. His pussy, hers.

7.41
That sense of the real, heightened, comes in meeting the Möbius strip. Negotiating excess without managing or recuperating it. Poetry is not an economy of anything but energy, potential, methodology.

7.411
The work of the morning is methodology; how to use oneself, and on what (Olson).

7.412
For *methodology* read *libido.* Read Bigmans with no apostrophe. The uncut possessive cock.

7.5
Oikos is prior to *nomos,* as it is prior to *logos,* centerless.

7.51
What's prior divides the apparent whole of the poem into the multiple.

7.52
The household is excessive, like Being, and vision is a possible relation, *heimlich* and *unheimlich*. It takes (more than) one to know (more than) one.

7.53
Counting to three by halves is sufficient for a catalog, for implication, the ten thousand things, the gesture inside the out of doors. The less than me counting for the subject, for the one who KNOWS.

8
That poetry makes NO THING happen in the reader, the unhousel'd.

9
That NO plus the THING makes the world.

The Moths

> Alfred North Whitehead: *It is more important that a proposition be interesting than that it be true.*

Begin again. In a spirit of pragmatism, taking language and the creatures of the imagination as things that obtain, that exist, fully as much as the pebble, the oyster, the cigarette; the high-pressure zone, the Precambrian, a bubble in the housing market. I am interested in these things, the beings-between, that they are a matter of my temperament, its line or lines of flight. Asking now what this assemblage of interests can *do*.

> Virginia Woolf: *The idea has come to me that I want to do now is to saturate every atom. I mean to eliminate all waste, deadness, superfluity: to give the moment whole; whatever it includes.*

In poetry this assemblage may empower a new practice, a practical poetics to be lived with and explored. Such a poetics undermines the impulse toward the made and returns attention to making. To be always beginning again, with the reader, asking what it is in the moment of making that poems do.

> Woolf: *Say that the moment is a combination of thought; sensation; the voice of the sea.*

Poetry as a practice of magic, of incantation, "a matter," says Robin Blaser, "of disturbance, entrance and passion, rather than abracadabra." A speech in which the speaker embeds himself, to which he is committed. A first person that gathers the moment, creating and being created by the otherness of what the poem includes. Call it naiveté. Call it nature.

> Woolf: *Waste, deadness, come from the inclusion of things that don't belong to the moment; this appalling narrative business of the realist: getting on from lunch to dinner: it is false, unreal, merely conventional.*

It is false, unreal, merely conventional; this appalling poetic business of the poet: how many poems merely encase and thwart experience? By their insistences poems obscure our vision of the actual, what William James called "pure experience." The actual may be a poem; it may be the western black rhino, declared extinct last week; it may be my daughter; it may be a feeling or a lure for feeling. We lose the actual when we lose the adventure of imagination.

> William James: *The world of wonders is limited at last to the parent's will (for will prospers where imagination is thwarted); intellectual appetites become no more than ambitions; curious minds become consciences; love, hatred, affection, and cruelty cease to be responses and become convictions. And the adventure of life becomes a self-improvement course.*

We can, in other words, know nothing in advance. The poem lies before us. We choose implication when we write it, when we read it. We are willing subjects in the wrong.

> Robert Duncan: *There is a stone chair on a dais. Seeing it is the King's chair or, even, in some dreamings of this dream, finding myself a lonely king in that chair, there is no one rightly there. A wave of fear seizes me. All things have gone wrong and I am in the wrong. Great doors break from their bars and hinges, and, under pressure, a wall of water floods the cavern.*

All writing in its will to expel what drives it outward tends toward Oedipus, toward *noir*. In a *noir* narrative the protagonist plunges more or less confidently into the heart of the expanding darkness of a bad collectivity, only to discover that the darkness is inside himself—that he is indistinguishable from its origin. *Noir* reverses the dialectic of innocence and experience. The detective is undone by his adventure, confronted by his own complicity in evil. He detects himself at the origin of the bad collectivity; a terrible innocence is born. This moment, the moment at the very end of the *noir* narrative, births our age.

> Walt Whitman: *I discover myself on the verge of the usual mistake.*

But we can bear in, imagining the darkness rather than willing it. Discovering fragility instead of frolicking in the ruins. Instead of a survivalist, a vulnerabilist. Utopia of wounds.

> Woolf: *Why admit anything to literature that is not poetry—by which I mean saturated? Is that not my grudge against novelists? that they select nothing?*

I betrayed poetry to write a novel with the Hegelian and Ginsbergian title *Beautiful Soul: An American Elegy.* It is a sentimental title for a narrative that struggles to emerge on the other side of sentimentality, as the protagonist, in her struggle with the past (the Holocaust, the Sixties) that composes her, tries to survive her own willed innocence of that past. The phrase "beautiful soul" is Hegelian (*schöne Seele*): "The beautiful soul maintains a split between self and world, an irresolvable chasm created by the call of conscience.... [it] cannot see that the evil it condemns is intrinsic to its existence—indeed, its very form as pure subjectivity *is* this evil." Pure subjectivity, unable to appear, unable to conjure in civic space.

> Duncan: *Medicine can cure the body. But soul, poetry, is capable of living in, longing for, choosing illness. Only the most fanatic researcher upon cancer could share with the poet the concept that cancer is a flower, an adventure, an intrigue with life.*

"Ecological politics has a *noir* form," Timothy Morton writes. "We start by thinking we can 'save' something called 'the world' 'over there,' but end up realizing that we ourselves are implicated. This is the solution to beautiful soul syndrome: reframing our field of activity as one for which we ourselves are formally responsible, even guilty." We are or ought to be fanatic cancer researchers, and the cancer is in us. *Is* us. We are caught up in the bad collectivity, capital, the Anthropocene. We are caught up in an intrigue with life.

> Woolf: *The poets succeeding by simplifying: practically everything is left out.*

Poems are not mimetic; they do not represent; they show nothing of states of affairs or states of mind. Poetry is the by-product of what Karen Barad calls "intra-action," "*the mutual constitution of entangled agencies* ... the notion of intra-action recognizes that distinct agencies do not precede, but rather emerge through, their intra-action." The poet is one agent entangled with innumerable other agents: black rhinos, Congressional Republicans, tornadoes, John Keats, Ebola, words. The particular moment of entanglement is the poet's experience. The record of that experience is the poem; liable, as Ezra Pound said of *The Cantos,* to be marked by "the defects inherent in a record of struggle."

> Duncan: *The poet's role is not to oppose evil, but to imagine it: what if Shakespeare had opposed Iago, or Dostoyevsky opposed Raskolnikov—the vital thing is that they created Iago and Raskolnikov.*

The poem itself is not mimetic but the struggle to produce it is microcosmic; as Whitehead says, "Each task of creation is a social effort, employing the whole universe." The defects of the poem mark its suffering of incompatible facts: "Insistence on birth at the wrong season is the trick of evil." Whitehead follows this claim with a gimcrack theodicy, assuring us that "in the advance of the world, particular evil facts are finally transcended." I can accept this only in the spirit of Kafka's mordant remark that there is plenty of hope in this universe, but not for us. Yet what John Keats calls "the poetical Character" must participate this hope if is not to be overwhelmed, or to retreat to the white guilt of the beautiful soul.

> Keats: *[I]t is not itself—it has no self—it is every thing and nothing—It has no character—it enjoys life and shade; it lives in gusto, be it foul or fair, high or low, rich or poor, mean or elevated—It has as much delight in conceiving an Iago as an Imogen.*

The *I* is embedded in, produces, and is produced by what it sees. "Environment" does not exist. There is a vibration and an overlapping and a revision. The poem ends, but the adventure does not. If the adventurer encounters evil, she tarries with it and becomes it for a while. "This thing of darkness I / Acknowledge mine." That is her obedience to the struggle.

> Keats: *A Poet is the most unpoetical of any thing in existence; because he has no Identity—he is continually in for—and filling some other Body—The Sun, the Moon, the Sea and Men and Women who are creatures of impulse are poetical and have about them an unchangeable attribute—the poet has none; no identity—he is certainly the most unpoetical of all God's Creatures.*

Keats is wrong about the unchangeable attributes of things, since all things are themselves entangled and intra-acting agents. He is right that a poet is willing to enter consciously and imaginatively into the contract of intra-action that binds the rest of us all, willing or unwilling in a state of blindness. That blindness is what makes us poetical creatures of impulse. The poet's vision makes blindness palpable. Choosing what Duncan called, "a little endarkenment."

> Woolf: *I want to put practically everything in: yet to saturate. That is what I want to do in "The Moths." It must include nonsense fact, sordidity: but made transparent.*

Moths are nocturnal insects, except when they are not. There is nothing so strange nor seemingly nonsensical as the life cycle of the luna moth, which molts five times in caterpillar form, eating the leaves of black walnut trees, until finally cocooning and emerging with a wingspan of four and a half inches. The luna moth has no mouth; its career as a gourmand is done. It lives for about a week, flying only by night (unlike the diurnal sphinx moth, the infant moth, the Panamanian tiger moth), the females releasing a chemical that attracts the males to mate with them. Then they lay several hundred eggs, and then they die. Moths are very common, except when they are not. Luna moths are endangered in many areas due to pollution from herbicides and insectisides, as well as habitat loss. Is this *saturated*? Is this *transparent*? Is the luna moth, selected for the purposes of this essay very nearly at random, something with which I am entangled in 2013, on a November night after a day of unseasonable warmth and torrential rain, during which at least seventy-seven tornadoes caused five reported deaths and untold property damage in the state of Illinois where I live? The lives of moths are fantastically brief. Does this writing bear the defects of a record of my struggle to imagine an order that is not an illusion or bad faith but an order of intra-action, of *noir*, of innocence trying to get organized?

> Duncan: *For she [H.D.] stood upon the threshold of an art where she was to take her place with Ezra Pound and William Carlos Williams in the adventure of the higher imagination, in the full risk of the poem in which divine, human, and animal orders must be revealed.*

The lives of moths are fantastically brief.

> Woolf: *Watching him, it seemed as if a fibre, very thin but pure, of the enormous energy of the world had been thrust into his frail and diminutive body.*

Translating Francis Ponge, I discover that the French *papillon* does not distinguish between butterfly and moth. "Mangy moths attack the candle when the moon, having vaporized the woods, flies too high." Beckett in L'*Innomable* calls them *les papillons de nuit*.

> Ponge: *Les papillons miteux l'assaillent de preference à la lune trop haute, qui vaporise les bois.*

Innocence survives experience, through experience. The innocence of the moth in its mouthless struggle for life. Millions of moths and the single life. The split nocturnal lyric underneath the epic day. The poem.

> Woolf: *Again, somehow, one saw life, a pure bead.*

Acknowledgments

While many of these pieces found their first life on one of my two blogs (joshcorey.blogspot.com, now joshua-corey.com/blog/), a number of them first appeared in print and online publications; most have been edited or altered for the purposes of this book. In roughly chronological order:

"Notes Toward the Dramatic Lyric": *sidereality*

"Notes Toward the Postmodern Baroque": Johannes Göransson, *Action Yes*

"Richard Hugo's Constructivist Moment": poets.org

"The Poet's Novel: On Ben Lerner's Fiction": Michelle Taransky, *Jacket 2*

"'Tansy City': Charles Olson and the Prospects for Avant-Pastoral": Franca Bellarsi, *Comparative American Studies*

"Robert Duncan's Visionary Ecology": Benjamin Friedlander, *Paideuma*

"The Moths": Jacob Ryan Syersak, *Cloud Rodeo*

"The Transcendental Circuit": Michael Theune and Kirstin Hotelling Zona, *Spoon River Poetry Review*

"The Golden Age of Poetry Blogging": Robert Archambeau and Daniel Lawless, *Plume*

I am deeply obliged to the late Reginald Shepherd's partner Robert Philen for his permission to reprint material from Reginald's blog and e-mails.

Thanks to Robert Archambeau and Marc Vincenz for their editorial vision and encouragement, and to Isabel McKenzie for her thoughtful comments. "Modes of Pastoral, Modes of Modernism" was originally published as "A Long Foreground: Exploring the Postmodern Pastoral" at arcadiaproject.net.

Thank you to my colleagues and students at Lake Forest College.

Thank you, Emily Grayson, for your constant faith and love. And thanks to our daughter, Sadie Gray Corey, for complementing and complicating my writing life in the very best of ways.

Finally, thanks to the many poets and bloggers and readers who helped to create the climate from which these writings emerged.

About the Author

JOSHUA COREY is a poet, critic, and novelist. With G.C. Waldrep he edited *The Arcadia Project: North American Postmodern Pastoral* (Ahsahta Press, 2012) and with Jean-Luc Garneau he translated Francis Ponge's first book as *Partisan of Things* (Kenning Editions, 2016). He is the author of several poetry collections including *Severance Songs* (Tupelo Press, 2011) and *The Barons* (Omnidawn Publishing, 2014), as well as a novel, *Beautiful Soul: An American Elegy*. *Hannah and the Master,* a poetic fantasia on the notorious romance between Martin Heidegger and Hannah Arendt, will be published in 2019 by Ahsahta Press. He lives in Evanston, Illinois, with his wife and daughter and teaches English at Lake Forest College.

www.ingramcontent.com/pod-product-compliance
Lightning Source LLC
Chambersburg PA
CBHW020324170426
43200CB00006B/266